FAVORITE BOOKS ACTIVITIES KIT

Ready-to-Use Quizzes, Projects and Activity Sheets for Grades 4-8

SUE JONES ERLENBUSCH, Ed.D.

THE CENTER FOR APPLIED RESEARCH IN EDUCATION
West Nyack, New York 10995

©1993 by

SUE JONES ERLENBUSCH

10 9 8 7 6 5 4 3

Library of Congress Cataloging-in-Publication Data

Erlenbusch, Sue Jones.
    Favorite books activities kit : ready-to-use quizzes, projects and activity sheets
for grades 4-8 / Sue Jones Erlenbusch.
        p.   cm.
    ISBN 0-87628-309-1
        1. Reading—United States—Aids and devices—Handbooks, manuals, etc.
2. Reading (Elementary)—United States—Handbooks, manuals, etc. 3. Children—
United States—Books and reading. 4. Activity programs in education—United States—
Handbooks, manuals, etc.
I. Title.
LB1573.39.E74   1993
372.4—dc20   92-46628
                                                                          CIP

ISBN 0-87628-309-1

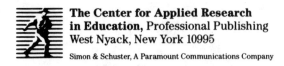
**The Center for Applied Research
in Education,** Professional Publishing
West Nyack, New York 10995
Simon & Schuster, A Paramount Communications Company

Printed in the United States of America

ABOUT THE AUTHOR

Sue Jones Erlenbusch, Ed.D. (University of Missouri), has taught for over twenty years—as a remedial and developmental reading teacher in grades 1 through 8 and as a clinical reading teacher at the high school level. She has also tutored both children and adults in a reading clinic setting. At present, Dr. Erlenbusch teaches reading at Berkeley Middle School in the Ferguson-Florissant School District in Florissant, Missouri.

Dr. Erlenbusch is the author of *Reading Activities for Every Month of the School Year* (The Center for Applied Research in Education, 1988) and *Ready-to Use Reading Activities Through the Year* (The Center for Applied Research in Education, 1992). She was one of the contributing authors of *The Primary Teacher's Ready-to-Use Activities Program* (The Center for Applied Research in Education, 1988) and acted as a consultant for *Horizons*, a book in the Globe Reading Comprehension Program.

A NOTE TO THE TEACHER

We all agree that teaching skills is important. We, however, must go beyond teaching skills: we have to instill in our students a love of reading. If we don't accomplish this, we are turning out—at best—a generation that is aliterate (people who <u>can</u> read, but choose <u>not</u> to do so). This book is designed to help you teach skills and motivate your students to develop the lifelong habit of reading for pleasure.

Favorite Books Activities Kit: Ready-to-Use Quizzes, Projects, and Activity Sheets for Grades 4–8 is a companion to *Ready-to-Use Reading Activities Through the Year.*

Ready-to-Use Reading Activities Through the Year presents activities based on the special days and events that occur throughout the year. A reading list correlated to these special days and events is given for each month. *Favorite Books Activities Kit* takes four books from those monthly reading lists and provides activities designed to improve comprehension, increase vocabulary, enhance writing skills, expand thinking skills, build self-concept, and develop a love of reading.

Each of the four monthly titles in *Favorite Books Activities Kit* has a summary, comprehension test, student activity sheet, and a list of projects. The monthly units are organized to follow the school year from September to August. Each student activity sheet has clear, easy-to-follow directions, and a complete answer key is provided at the back of the book. Also included are a Class Reading Record and a Personal Reading Record. Make as many copies of these forms as you need for yourself and your students to keep track of the books read, tests taken, and activities and projects completed.

All of these activities have been used in the classroom and have proven effective in helping students develop basic skills while acquiring a love of reading.

Sue Jones Erlenbusch

HOW TO USE THIS BOOK

Each month's list of favorite books provides you with the following information and worksheets.

Summaries

A summary of each book title is given so that you may quickly familiarize yourself with the story line. Remember, summaries are poor substitutes for actually reading the books: Only by reading a book can you become so excited that you're able to "sell" a student on the idea of reading it too. Only by reading a book can you share your thoughts and feelings about it with your students.

Although reading books takes time, you will be amply rewarded when you watch one student's eyes light up, a tear trickle down another's cheek, or hear another's voice crack with emotion while relating an incident from a story!

Reading levels are provided for all the books and the Newbery award winners are indicated.

Comprehension Tests

Three comprehension tests (A, B, and C) are given for each book. This allows you to choose one test for a student and assures that not every student reading a title has to take the same test. If you are using a computer program such as Electronic Bookshelf™, you may decide to set up a disk for each month of the year and type all thirty questions for each of the four selections. The program will randomly select ten test items out of this bank of thirty. Taking the time to put the questions on the computer gives you the option of allowing students to choose whether they want to take a test on the computer or with paper and pencil. In either case, a score of 80 percent is considered passing.

Reading Motivators. Here are some tips on how to motivate students to read the entire book they have chosen so they do well on the comprehension tests.

- Make a large classroom chart listing each book title. Record scores on this classroom chart. The class that reads the most books by the end of a specified period receives a reward, such as a pizza party.

- Make a smaller chart entitled "Members of the 100 Club." Each time a student gets a score of 100 percent, place a gold star next to his or her name. Organize contests for members of this elite club.

- Designate each student who earns a score of 100 percent for the first time as a "Superstar Reader." Take an instant photo of each Superstar Reader. Mount the photo on a large star and display it under a (computer) banner that reads "SUPERSTAR

READER." (If you are going to use the wall in the hallway outside of your classroom for this display, be sure to laminate the mounted pictures first. It's also better to cut the large stars out of patterned paper. It seems that light-colored stars on plain paper send out an invitation to be written on by passersby.

- Set up a system of rewards according to the score achieved on the tests. For instance, we use "Pride" points in our school. A score of 80 percent earns five Pride points, a score of 90 percent earns ten Pride points, and a score of 100 percent earns fifteen Pride points. Pride points may be used at the snack bar during lunch break or they may be used to purchase items from the Pride Store. Items in the Pride Store include pencils, notebooks, erasers, posters, books, T-shirts, caps, radios, basketballs, novelty items, and so on. If you don't want to set up a store, you might choose to hold an auction of similar items at the end of each quarter or semester.

Activity Sheets

In order to teach basic reading, writing, listening, speaking, and thinking skills, you are probably already using a wide variety of materials such as newspapers, magazines, worktexts, a basal, filmstrips, videos, old radio shows, and so on. The activity sheets in this book have been designed to reinforce and supplement the basic skills being taught.

Some of the activity sheets give students an opportunity to do a creative writing assignment, such as a bio-poem. Turn these assignments into published works that are displayed in your classroom's reading center. For example, in September an activity sheet for *It's Like This, Cat* directs students to write a pet bio-poem. Have students write their final draft with black pen on a 5-inch-by-8-inch card and draw an illustration of their pet. Laminate each card, punch two holes in the top, place the cards between laminated book covers, and secure with metal rings. The title of such a book could be *You and Your Pet* or *Pet Pals*. You can draw the cover illustration yourself or use a picture from a magazine. Better yet, "commission" a student to draw the illustration for the cover. Make sure to acknowledge the illustrator on the front cover.

You may be wondering why it's suggested that this first student book should be done with black pen instead of on the computer. The reason is that students need time to learn the basics of AppleWorks™ and to practice their keyboarding skills with a program such as MECC CommuniKeys™ before doing writing projects on the computer. They should be ready by October. Why should you take valuable classroom time to teach students keyboarding skills? Because the time spent in September on keyboarding skills will easily be made up over the course of the school year. (And, can you honestly think of one valid reason for students to require one or more class periods to hunt and peck their way through something as short as a bio-poem?)

Projects

Each book title is accompanied by a list of possible projects and space for students to design their own projects. These projects allow students to unleash their creativity. Projects may be done on an individual basis or—if you use literature study groups—the group may work on a project together.

The projects accomplish at least two important things. Sharing a completed project with classmates improves the self-concept of the student who did the project, and displaying projects around the room makes others interested in reading the book upon which the project is based. Getting students interested in reading books is one of the most important challenges we face!

CLASS READING RECORD

PERIOD _____

STUDENT

Section 1 (September)

- TEST: The Indian in the Cupboard
- ACTIVITY
- PROJECT
- TEST: It's Like This, Cat
- ACTIVITY
- PROJECT
- TEST: Thimble Summer
- ACTIVITY
- PROJECT
- TEST: Where the Red Fern Grows
- ACTIVITY
- PROJECT

Section 2 (October)

- TEST: Bunnicula
- ACTIVITY
- PROJECT
- TEST: Just One Friend
- ACTIVITY
- PROJECT
- TEST: Leif the Unlucky
- ACTIVITY
- PROJECT
- TEST: M.C. Higgins, the Great
- ACTIVITY
- PROJECT

CLASS READING RECORD (continued)

PERIOD ____ STUDENT	Section 3 (November)												Section 4 (December)											
	TEST: The Great Gilly Hopkins	ACTIVITY	PROJECT	TEST: How to Eat Fried Worms	ACTIVITY	PROJECT	TEST: Sarah, Plain and Tall	ACTIVITY	PROJECT	TEST: Tales of a Fourth Grade Nothing	ACTIVITY	PROJECT	TEST: Anne Frank	ACTIVITY	PROJECT	TEST: The Best Christmas Pageant Ever	ACTIVITY	PROJECT	TEST: Johnny Tremain	ACTIVITY	PROJECT	TEST: Racso and the Rats of NIMH	ACTIVITY	PROJECT

CLASS READING RECORD (continued)

PERIOD ___

STUDENT

Section 5 (January)

- TEST: Across Five Aprils
- ACTIVITY
- PROJECT
- TEST: From the Mixed-Up Files...
- ACTIVITY
- PROJECT
- TEST: In the Year of the Boar and Jackie Robinson
- ACTIVITY
- PROJECT
- TEST: The Slave Dancer
- ACTIVITY
- PROJECT

Section 6 (February)

- TEST: Roll of Thunder, Hear My Cry
- ACTIVITY
- PROJECT
- TEST: Sounder
- ACTIVITY
- PROJECT
- TEST: To Be a Slave
- ACTIVITY
- PROJECT
- TEST: With You and Without You
- ACTIVITY
- PROJECT

CLASS READING RECORD (continued)

PERIOD ___		Section 7 (March)									Section 8 (April)									
STUDENT	TEST: The Cat Ate My Gymsuit	ACTIVITY	PROJECT	TEST: James and the Giant Peach	ACTIVITY	PROJECT	TEST: Julie of the Wolves	ACTIVITY	PROJECT	TEST: One Fat Summer	ACTIVITY	PROJECT	TEST: Charlie and the Chocolate Factory	ACTIVITY	PROJECT	TEST: Frankenstein	ACTIVITY	PROJECT	TEST: My Brother Sam Is Dead	ACTIVITY	PROJECT	TEST: The War Between the Pitiful Teachers ...	ACTIVITY	PROJECT

CLASS READING RECORD (continued)

PERIOD ____		TEST: All-of-a-Kind Family	ACTIVITY	PROJECT	TEST: Call It Courage	ACTIVITY	PROJECT	TEST: Dirt Bike Racer	ACTIVITY	PROJECT	TEST: Homesick: My Own Story	ACTIVITY	PROJECT	TEST: Animal Farm	ACTIVITY	PROJECT	TEST: The Boat Who Wouldn't Float	ACTIVITY	PROJECT	TEST: The Summer of the Swans	ACTIVITY	PROJECT	TEST: Tiger Eyes	ACTIVITY	PROJECT
STUDENT		Section 9 (May)													Section 10 (June)											

CLASS READING RECORD (continued)

PERIOD ____ STUDENT	TEST: Summer of My German Soldier	ACTIVITY	PROJECT	TEST: Summer of the Monkeys	ACTIVITY	PROJECT	TEST: Pursuit	ACTIVITY	PROJECT	TEST: Wuthering Heights	ACTIVITY	PROJECT	TEST: The Hero and the Crown	ACTIVITY	PROJECT	TEST: Hitty: Her First Hundred Years	ACTIVITY	PROJECT	TEST: National Velvet	ACTIVITY	PROJECT	TEST: The Red Pony	ACTIVITY	PROJECT

Section 11 (July) — Section 12 (August)

Name _____ Period _____

PERSONAL READING RECORD

BOOK	TEST	ABC	DATE	ACTIVITY	PROJECT
THE INDIAN IN THE CUPBOARD					
IT'S LIKE THIS, CAT					
THIMBLE SUMMER					
WHERE THE RED FERN GROWS					
BUNNICULA: A RABBIT TALE OF MYSTERY					
JUST ONE FRIEND					
LEIF THE UNLUCKY					
M.C. HIGGINS, THE GREAT					
THE GREAT GILLY HOPKINS					
HOW TO EAT FRIED WORMS					
SARAH, PLAIN AND TALL					
TALES OF A FOURTH GRADE NOTHING					
ANNE FRANK: DIARY OF A YOUNG GIRL					
THE BEST CHRISTMAS PAGEANT EVER					
JOHNNY TREMAIN					
RACSO AND THE RATS OF NIMH					
ACROSS FIVE APRILS					
FROM THE MIXED-UP FILES OF MRS. BASIL E. FRANKWEILER					
IN THE YEAR OF THE BOAR AND JACKIE ROBINSON					
THE SLAVE DANCER					
ROLL OF THUNDER, HEAR MY CRY					
SOUNDER					
TO BE A SLAVE					
WITH YOU AND WITHOUT YOU					

COMMENTS: _____

_____

_____

_____

_____

_____

Name _____ Period _____

PERSONAL READING RECORD (continued)

BOOK	TEST	ABC	DATE	ACTIVITY	PROJECT
THE CAT ATE MY GYMSUIT					
JAMES AND THE GIANT PEACH					
JULIE OF THE WOLVES					
ONE FAT SUMMER					
CHARLIE AND THE CHOCOLATE FACTORY					
FRANKENSTEIN					
MY BROTHER SAM IS DEAD					
THE WAR BETWEEN THE PITIFUL TEACHERS AND THE SPLENDID KIDS					
ALL-OF-A-KIND FAMILY					
CALL IT COURAGE					
DIRT BIKE RACER					
HOMESICK: MY OWN STORY					
ANIMAL FARM					
THE BOAT WHO WOULDN'T FLOAT					
THE SUMMER OF THE SWANS					
TIGER EYES					
SUMMER OF MY GERMAN SOLDIER					
SUMMER OF THE MONKEYS					
PURSUIT					
WUTHERING HEIGHTS					
THE HERO AND THE CROWN					
HITTY: HER FIRST HUNDRED YEARS					
NATIONAL VELVET					
THE RED PONY					

COMMENTS: _____

CONTENTS

Section 1
_____

FAVORITE BOOKS FOR SEPTEMBER
1

The Indian in the Cupboard by Lynne Reid Banks

It's Like This, Cat by Emily Neville

Thimble Summer by Elizabeth Enright

Where the Red Fern Grows by William Rawls

Section 2

FAVORITE BOOKS FOR OCTOBER
25

Section 3

FAVORITE BOOKS FOR NOVEMBER
47

Section 4

FAVORITE BOOKS FOR DECEMBER
69

Section 5

FAVORITE BOOKS FOR JANUARY
91

Section 6

FAVORITE BOOKS FOR FEBRUARY
115

Section 7

FAVORITE BOOKS FOR MARCH
137

The Cat Ate My Gymsuit by Paula Danziger

7-1	Comprehension Test A
7-2	Comprehension Test B
7-3	Comprehension Test C
7-4	Activity Sheet
7-5	Projects

James and the Giant Peach by Roald Dahl

7-6	Comprehension Test A
7-7	Comprehension Test B
7-8	Comprehension Test C
7-9	Activity Sheet
7-10	Projects

Julie of the Wolves by Jean Craighead George

7-11	Comprehension Test A
7-12	Comprehension Test B
7-13	Comprehension Test C
7-14	Activity Sheet
7-15	Projects

One Fat Summer by Robert Lipsyte

7-16	Comprehension Test A
7-17	Comprehension Test B
7-18	Comprehension Test C
7-19	Activity Sheet
7-20	Projects

Section 8

FAVORITE BOOKS FOR APRIL
161

Charlie and the Chocolate Factory by Roald Dahl

8-1	Comprehension Test A

Section 9

FAVORITE BOOKS FOR MAY
185

Section 10

FAVORITE BOOKS FOR JUNE
207

Tiger Eyes by Judy Blume

Section 11

FAVORITE BOOKS FOR JULY
229

Summer of My German Soldier by Bette Greene

Summer of the Monkeys by Wilson Rawls

Pursuit by Michael French

Wuthering Heights by Emily Brontë

Section 12

FAVORITE BOOKS FOR AUGUST
253

ANSWER KEYS

275

Section 1

FAVORITE BOOKS
FOR
SEPTEMBER

The following books are on "September Book List B" in *Ready-to-Use Reading Activities Through the Year.*

Activity Sheets	Book Title	Reading Level	Award
1-1 to 1-5	**The Indian in the Cupboard**	5	
1-6 to 1-10	**It's Like This, Cat**	5	Newbery Medal
1-11 to 1-15	**Thimble Summer**	4.9	Newbery Medal
1-16 to 1-20	**Where the Red Fern Grows**	6	

The Indian in the Cupboard by Lynne Reid Banks.
New York: Avon, 1980. 181 pages.

For his birthday, Omri receives a plastic figure of an Indian from his friend, a cupboard from his brother, and an old key from his mother. He places the plastic Indian in the cupboard and turns the key in the door before going to sleep. Omri awakens to hear muffled sounds coming from inside the cupboard. Imagine his surprise when he opens the cupboard and finds a live Indian who is only 3½ inches high! Omri discovers that the cupboard can magically make anything plastic become real. For a little while, Omri keeps the wondrous secret of the Indian Little Bear to himself. Then he tells his best friend Patrick. Patrick convinces Omri to put a plastic cowboy in the cupboard. A cowboy named Boone appears in a few seconds. At first, Patrick is selfish and inconsiderate toward Boone and Little Bear. This strains his friendship with Omri—almost to the breaking point—before he learns that turning plastic figures into real people means he has a responsibility to put his own feelings aside and do what is best for them.

It's Like This, Cat by Emily Neville.
New York: Harper & Row, 1963. 180 pages.

Dave Mitchell is a teenager growing up in New York City in the 1960s. He and his father are a lot alike, which leads to many heated arguments. When they start yelling, Dave's mom starts wheezing. Dave and his father decide they have to learn to get along so they stop setting off Mom's asthma attacks. Dave's friend, whom he calls Aunt Kate, gives him a stray cat. Cat moves in against Pop's wishes. Cat runs off and is rescued by Tom, who becomes a family friend. Next, Cat helps Dave meet Mary, who becomes his first girlfriend. Dave, an only child, realizes how lonely he has been as Cat starts collecting people to be part of Dave's family, just as Aunt Kate collects stray cats to be her family. Cat and Dave's friends help him come to better understand himself, his family, and others.

Thimble Summer by Elizabeth Enright.
New York: Dell, 1938. 136 pages.

Garnet is growing up on a Wisconsin farm in the early 1900s. When she finds a silver thimble, she thinks it has magical properties. Her joyous summer unfolds as she and her best friend Citronella get locked in the library, build a treehouse, and listen to great-grandmother Eberhardt tell about her childhood. While Garnet is helping her family make lime at the kiln, an orphan named Eric comes out of the woods and is quickly made one of the family. Eric is a welcome addition because he is a jack-of-all-trades and gets along with everyone. When Garnet's older brother Jay belittles her during the barn-raising, she runs away. She hitchhikes to a town 18 miles away, shops, and hitchhikes back home before anyone but Mr. Freebody, a family friend, misses her. Mr. Freebody says he never knew a child with more spirit and he guesses he has to expect her to get into mischief once in a while. Then he tells her he wouldn't have her change for the world. At the end of Garnet's magical summer, she attends the State Fair with her family and friends. The highlight of the day is when Timmy, her beloved pig, wins a blue ribbon. Garnet returns home so bubbling over with joy that she turns a series of handsprings in the pasture. Garnet's joy in living makes readers bubble over with joy, too. Maybe the thimble wasn't magic, but the book is!

Where the Red Fern Grows by Wilson Rawls.
New York: Bantam, 1961. 212 pages.

Ten-year-old Billy wants two hunting dogs more than anything else in the world. His mother and father would love to give him the dogs, but times are hard and money is scarce. At first, Billy is miserable because his parents won't give him the dogs. He decides to buy the dogs himself. He sees an ad in a newspaper that gives the price of two pups. Billy starts picking berries and doing odd jobs to earn money. It takes him two years to save enough. His grandfather helps him send away for the puppies. From the second he sets eyes on them at the train station, Billy knows the two dogs and he will have a very special relationship. From that time on, one boy plus two dogs equals companionship, love, laughter, adventure, sacrifice, and tears. Billy, Old Dan, and Little Ann will snuggle up in a warm, cozy place in your heart and stay with you forever.

THE INDIAN IN THE CUPBOARD
Comprehension Test A

Directions: Read each question carefully. Circle the letter of the choice that best answers each question.

1. Who wrote this book?
   a. E.B. White   *b.* Robert Newton Peck   *c.* Lynne Reid Banks

2. Little Bear told Omri to give him _____.
   a. a tepee, firewater, and food
   b. a blanket, food, and fire
   c. a longhouse, meat, and weapons

3. Omri said he would give Little Bear a horse, and a bow and arrows, but no _____.
   a. gun   *b.* tomahawk   *c.* crossbow

4. Why did Omri bring a knight to life?
   a. so he could get clothes for Little Bear to wear
   b. so he could get Little Bear a friend
   c. so he could get an ax for Little Bear

5. What did Patrick threaten to do to Omri if he took his cowboy?
   a. tell his parents so he'd get in trouble
   b. throw his Indian down the stairs
   c. bash him

6. Why did Patrick show Boone and Little Bear to the headmaster of the school?
   a. to keep the headmaster from calling his father
   b. to get even with Omri
   c. to impress the headmaster

7. Why did Omri's brother hide the cupboard under piles of junk in the attic?
   a. to get even with Omri for going into his room
   b. he thought Omri had hidden his gym shorts
   c. to make Omri pay a ransom to get it back

8. Why did Gillon's pet rat gnaw on the electric cord of Omri's lamp?
   a. for insulation for a nest
   b. for food
   c. so he could wear down his front teeth

9. Tommy thought he saw Omri, Patrick, Boone, and Little Bear in a _____.
   a. hallucination   *b.* dream   *c.* nightmare

10. Who was Bright Stars?
    a. Boone's horse   *b.* Little Bear's horse   *c.* the Indian girl

THE INDIAN IN THE CUPBOARD
Comprehension Test B

Directions: Read each question carefully. Circle the letter of the choice that best answers each question.

1. What did Patrick give Omri for his birthday?
   a. a plastic cowboy   b. a plastic Indian   c. a plastic horse

2. When Omri put a plastic tepee and a matchbox car into the cupboard, why didn't the car become real?
   a. It had too many working parts.
   b. It wasn't plastic.
   c. The cupboard lost its magic.

3. When Little Bear's leg was bleeding, Omri poured _____ into water to use as a disinfectant.
   a. iodine   b. hydrogen peroxide   c. Listerine®

4. When Omri brought the Indian chief to life, why did he fall over?
   a. He fainted.   b. He died.   c. He fell asleep.

5. Omri made Little Bear promise not to attack the cowboy or Omri wouldn't _____ .
   a. get him a wife   b. bring him any more food   c. take him to school

6. Omri told Patrick he couldn't have Little Bear and Boone any longer because _____.
   a. he used them and you can't use people
   b. he almost drowned them in the basin
   c. his pocket wasn't large enough

7. After Omri found the cupboard in the attic, why didn't the magic still work?
   a. The key was lost.
   b. The cupboard door fell off.
   c. The spell was broken when the cupboard got moved.

8. Omri call Gillon's pet a "pink-eyed, needle-toothed, omnivorous, giant rat." *Omnivorous* means _____.
   a. eating only animal food
   b. eating both animal and vegetable food
   c. eating only vegetable food

9. Omri told Little Bear that when Boone recovered from his wounds, they had to _____.
   a. become blood brothers
   b. go live with Patrick
   c. go back to being plastic

10. Why did they have a feast before going back into the cupboard for the last time?
    a. as a going away party
    b. to celebrate Boone's recovery
    c. to celebrate becoming blood brothers

THE INDIAN IN THE CUPBOARD
Comprehension Test C

Directions: Read each question carefully. Circle the letter of the choice that best answers each question.

1. Why was Omri so excited the morning after his birthday?
   a. The Indian in the cupboard had come to life.
   b. He was going to skip school and go shopping with his birthday money.
   c. His family was leaving on a camping trip.

2. Little Bear said he didn't take English scalps because the English helped the Iroquois _____.
   a. become allies of the French
   b. fight their Algonquin enemies
   c. escape from the Continental soldiers

3. Who did Omri bring to life to help bandage Little Bear's leg?
   a. a World War I medical orderly
   b. a World War II doctor
   c. a Korean War medic

4. With whom did Omri share the secret of his Indian?
   a. his two brothers   b. Patrick   c. his teacher

5. Omri convinced Boone to declare a truce for breakfast or he would _____.
   a. refuse to take him to school
   b. not bring him any coffee
   c. tell Little Bear his nickname was Boohoo

6. Omri's two brothers were named _____.
   a. Robert and Patrick   b. Gillon and Adiel   c. Gilbert and Albert

7. While they were all watching a cowboy and Indian movie on TV, _____.
   a. Boone spit tobacco on Patrick's shirt
   b. Little Bear shot Boone with his bow and arrow
   c. Boone shot Little Bear with his pistol

8. Tommy explained that a Minnie was the nickname for a Minnenwerfer, which was a German _____.
   a. tank   b. airplane   c. shell

9. Boone convinced Omri that his wound would heal faster if he had _____.
   a. some penicillin   b. some whiskey   c. a good doctor

10. When Omri put them in the cupboard for the last time, he told Little Bear _____.
    a. to hold onto Bright Starts, but not Boone
    b. to hold onto Bright Stars, Boone, and his horse
    c. not to hold onto anyone or anything

THE INDIAN IN THE CUPBOARD

I. *Directions:* Put these events in the correct order. Write the numeral 1 in front of the event that happened first. Continue numbering the remaining items.

_____ The key falls under the floorboards in Omri's room.

_____ Gillon gives Omri a cupboard he found in the alley.

_____ The owner of Yapp's accuses Omri of stealing.

_____ Patrick gives Omri a plastic Indian for his birthday.

_____ Mr. Johnson sees Little Bear and Boone.

_____ Tommy helps stitch up Boone's wound.

_____ Omri returns Little Bear, Boone, and Bright Stars to their own time.

II. *Directions:* Several words from the story are in the bottom drawer of the cupboard. Place each word in the correct category. You may use a dictionary.

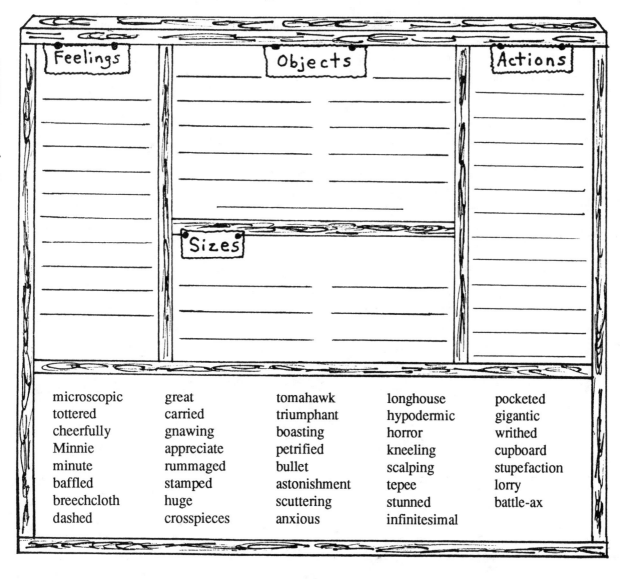

Feelings	Objects	Actions
	Sizes	

microscopic	great	tomahawk	longhouse	pocketed
tottered	carried	triumphant	hypodermic	gigantic
cheerfully	gnawing	boasting	horror	writhed
Minnie	appreciate	petrified	kneeling	cupboard
minute	rummaged	bullet	scalping	stupefaction
baffled	stamped	astonishment	tepee	lorry
breechcloth	huge	scuttering	stunned	battle-ax
dashed	crosspieces	anxious	infinitesimal	

PROJECTS FOR *THE INDIAN IN THE CUPBOARD*

Directions: Choose one of the following projects or design your own. If you design your own project, fill out the form below and submit it to your teacher for approval.

1. Omri and Patrick wished they could become the same size as Little Bear, Boone, and Bright Stars. What if their wish came true? Write an adventure for the five friends.

2. Look at the illustration of the longhouse that Little Bear built. Bring this illustration to life by building this longhouse to scale. Place it in a shallow cardboard box filled with tamped-down earth. Add plastic figures of an Indian and a horse.

3. Boone drew a picture of his hometown. Reread this description; then recreate this scene. Enlarge the scale and draw the picture on banner paper or posterboard.

4. At first, Patrick was selfish and uncaring in his actions toward Little Bear and Boone. Tell how Patrick changed by the end of the story. What do you think brought about this change?

5. Boone described how the doctor in his town treated wounds and illnesses. Research medical practices in the American West in the late 1800s. Write a report contrasting medical practices of the settlers with those of Indians. In what ways were their medical practices similar? In what ways were their medical practices different?

PROJECT PROPOSAL

Name _____ Beginning Date _____ Completion Date _____

Describe the project in detail: _____

_____

Why do you want to do this project? _____

_____

What will the final product be? _____

_____

How will you share your final product? _____

_____

Comments: _____

_____

IT'S LIKE THIS, CAT
Comprehension Test A

Directions: Read each question carefully. Circle the letter of the choice that best answers each question.

1. Who wrote this book?
   a. Cynthia Voight   *b.* Elizabeth George Speare   *c.* Emily Neville

2. Who was Dave's best friend since kindergarten?
   a. Mick   *b.* Nick   *c.* Dick

3. Where did Dave go on his first date?
   a. to the roller rink
   b. to the bowling alley
   c. to the movies

4. Dave says streets in Manhattan run pretty regularly north and south, but Brooklyn streets _____.
   a. run in circles and angles
   b. run east and west
   c. have no plan

5. Where did Dave and Mary go on their first date?
   a. to the beach   *b.* to a play   *c.* to the movies

6. When the car was stalled in traffic, what did Cat do?
   a. had heat stroke
   b. scratched Dave's dad on the back of the neck
   c. jumped out of the car

7. The encyclopedia told Ben and Dave that salamanders are amphibians and have _____.
   a. thick, dry skin and claws
   b. scales and claws
   c. thin, moist skin and no claws

8. Where did Dave and Mary meet on Columbus Day?
   a. Coney Island   *b.* Bronx Zoo   *c.* Metropolitan Museum of Art

9. On Thanksgiving Day, Kate got a telegram saying _____.
   a. she had inherited a million dollars
   b. she had been evicted
   c. her brother was dead

10. Why did Mary call Dave from Macy's?
    a. She wanted to find out why he stood her up.
    b. Her mother forgot to pick her up and she didn't have any money.
    c. She wanted Dave to go Christmas shopping with her.

IT'S LIKE THIS, CAT
Comprehension Test B

Directions: Read each question carefully. Circle the letter of the choice that best answers each question.

1. Why did Dave Mitchell decide to get a cat instead of a dog?
    a. His father wanted him to have a dog.
    b. His father wanted him to have a cat.
    c. He was afraid of dogs.

2. Where did Cat discover sand crabs?
    a. Central Park   b. Coney Island   c. Hudson River

3. Dave says Tom is by himself so much he is sort of like _____.
    a. an island   b. a hermit   c. a nerd

4. Why did Tom get thrown out of New York University?
    a. He flunked a French exam and yelled at a professor.
    b. He got caught cheating.
    c. His father wouldn't pay damages for a water fight.

5. What did Tom discover when he wrote to his father?
    a. His father was dead.
    b. His father was in prison.
    c. His father had moved and left no forwarding address.

6. At the Bronx Zoo, Dave and Ben found a _____, which is native to New York City.
    a. raccoon   b. newt   c. woodchuck

7. What did Cat do when left alone with Redskin and Brownie?
    a. killed Brownie   b. killed Redskin   c. killed both of them

8. The howling wind and gray, powerful water made Dave want _____.
    a. to be inside where it's warm and quiet
    b. to be out in a boat
    c. to go see *The Old Man and the Sea* at the movies

9. When the newspaper reporters were badgering Kate, what terrible thing happened?
    a. A reporter accidentally killed a kitten.
    b. Kate had a nervous breakdown.
    c. Kate's cats all ran off.

10. Tom tells Dave the reason he fights with his father so much is because _____.
    a. they like to see Dave's mom wheeze
    b. they're so different
    c. they're so much alike

IT'S LIKE THIS, CAT
Comprehension Test C

Directions: Read each question carefully. Circle the letter of the choice that best answers each question.

1. Where did Dave get Cat?

   a. at the pet store   *b.* at the city pound   *c.* at Aunt Kate's

2. What is it about Nick that gripes Dave?

   a. Nick hates cats.

   b. Nick complains about everything.

   c. Nick always has to think up all the plans.

3. What kind of sandwiches did Dave and Tom take to Inwood Park?

   a. salami   *b.* lasagna   *c.* spaghetti

4. Why did Dave decide to get Cat altered?

   a. so Cat wouldn't go out at night and fight so much

   b. so Cat's personality would improve

   c. because his father ordered him to do it

5. The first indication that Dave's dad likes Cat is when he tells Tom, _____.

   a. "You've got nothing to worry about. Cat's on your side."

   b. "Don't worry. Cat likes you."

   c. "Why not take Cat to live with you?"

6. Ben's pets were _____.

   a. lizards   *b.* salamanders   *c.* snakes

7. The encyclopedia told Dave that cats are of the species _____.

   a. Felis domesticus

   b. Canis familiaris

   c. Triturus viridescens

8. Mary and Dave took the ferry from Brooklyn to _____.

   a. Coney Island   *b.* Staten Island   *c.* Manhattan

9. Kate said there were a lot of stray children in New York City, so she might _____.

   a. bring some home to live with her

   b. buy them bus tickets to Brooklyn

   c. leave some money to Children's Aid

10. Tom, Hilda, Dave, Mom, and Pop all drink a toast to _____.

    a. Kate   *b.* Cat   *c.* Susan

IT'S LIKE THIS, CAT

Directions: Ben and Dave looked up information about their pets in an encyclopedia. They could have used this information to write a pet bio-poem. In a pet bio-poem, you are told what to write on each line. Read the seven bio-poem lines below. Then, read the examples. Next, fill in the form to write a bio-poem about your pet. You may need to use an encyclopedia for lines 3, 6, and 7.

Bio-Poem

Line 1	Name,
Line 2	Three adjectives that describe this pet,
Line 3	Member of what food class,
Line 4	Who feeds on (three things),
Line 5	Who lives·in (three places),
Line 6	Who belongs to the class of _____,
Line 7	Scientific name.

Examples

Puff,
Sneaky, sleek, independent,
Carnivore,
Who feeds on steak, Tender Vittles®, and ham,
Who lives in my friend's house, in our kitchen, and around,
Who belongs to the class of mammals,
Felis Domesticus.

Taffy
Cuddly, funny, friendly,
Carnivore,
Who feeds on pizza, hamburgers, and hot dogs,
Who lives in his own doghouse, in our backyard, and at the kennel,
Who belongs to the class of mammals,
Canis familiaris.

_____,

_____, _____, _____,

_____,

Who feeds on _____, _____, and _____,

Who lives in _____, _____, and _____,

Who belongs to the class of _____,

_____,

PROJECTS FOR *IT'S LIKE THIS, CAT*

Directions: Choose one of the following projects or design your own. If you design your own project, fill out the form below and submit it to your teacher for approval.

1. Dave told Mary's mother that his class was studying metaphors and similes by reading "The Highwayman" and "The Wreck of the Hesperus." Read these two poems. Pay particular attention to the way the authors use metaphors and similes. Write a poem of your own using both metaphors and similes.

2. Kate inherited an enormous amount of money and a big, old house in Brooklyn. What if her landlord evicted her? Write a story telling what Kate might do.

3. Dave's father accused him of going to a Twist Parlor. This story took place in the 1960s when a dance called the Twist was the fad. Prepare a list of at least five popular Twist songs. Have someone who was a teenager in the 1960s teach you how to do the Twist. Demonstrate this dance to your class. Ask your teacher if your class can have a Twist Contest. For the contest, wear outfits that would have been seen in a typical Twist Parlor.

4. Make clay replicas of Cat, Redskin, and Brownie. Show the figures to your class and explain what happened when these three pets met for the first and last time.

PROJECT PROPOSAL

Name _____ Beginning Date _____ Completion Date _____

Describe the project in detail: _____

_____

Why do you want to do this project? _____

_____

What will the final product be? _____

_____

How will you share your final product? _____

_____

Comments: _____

_____

THIMBLE SUMMER
Comprehension Test A

Directions: Read each question carefully. Circle the letter of the choice that best answers each question.

1. Who wrote this book?
    a. Lynne Reid Banks   *b.* Elizabeth Enright   *c.* Judy Blume

2. Why did Garnet's father sit up late at night?
    a. He was trying to figure out how to pay the bills.
    b. It was too hot to sleep.
    c. He was reading a good book.

3. What was Elly Gensler's Emporium?
    a. a general store   *b.* a restaurant   *c.* a grocery store

4. The kiln was fired for three days and nights to make lime for _____.
    a. bricks   *b.* cement   *c.* pottery

5. Citronella and Garnet accidentally got locked in the _____.
    a. post office   *b.* general store   *c.* library

6. Why did Garnet run away from home?
    a. She had a fight with Citronella.
    b. Jay yelled at her and treated her like a baby.
    c. Eric tore down her treehouse.

7. What did the truck driver give Garnet when he dropped her off by the mailboxes?
    a. a black chicken   *b.* a dime   *c.* a circus handbill

8. Why did Timmy smell?
    a. He tangled with a skunk.
    b. He had been rolling around in the mud.
    c. He had a bath with scented soap.

9. Mrs. Zangl won a blue ribbon for her _____.
    a. crocheted afghan   *b.* hooked rug   *c.* quilt

10. When Garnet and Citronella rode the Ferris wheel, _____.
    a. Citronella threw up on Garnet's blue dress
    b. they got so scared that they started crying
    c. they got stuck on top for more than half an hour

THIMBLE SUMMER
Comprehension Test B

Directions: Read each question carefully. Circle the letter of the choice that best answers each question.

1. Garnet's last name was _____.

    a. Hauser   *b.* Linden   *c.* Schoenbecker

2. Citronella's great-grandmother told the girls about the long winters her family endured when _____.

    a. wild animals used to come into the house at night to escape the cold

    b. Indians used to come in and sleep before the fire

    c. they went without a fire for days at a time

3. Why did Fanny Eberhardt leave her little brother Thomas alone in the woods?

    a. She wanted to walk to town and buy a coral bracelet.

    b. She wanted to go to a party with her friends.

    c. She got tired of baby-sitting him all the time.

4. When the hair on Major's neck rose and he stood growling at the thicket, who or what emerged?

    a. a skunk   *b.* another dog   *c.* a boy

5. Mr. Freebody called Garnet and Citronella _____.

    a. busybodies   *b.* pests   *c.* bookworms

6. While Garnet was in the dime store, she thought her stomach was as empty as _____.

    a. a hollow log   *b.* a ragpicker's pocket   *c.* an empty purse

7. What did Garnet name the black chicken?

    a. Brunnhilde   *b.* Beauty   *c.* Betsy

8. Garnet was so nervous on the day of the fair, she said _____.

    a. she felt like she had a pinwheel in her stomach

    b. she thought she was going to be sick all over the truck cab

    c. she wanted to stay home in bed

9. Eric said Zara, the Jungle Dancer, forgot to take off her _____.

    a. gold watch   *b.* sneakers   *c.* eyeglasses

10. The judges awarded Timmy a _____.

    a. blue ribbon

    b. red ribbon

    c. green ribbon

THIMBLE SUMMER
Comprehension Test C

Directions: Read each question carefully. Circle the letter of the choice that best answers each question.

1. Citronella was Garnet's _____.

   a. sister   *b.* friend   *c.* cousin

2. What were the only kind of shoes Garnet liked to wear?

   a. sandals   *b.* thongs   *c.* moccasins

3. Garnet liked to go to Citronella's house because there were always _____.

   a. cake and cookies

   b. singing and dancing

   c. lots of children to play with

4. Eric's father died of _____.

   a. old age   *b.* blood poisoning   *c.* a heart attack

5. When Garnet was operating the thresher, she _____.

   a. turned it over

   b. fell asleep at the wheel

   c. ran into the new barn

6. Garnet hitched a ride from New Conniston on a truck carrying _____.

   a. cows   *b.* pigs   *c.* chickens

7. Who worried all day when Garnet ran away?

   a. Mr. Hauser   *b.* Mr. Freebody   *c.* Mr. Swanstrom

8. Why did Citronella start feeling sick after a ride on the whip cars?

   a. She was nervous.

   b. She was dizzy.

   c. She ate and drank too much.

9. What did Mrs. Hauser win at the coconut shy and the weight-lifting booths?

   a. two teddy bears

   b. two Kewpie dolls

   c. two dollars

10. Why did Garnet say she was going to call this summer "the thimble summer"?

   a. She learned that the thimble she found was very valuable.

   b. Nice things began to happen after she found the thimble.

   c. She always wore the thimble on a chain around her neck for good luck.

THIMBLE SUMMER

I. *Directions:* A simile compares two things by saying that one thing is *like* the other thing. Elizabeth Enright, the author of ***Thimble Summer***, is a master at using similes. Below are some similes from the book. Match column A to column B by writing the letters on the correct lines.

Column A

_____ 1. The rain was like

_____ 2. The huge raindrops were dropping like

_____ 3. The many-branched lightning stood for an instant like

_____ 4. The teapot purred like

_____ 5. The thresher had a long neck like

_____ 6. The kiln door was red hot and glowing like

_____ 7. The grasshoppers popped and scattered like

_____ 8. The telephone poles rushed by like

_____ 9. She scrubbed her face till it had a shine like

_____ 10. I wore so many petticoats I must have looked like

Column B

a. a dinosaur.

b. a kitten.

c. sparks from a fire.

d. pennies on the roof.

e. tall giraffes in a hurry.

f. shellac.

g. the eye of a dragon.

h. a tree on fire.

i. a cabbage wrong-side up.

j. a sea turned upside down.

II. *Directions:* A metaphor compares two things by saying that one thing *is* the other thing. Elizabeth Enright wrote, "The watermelons in their patch were little green whales in a sea of frothy leaves." Write a metaphor that the author could have used in ***Thimble Summer***.

_____

_____

_____

_____

_____

III. *Directions:* The author is also a master at using vivid verbs. A verb is a word that shows action. By using vivid verbs, the author helps the reader "see" the action clearly. Here are some vivid verbs from the story: *boomed, commanded, gobbled, hissed, jostled, quivered, rocketed, slopped, splashed, shattered, snatched, sniffled, sputtered, thumped.* On a separate sheet of paper, use at least six of these vivid verbs in a paragraph about your life.

PROJECTS FOR *THIMBLE SUMMER*

Directions: Choose one of the following projects or design your own. If you design your own project, fill out the form below and submit it to your teacher for approval.

1. Fill a coffee can with sand and place a twig in the center. Build a miniature treehouse in the branches of the twig. Place figures representing Garnet and Citronella in the treehouse.

2. What if Garnet had found a $5.00 bill lying on the sidewalk when she was in New Conniston? Write a diary entry telling what she would have done.

3. The author does not tell us what year the story takes place. Look at this list of clues from the story: they had no electricity in the house; they used a room in the basement to keep food cold; spoons were kept in a tumbler in the center of the table; they had a very high, narrow Ford; they had Coca-Cola®; the library had gas lights; Mrs. Hauser won two Kewpie dolls; they used tractors; Mrs. Hauser had a balloon shaped like Micky Mouse and one shaped like a Zeppelin; all the kitchen utensils in the window of the store had green handles. Now it's time to be a detective and use these clues to guess the decade when this story most likely occurred. How do you get started? Look in a book on dolls to find out when Kewpie dolls were popular. After you have assigned a time period to as many of the clues as possible and guessed the decade when the story took place, explain your choice to the class.

PROJECT PROPOSAL

Name _____ Beginning Date _____ Completion Date _____

Describe the project in detail: _____

_____

Why do you want to do this project? _____

_____

What will the final product be? _____

_____

How will you share your final product? _____

_____

Comments: _____

_____

WHERE THE RED FERN GROWS
Comprehension Test A

Directions: Read each question carefully. Circle the letter of the choice that best answers each question.

1. Who is the author of this story?
   a. Matt Christopher   *b.* Scott O'Dell   *c.* Wilson Rawls

2. Who was the first animal to get caught in the steel trap?
   a. Sloppy Ann, a hog
   b. Mister Ringtail, a coon
   c. Samie, a cat

3. Who came to Billy's aid when the town bully and his friends were beating him up?
   a. the marshall   *b.* the stationmaster   *c.* a teacher

4. Why did the coon stay up in the tree after Billy went home?
   a. The dogs stayed there all night.
   b. Billy's father stayed there all night.
   c. Grandpa and the scarecrow stayed there all night.

5. What happened when Billy hunted the ghost-coon with the Pritchard brothers?
   a. Rainie fell on the ax.
   b. Rubin fell on the ax.
   c. Billy fell on the ax.

6. Who fell down in the blizzard and injured his ankle?
   a. Papa   *b.* Old Dan   *c.* Grandpa

7. What did Billy get besides money when he won the coon hunting contest?
   a. a gold coin   *b.* a gold cup   *c.* a silver chalice

8. Why did Old Dan die?
   a. He grieved over the death of Little Ann.
   b. A mountain lion badly wounded him.
   c. He was accidentally shot.

9. Who earned enough money for the family to move to town?
   a. Billy and Grandpa   *b.* Little Ann and Old Dan   *c.* Mama

10. When Billy went to say a last good-bye to his dogs, he discovered that a red fern _____.
   a. had grown between their graves
   b. was growing in the woods near the graves
   c. had grown next to the doghouse

WHERE THE RED FERN GROWS
Comprehension Test B

Directions: Read each question carefully. Circle the letter of the choice that best answers each question.

1. Where did this story take place?

    a. in the Rockies   *b.* in the Ozarks   *c.* in the Alps

2. How long did it take Billy to save fifty dollars to buy the two hounds?

    a. two years   *b.* three years   *c.* four years

3. When Billy was taking his puppies home, what tried to attack them in the cave?

    a. a mean group of kids   *b.* a mountain lion   *c.* a coyote

4. What did Billy do with his first coon hide?

    a. He traded it for a Missouri mule.

    b. He sold it to save the family farm.

    c. He had his mother make it into a hat for him.

5. Why did Billy go ghost-coon hunting with the Pritchard boys?

    a. They goaded Billy's father into making a bet.

    b. They goaded Billy's grandfather into making a bet.

    c. They goaded Billy into making a bet.

6. Why did Old Dan and Little Ann run around a tree all night?

    a. to keep from freezing

    b. to keep the coon from jumping down and running off

    c. because they were playing tag

7. Why did Billy win a silver cup?

    a. Old Dan won a race.   *b.* His dogs treed the most coons.   *c.* Little Ann won a beauty contest.

8. Why did Little Ann die?

    a. She grieved over the death of Old Dan.

    b. A mountain lion badly wounded her.

    c. She was accidentally shot.

9. Billy's father said God took his dogs _____.

    a. so the family could stay together

    b. so Billy would stop hunting once and for all

    c. to punish Billy

10. Indian legend said angels planted the seeds of a red fern, and where one grew _____.

    a. the spot became a tourist attraction

    b. the spot was off limits to everyone

    c. the spot was sacred

WHERE THE RED FERN GROWS
Comprehension Test C

Directions: Read each question carefully. Circle the letter of the choice that best answers each question.

1. The narrator of the story says he was a young _____.
   a. Kit Carson   *b.* Daniel Boone   *c.* Davy Crockett

2. Why did Billy walk so far to pick up his dogs?
   a. He couldn't get a ride.
   b. His dad's truck broke down.
   c. He couldn't wait for his dogs any longer.

3. The first time they went coon hunting, Old Dan and Little Ann _____.
   a. had no luck at all
   b. got lost and howled at the moon
   c. ran a coon up a big tree

4. When Old Dan was stuck up in a tree, how did Billy get him down?
   a. He climbed the tree and stuffed Old Dan down the hollow trunk.
   b. He called the fire department.
   c. He got several neighbors to help.

5. How many coons did Old Dan and Little Ann have to tree a day to stay in the contest?
   a. two   *b.* three   *c.* four

6. How much money did Billy get when he won the coon hunting contest?
   a. about $100.00   *b.* about $200.00   *c.* about $300.00

7. What was the last animal that Old Dan and Little Ann treed?
   a. a mountain lion   *b.* a coon   *c.* a squirrel

8. What was Mama's greatest wish?
   a. to help Billy get job training
   b. to buy a car
   c. to move to town so the children could get an education

9. Who buried Old Dan and Little Ann?
   a. Billy and his father   *b.* Billy   *c.* Billy and his mother

10. Why did Billy stop hurting so much over the loss of his dogs?
    a. He thought God made a special place in heaven for all good dogs.
    b. His father gave him a new puppy.
    c. He bought two new coon hounds.

WHERE THE RED FERN GROWS

Directions: All of the clues in the puzzle are from the book. Read the clues and fill in the puzzle.

ACROSS

1. Billy's family lived in _____ country.
3. Only an _____ can plant seeds of a red fern.
6. The first thing Billy trapped was the house _____.
10. They lived near the _____ River.
11. A large piece of candy.
12. "God helps those who help _____."
14. Mother made butter in a _____.
15. Meat was cured in a _____.
18. Little _____.
19. The ad was found in a sportsman's _____.
20. Billy walked _____ miles to pick up his puppies and take them home.

DOWN

2. They lived in the _____.
4. Billy took an ax and a _____ when he went hunting.
5. Billy said he suffered from dog-wanting _____.
7. The dogs had a _____ of their own.
8. Old _____.
9. Billy bought two _____ coon hound pups.
13. Mountain _____.
14. " Mama! Mama! _____ here!"
16. Billy carried the puppies _____ in a sack.
17. Billy had to earn _____ dollars to buy the pups.

_____

Illustration based on 1880s cast iron pull toy. The boy enters the trunk when the toy is pulled forward. The bell rings to warn the raccoon.

PROJECTS FOR *WHERE THE RED FERN GROWS*

Directions: Choose one of the following projects or design your own. If you design your own project, fill out the form below and submit it to your teacher for approval.

1. Reread the poem about Little Ann on page 180. Write a poem about Old Dan.

2. The story of the red fern is an old Cherokee legend. Research other Indian legends. Write a report about three of them.

3. Billy's father gave him three small steel traps. Billy used these traps to catch animals so he could make money by selling their hides. Today, animal rights activists argue against the use of steel traps. If Billy had set his mind to it, he probably could have designed a more humane trap. Make such a trap.

4. Billy sold his coonskins for a good price because of the fad back East for wearing coonskin coats. Animal rights activists argue against wearing fur. Form a debate team. Hold a debate presenting sound arguments for and against the killing of animals for their skins. Each side should design a large poster illustrating their point of view. The posters should be displayed as a backdrop during the debate. Videotape the debate.

PROJECT PROPOSAL

Name _____ Beginning Date _____ Completion Date _____

Describe the project in detail: _____

_____

Why do you want to do this project? _____

_____

What will the final product be? _____

_____

How will you share your final product? _____

_____

Comments: _____

_____

Section 2

FAVORITE BOOKS FOR *OCTOBER*

The following books are on "October Book List B" in *Ready-to-Use Reading Activities Through the Year*.

Activity Sheets	Book Title	Reading Level	Award
2-1 to 2-5	*Bunnicula: A Rabbit Tale of Mystery*	6	
2-6 to 2-10	*Just One Friend*	6.5	
2-11 to 2-15	*Leif the Unlucky*	7	
2-16 to 2-20	*M.C. Higgins, the Great*	4.9	Newbery Medal

Bunnicula: A Rabbit Tale of Mystery by Deborah Howe and James Howe. New York: Avon, 1979. 98 pages.

On a dark and stormy night, Mr. and Mrs. Monroe take their sons Toby and Pete to a Dracula movie. They return with a bunny that had been abandoned in the theater. They name him Bunnicula. Chester, the Monroes' cat, suspects that Bunnicula is a vampire when he sees fangs where his two front teeth should be and the strange markings on his fur in the shape of a cape. Chester starts gathering evidence to try to convince Harold, the family dog, that they have a vampire living with them in their happy home. Chester's antics cause Harold and Bunnicula to become friends and the family to call a cat psychiatrist.

Just One Friend by Lynn Hall.
New York: Collier, 1985. 118 pages.

Doreen thinks she is dumb and built like a sack of potatoes. She wishes she were smarter and had a better figure. But more than anything else, she wishes she had a friend—just one friend. The friend she wants is Robin, but Robin already has a best friend, Meredith. Because she is so desperately lonely, Dory begins planning ways to break up Robin and Meredith's friendship. She succeeds, but with tragic results.

Leif the Unlucky by Erik Christian Haugaard.
Boston: Houghton Mifflin, 1982. 206 pages.

Erik the Red and his followers settle Greenland in 986. Their descendants manage to survive on the barren, ice-covered island for several hundred years. Then, in the fourteenth century, the weather changes. The climate becomes colder. The winters become more severe and the summers shorter. It is more and more difficult to grow enough food for both people and animals. Many die of hunger and sickness. The people of the older generation spend their days longing for a ship to arrive and take them away to Norway. The younger generation is obsessed with the daily struggle to survive the harsh climate. Egil is the exception. He resents his lowly station in life and wants to grab power, prestige, possessions, land, and silver. Leif, the son and nephew of great chieftains, has what Egil covets. The life-and-death struggle between these two young men is set against a tragic background of desperation and despair.

M.C. Higgins, the Great by Virginia Hamilton.
New York: Collier, 1974. 278 pages.

Thirteen-year-old M.C. Higgins and his family live on an outcropping on Sarah's Mountain. M.C. takes care of his two brothers and little sister while his mother and father eke out a meager living whenever and wherever they can find work. M.C. dreams of the day he can move his family off the mountain before the mining company's slag heap, which hangs over their outcropping, finally gives way and cascades down the mountain burying them all under tons of refuse. When M.C. realizes that his dream of escaping isn't going to come true, he sets to work trying to make his home and family safe.

BUNNICULA: A RABBIT TALE OF MYSTERY
Comprehension Test A

Directions: Read each question carefully. Circle the letter of the choice that best answers each question.

1. Who helped write this story?
   a. James Howe   *b.* Scott O'Dell   *c.* Matt Christopher

2. Harold's friend Chester is a _____.
   a. bunny   *b.* boy   *c.* cat

3. The violin music that Chester and Bunnicula heard was made by _____.
   a. a band of gypsies camped nearby
   b. Toby's radio
   c. Professor Mickelwhite, a neighbor

4. When Mrs. Monroe found white beans, peas, squash, tomatoes, lettuce, and zucchini, _____.
   a. she returned them to the grocery store and complained to the manager
   b. Peter told her it was because DDT had been sprayed on them
   c. she wanted Mr. Monroe to call the doctor

5. What renders vampires immobile according to Chester?
   a. steak   *b.* garlic   *c.* catnip

6. Chester read that if a vampire is immersed in water, it _____.
   a. will shrivel and disappear
   b. will leave forever
   c. loses its powers

7. Harold tried to feed Bunnicula by _____.
   a. dragging the salad bowl over to his cage
   b. giving him a green sourball
   c. placing him on the dining room table

8. The vet said that Chester suffered from a case of _____.
   a. severe starvation   *b.* sibling rivalry   *c.* depression

9. The Monroes believed _____.
   a. they were victims of a curious vegetable blight
   b. they owned a vampire bunny
   c. Chester needed to see a physical therapist

10. When Harold heard the most awful noise coming from the basement, he assumed _____.
    a. Bunnicula finally made contact with Chester's neck
    b. a burglar stepped on the mousetrap
    c. it was Chester doing scream therapy

BUNNICULA: A RABBIT TALE OF MYSTERY
Comprehension Test B

Directions: Read each question carefully. Circle the letter of the choice that best answers each question.

1. This story is told from the point of view of _____.
   a. Bunnicula   *b.* Toby   *c.* Harold

2. After the family was asleep, Chester liked to _____.
   a. chase mice   *b.* read books   *c.* tease the parakeet

3. When the family found a white tomato in the refrigerator, _____.
   a. Pete got in trouble for using it in an experiment
   b. Mrs. Monroe said she should clean out the refrigerator more often
   c. Chester said it showed the mark of a vampire

4. Mrs. Monroe thought Chester might be cold, so she _____.
   a. pinned a towel around him
   b. tied a bandanna around his throat
   c. buttoned him into a kitty sweater

5. When Harold tried to get Bunnicula out of his cage, _____.
   a. he got bit on the nose
   b. he got his head stuck
   c. Chester bit him on the tail

6. Bunnicula was getting sick because _____.
   a. nobody seemed to like him
   b. Chester wouldn't let him eat
   c. Chester sneaked garlic into his cage

7. Toby was reading an exciting book called _____.
   a. Robinson Crusoe   *b. Treasure Island*   *c. Kidnapped*

8. The vet gave Harold a pat on the head and a _____.
   a. doggie-pop   *b.* green sourball   *c.* Twinkie®

9. Chester used to love to read _____ at night.
   a. Stephen King   *b. Dracula*   *c.* Edgar Allan Poe

10. Bunnicula and Harold began taking long _____ together.
    a. snoozes   *b.* walks   *c.* baths

BUNNICULA: A RABBIT TALE OF MYSTERY
Comprehension Test C

Directions: Read each question carefully. Circle the letter of the choice that best answers each question.

1. The Monroes went to the theater and returned with _____.
   a. an abandoned bunny   *b.* stomach aches   *c.* pizza and ice cream

2. Bunnicula had a dark colored patch of fur in the shape of a _____.
   a. tomato   *b.* cape   *c.* bat

3. One of Harold's favorite snacks was _____.
   a. chocolate cupcakes with cream filling
   b. peanut butter and banana sandwiches
   c. green sourballs

4. The odor of _____ woke Harold up in the middle of the night.
   a. popcorn   *b.* garlic   *c.* bacon

5. Chester tried to destroy the vampire bunny by _____.
   a. dragging him outside into the sunlight
   b. driving a stake through his heart
   c. pounding a sharp steak into his heart

6. Harold decided that Bunnicula really was _____.
   a. a killer vampire
   b. a threat to the safety of the family
   c. kind of harmless

7. Harold lost sleep one night worrying about _____.
   a. the next morning's visit to the vet
   b. how sick Bunnicula was
   c. how he could get Chester to leave Bunnicula alone

8. The vet prescribed a diet of _____ for Bunnicula.
   a. meat and potatoes   *b.* baby food   *c.* liquefied vegetables

9. Chester told Harold that he was trying to get in touch with his _____.
   a. you-ness   *b.* kittenhood   *c.* mother

10. Harold ended his story when he heard _____.
    a. the refrigerator door open
    b. toenails clicking across the floor
    c. the crinkle of cellophane

BUNNICULA: A RABBIT TALE OF MYSTERY

I. Directions: Chester was convinced that Bunnicula was a vampire bunny. Maybe Chester had been watching too many monster movies on TV or reading too many books about monsters. Write a monster cinquain. In a cinquain you are told what to write on each line. First, read all five lines. Next, read the examples. Then, fill in the form to write your own monster poem.

Cinquain

Line 1	one noun (a subject)
Line 2	two adjectives that describe the subject
Line 3	three verbs about the subject, usually ending in -ing
Line 4	a four-word phrase or a sentence telling your feelings about the subject
Line 5	a synonym for the subject

Examples

Vampire
scary, dangerous
flying, chasing, swooping
He bit my neck!
Bat

Werewolf
mysterious, deadly
growling, slobbering, coming
I'm struggling for my life!
Carnivore

Line 1 _____

Line 2 _____

Line 3 _____

Line 4 _____

Line 5 _____

II. Directions: Show your poem to your teacher. Make any necessary corrections. Print or type your poem on a new sheet of paper. Illustrate your poem. Give this new copy to your teacher so it can be bound into a class monster book.

PROJECTS FOR *BUNNICULA: A RABBIT TALE OF MYSTERY*

Directions: Choose one of the following projects or design your own. If you design your own project, fill out the form below and submit it to your teacher for approval.

1. Make a papier-mâché or clay model of Bunnicula.

2. Write the scene in which Chester first visits his psychologist. Remember, the psychologist tells Chester that he must get in touch with his kittenhood.

3. Harold, the family dog, "wrote" this story. What if Bunnicula could also write and had kept a diary? Write Bunnicula's diary from the time right before he was abandoned in the theater until Chester had to visit a shrink.

4. Create a monster word search. Use monsters from books, movies, radio, and TV.

5. Make a mobile featuring Harold, Chester, and Bunnicula.

6. Make a bibliography of at least twelve books about animals. Write the book titles and authors on a large poster. Draw a box in front of each title. For each book that you have read, write a number in the box indicating how you would rate it on a scale of 1 to 10 (with 10 being the highest rating). Ask other class members to rate books that you have not read.

PROJECT PROPOSAL

Name _____ Beginning Date _____ Completion Date _____

Describe the project in detail: _____
_____

Why do you want to do this project? _____
_____

What will the final product be? _____
_____

How will you share your final product? _____
_____

Comments: _____
_____

JUST ONE FRIEND
Comprehension Test A

Directions: Read each question carefully. Circle the letter of the choice that best answers each question.

1. Who wrote this book?
    a. Lynn Hall   *b.* Lynne Reid Banks   *c.* Elizabeth Enright

2. Dory wanted _____ to be her best friend.
    a. Meredith   *b.* Jeckel   *c.* Robin

3. Robin's best friend was _____.
    a. Meredith   *b.* Doreen   *c.* Eldean

4. In sixth grade, Doreen was _____.
    a. sent to a special school
    b. mainstreamed
    c. placed in a resource room for three periods a day

5. Doreen's goal after graduation was to become a _____.
    a. secretary   *b.* waitress   *c.* nurse

6. Mrs. Osborne washed and dried Dory's dress for the fair and offered her _____.
    a. a pair of matching sandals
    b. a bubble bath
    c. lunch

7. Meredith didn't watch Robin and Jeckel in the dog show because she _____.
    a. fell asleep
    b. was flirting with a boy
    c. was busy brushing her hair and putting on makeup

8. On the first day of high school, Dory _____.
    a. had to have Robin help her all day
    b. stayed home because she was too scared to go
    c. found her classes by herself

9. Dory's cottage parents were Mr. and Mrs. _____.
    a. Joker   *b.* Card   *c.* Ace

10. Meredith's parents thought her death was _____.
    a. murder   *b.* due to carelessness   *c.* a terrible accident

JUST ONE FRIEND
Comprehension Test B

Directions: Read each question carefully. Circle the letter of the choice that best answers each question.

1. This story is told from the point of view of _____.
   a. Dory   b. Robin   c. Meredith

2. Dory thought she was _____.
   a. talented   b. popular   c. dumb

3. This story takes place in Nordness, _____.
   a. Indiana   b. Illinois   c. Iowa

4. In eighth grade, Doreen was _____.
   a. sent to a special school
   b. mainstreamed
   c. placed in a resource room for three periods a day

5. Doreen's brother was sent to the Boys Training School because he was caught _____.
   a. breaking into the school building to steal money from the office
   b. robbing a convenience store
   c. stealing cars

6. Robin's father paid Dory's way into the fair because _____.
   a. it was her reward for helping train Jeckel
   b. it was her birthday
   c. he didn't think she could afford it

7. Dory begged Eldean _____.
   a. to pull the wires in Meredith's car so it wouldn't run
   b. for money to buy a new dress for the first day of school
   c. to take her to the school and show her around

8. Dory had a nervous breakdown and got sent to the _____.
   a. State Training School for Girls
   b. state penitentiary
   c. state mental hospital

9. Dory's mother was _____.
   a. schizophrenic   b. abusive   c. an alcoholic

10. Doreen lost a lot of weight when _____.
    a. her mother's AFDC checks stopped coming
    b. she had her nervous breakdown
    c. she became anorexic

JUST ONE FRIEND
Comprehension Test C

Directions: Read each question carefully. Circle the letter of the choice that best answers each question.

1. Robin trained Jeckel to be a good _____.
   - *a.* show dog
   - *b.* cattle herding dog
   - *c.* coon hunting dog

2. Dory's brother was named _____.
   - *a.* Eldean
   - *b.* Elvis
   - *c.* Elfred

3. Dory remembered how embarrassed she felt on the first day of school when she _____.
   - *a.* threw up on the teacher's desk
   - *b.* wet her pants
   - *c.* fell face down in a mud puddle at recess

4. Doreen decided she couldn't drop out of school because she wanted to be better than her _____.
   - *a.* brothers and sisters
   - *b.* mother
   - *c.* friends

5. Doreen decided the most important thing she had to do was _____.
   - *a.* learn to coon hunt so she could earn some money
   - *b.* find out how to be popular in her new school
   - *c.* break up Robin and Meredith's friendship

6. At the dog show, Robin and Jeckel won _____.
   - *a.* third place
   - *b.* second place
   - *c.* first place

7. Dory hit Meredith while she was driving and _____.
   - *a.* the car slid into a ditch
   - *b.* Meredith said she'd never take Dory riding again
   - *c.* they got suspended for fighting

8. Meredith died from _____.
   - *a.* asthma
   - *b.* asphyxiation
   - *c.* acute appendicitis

9. When Dory was talking to her counselor, she kept losing her train of thought because the counselor _____.
   - *a.* wrote things down
   - *b.* kept interrupting
   - *c.* kept answering the phone

10. Dory discovered that _____ wanted her for a friend.
    - *a.* Lori
    - *b.* Robin
    - *c.* Wendy

JUST ONE FRIEND

I. *Directions:* Dory yearned for just one friend. The friend she wanted lived just down the road, but Dory would have traveled a long way to visit a friend. Help Dory reach her goal by drawing a continuous line through all the words that describe her.

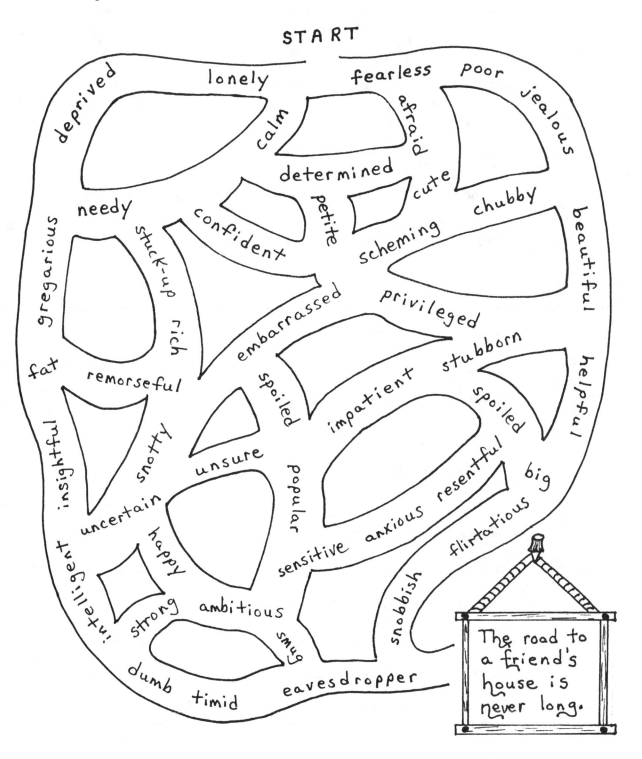

II. What does this saying mean to you? Write your answer on a separate sheet of paper.

PROJECTS FOR *JUST ONE FRIEND*

Directions: Choose one of the following projects or design your own. If you design your own project, fill out the form below and submit it to your teacher for approval.

1. Write a diary entry for the first day of school from Robin's or Meredith's point of view.

2. Doreen was desperately lonely and needed someone to talk to. What if she had written to "Dear Abby" for advice? Write this letter for Dory.

3. If Dory had found enough courage, what could she have done when she and Eldean were standing inside the school and a teacher came up and told them that students were not allowed in the building until the next day? Rewrite this scene using dialogue and narration.

4. Prepare a bibliography of other books about adolescents coming to terms with their problems. Include at least ten books in this bibliography.

5. What if Dory had advertised in the newspaper for a friend? Write this ad for her.

6. What if Dory received three new outfits when she was released from the State Training School for Girls? Draw three outfits on a large sheet of paper. Color the designs.

PROJECT PROPOSAL

Name _____ Beginning Date _____ Completion Date _____

Describe the project in detail: _____
_____

Why do you want to do this project? _____
_____

What will the final product be? _____
_____

How will you share your final product? _____
_____

Comments: _____
_____

LEIF THE UNLUCKY
Comprehension Test A

Directions: Read each question carefully. Circle the letter of the choice that best answers each question.

1. Who wrote this book?
   a. Erik Christian Haugaard   *b.* Wilson Rawls   *c.* Lloyd Alexander

2. A *hird* is a _____.
   a. flock of sheep   *b.* group of children   *c.* litter of puppies

3. As soon as Leif set eyes on _____, he knew they were enemies.
   a. Egil   *b.* Flose   *c.* Bjarne

4. Leif said he made a cairn to bury the old people so _____.
   a. they wouldn't come back to haunt anyone
   b. he could inherit their money
   c. the foxes wouldn't make a meal of them

5. What covered the windows of the house?
   a. sheep's bladders   *b.* glass   *c.* oil cloth

6. Ingeborg's father thought that showing affection was the sign of a _____.
   a. weakling   *b.* strong man   *c.* kind person

7. Why did Egil capture Ulv?
   a. to bring Leif out of hiding
   b. to offer him as a human sacrifice
   c. to force Ingeborg to marry him

8. Why did Egil demand a meeting with Leif at the pass?
   a. so he could tease and taunt him
   b. so his hird could raid Leif's home
   c. to give him one last chance to give up

9. Why had Bera never liked her brother Egil?
   a. He always bossed her around.
   b. He reminded her of their weak-willed father.
   c. He killed her pet sparrow when she was young.

10. Who called Leif Magnusson, Lief the Unlucky?
    a. Leif   *b.* Odd   *c.* Egil

LEIF THE UNLUCKY
Comprehension Test B

Directions: Read each question carefully. Circle the letter of the choice that best answers each question.

1. This story is told from the point of view of _____.
   - *a.* Erik the Red
   - *b.* Leif Magnusson
   - *c.* Ingeborg Gudrinsdaughter

2. Ravn Eriksen was Leif Magnusson's _____.
   - *a.* uncle
   - *b.* father
   - *c.* cousin

3. Where did Odd get the firebow he used to start fires?
   - *a.* from the little people
   - *b.* from a ghost
   - *c.* from old Mother Hildegun

4. Why did Egil and his hird raid Leif's farm while he was away?
   - *a.* to take the tools
   - *b.* to steal some hay
   - *c.* to rustle the cattle

5. What position did Gunner Ulfson hold that Egil wanted?
   - *a.* King of Greenland
   - *b.* Earl of Norway
   - *c.* Chieftain of Brattahlid

6. Egil wanted the Norsemen to stop worshipping Christ and return to the worship of _____.
   - *a.* Zeus and Isis
   - *b.* Odessa and Venus
   - *c.* Odin and Thor

7. Ingeborg insulted Egil by saying that his great-grandfather was _____.
   - *a.* a thief
   - *b.* a cattle rustler
   - *c.* born a slave

8. Why did Magnus Eriksen die?
   - *a.* He died of a broken heart.
   - *b.* He died of the plague.
   - *c.* He was mortally wounded during a robbery.

9. Egil got Geir from Gardar to do what he wanted by _____.
   - *a.* promising him Isafjord
   - *b.* using blackmail
   - *c.* making him fear Egil's temper

10. What was the Tinge?
    - *a.* the general store where everyone gathered to gossip
    - *b.* where the wisest and most powerful men met to decide law and justice
    - *c.* a private school for the children of rich landholders

LEIF THE UNLUCKY
Comprehension Test C

Directions: Read each question carefully. Circle the letter of the choice that best answers each question.

1. The people of Greenland kept waiting for _____.
- *a.* warmer weather and good crops
- *b.* a rise in the prices of goods they exported
- *c.* a longship from Norway

2. Why was Leif so angry when a servant broke the wooden handle of one of the rakes?
- *a.* he didn't have enough money to buy a new one
- *b.* the servant had been warned not to be so clumsy
- *c.* there were no trees nearby

3. Who did Leif want for his friend?
- *a.* Odd   *b.* Egil   *c.* Bjarne

4. Ingeborg sent _____ to warn Leif that Egil would try to kill him.
- *a.* Katla   *b.* Bera   *c.* Ingrid

5. The boats of the little people were _____.
- *a.* kayaks   *b.* canoes   *c.* pontoons

6. Who was the last Christian in Greenland?
- *a.* Ingeborg Gudrinsdaughter
- *b.* Olaf Ulfson
- *c.* Magnus Eriksen

7. Why did Ingeborg's father visit his dead brother's hut?
- *a.* to steal the silver cross he wore around his neck
- *b.* to pay his last respects
- *c.* to hold a wake

8. Odd's father died _____.
- *a.* of a broken heart
- *b.* while defending Leif's father
- *c.* in a boating accident

9. Berserks were _____.
- *a.* Norsemen who killed for pleasure
- *b.* Vikings who sacked and looted
- *c.* people who had become insane

10. How did Egil die?
- *a.* Bera poisoned him.
- *b.* He fell through the ice.
- *c.* Leif killed him in a duel.

LEIF THE UNLUCKY

Directions: Erik the Red and 500 followers settled Greenland in 986. Write a historical figure bio-poem about Erik the Red, his son Leif Erikson, or another famous person in history. In a bio-poem, you are told what to write on each line. First, read all nine lines. Next, read the example. Then, fill in the form to write your own Historical Figure Bio-Poem.

Historical Figure Bio-Poem

Line 1	Historical figure's first name,
Line 2	four adjectives that describe the person,
Line 3	Friend of (2 people),
Line 4	Who liked (3 things),
Line 5	Who felt (3 things),
Line 6	Who feared (3 things),
Line 7	Who wanted to see (3 things),
Line 8	Resident of (city, state and/or country),
Line 9	Person's last name.

Example

Christopher,

Curious, adventuresome, bold, dauntless,

Friend of King Ferdinand and Queen Isabella,

Who liked adventure, exploration, and sailing,

Who felt frustrated that it took so long to get money for his voyage, anxious to find a new route to Asia, determined to prove he could reach Asia by sailing west,

Who feared running out of food and water on the voyage, violent storms, mutiny by the crew,

Who wanted to see the voyage end in success, gold and riches in the new land, honors given to him when he returned to Spain,

Resident of Spain,

Columbus.

_____,

_____, _____, _____, _____,

Friend of _____ and _____,

Who liked _____, _____, and _____,

Who felt _____, _____, _____,

Who feared _____, _____, _____,

Who wanted to see _____, _____, _____,

Resident of _____,

_____.

PROJECTS FOR *LEIF THE UNLUCKY*

Directions: Choose one of the following projects or design your own. If you design your own project, fill out the form below and submit it to your teacher for approval.

1. Make costumes for Leif and Ingeborg. Display the costumes on Barbie™ and Ken™ dolls or other larger dolls. As an alternative, take an old pillow case, draw Leif and Ingeborg on one side, stitch the outlines, cut around the outlines, and stuff with batting. Display the costumes on these figures.

2. Pretend that you live in Greenland at the same time as Leif and Ingeborg. Prepare a family tree. Remember that sons take the father's first name and add "son" to get their last name. Daughters take their mother's first name and add "daughter" to get their last name. For example, Leif's father was Magnus, so Leif became Leif Magnusson. Ingeborg's mother was Gudrin, so Ingeborg became Ingeborg Gudrinsdaughter.

3. Both Ingeborg and Bera wanted to marry Leif. Leif became uncertain about who he wanted to marry. What if Ingeborg hadn't died? Write about this love triangle and how it might have been resolved.

4. Leif couldn't find out how to make iron. How did people make iron in the fourteenth century? Research this topic and write a step-by-step description of the process.

PROJECT PROPOSAL

Name _____ Beginning Date _____ Completion Date _____

Describe the project in detail: _____

_____

Why do you want to do this project? _____

_____

What will the final product be? _____

_____

How will you share your final product? _____

_____

Comments: _____

_____

M.C. HIGGINS, THE GREAT
Comprehension Test A

Directions: Read each question carefully. Circle the letter of the choice that best answers each question.

1. Who wrote this book?
   a. Paula Danziger   *b.* Virginia Hamilton   *c.* Lois Lowry

2. How did M.C. hope to move his family off the mountain?
   a. by trapping animals and selling their hides for money
   b. by getting a summer job and saving his money
   c. by helping his mother become a famous singer

3. How did M.C. get the pole that he loved to sit on?
   a. It was the prize for winning the spelling bee.
   b. It was the prize for a talent contest.
   c. It was the prize for swimming the Ohio River.

4. Why did James K. Lewis come up Sarah's Mountain?
   a. to get Banina's voice on tape
   b. to try to buy the mining rights from Jones
   c. to film M.C. doing stunts on his pole

5. Why did M.C. bring Lurhetta home after they went through the tunnel?
   a. because she was hungry
   b. to meet his mother and father
   c. to show her how to climb the pole

6. Why were the Killburns said to be witchy?
   a. They had twelve fingers and twelve toes.
   b. They had yellowish skin, red hair, and gray eyes.
   c. Both of the above.

7. James K. Lewis told M.C. that Banina wouldn't fit on a stage because _____.
   a. they'd try to change her   *b.* she was too fat   *c.* she was too shy

8. Lewis told M.C. that he never _____.
   a. sold many taped songs
   b. earned much with his cassette
   c. paid people very much to sing into his recorder

9. What did Jones give M.C. to help make the wall strong?
   a. the pole   *b.* Great-grandmother Sarah's gravestone   *c.* car parts

10. Ben's father put green _____ in a barrel in the barn.
    a. snakes   *b.* tomatoes   *c.* apples

M.C. HIGGINS, THE GREAT
Comprehension Test B

Directions: Read each question carefully. Circle the letter of the choice that best answers each question.

1. What did the initials M.C. stand for?

   a. Michael Crawford   *b.* Moses Corey   *c.* Mayo Cornelius

2. Who was M.C.'s best friend?

   a. Ben Killburn   *b.* Ben Kettle   *c.* Ben Killdare

3. Which of M.C.'s relatives ran away from slavery and came to live on the mountain?

   a. his Great-great-grandfather Lewis

   b. his Great-grandmother Sarah

   c. his Grandfather Jones

4. How many brothers and sisters did M.C. have?

   a. two   *b.* three   *c.* four

5. When M.C. brought Lurhetta home, she told Jones that _____.

   a. her name was Lurhetta Outlaw

   b. she was a runaway

   c. she was running from the law

6. Ben took Lurhetta to his house because she said she needed _____.

   a. food   *b.* water   *c.* a telephone

7. What did Lurhetta leave M.C. when she left the mountain?

   a. her tent   *b.* money to pay for lunch   *c.* her knife

8. Ben told M.C. and Lurhetta there were _____ children living on the mound.

   a. 13   *b.* 23   *c.* 33

9. M.C. caught a _____ in one of his traps and freed it.

   a. skunk   *b.* squirrel   *c.* coon

10. Members of Ben's family were _____.

    a. farmers

    b. miners

    c. teachers

M.C. HIGGINS, THE GREAT
Comprehension Test C

Directions: Read each question carefully. Circle the letter of the choice that best answers each question.

1. Why did M.C. want to move his family off the mountain?
   a. The pile of rubble left from strip mining made the area dangerous.
   b. He wanted to go live in town and get his own car.
   c. He wanted to travel and see more of the world.

2. M.C. wasn't allowed to go near the Killburns because they were said to be _____.
   a. witchy   *b.* afflicted   *c.* mean

3. Who held the title to the part of the mountain slope M.C. and his family lived on?
   a. the mining company   *b.* his father   *c.* the town of Harenton

4. Why did M.C. and Lurhetta almost drown going through the tunnel?
   a. She wanted to be the leader.
   b. She panicked when the fish touched her.
   c. She couldn't swim.

5. Why did three Killburn men come to M.C.'s house?
   a. to deliver ice   *b.* to cast a spell   *c.* to pick a fight

6. Ben's mother fed them _____ pie hot from the oven.
   a. peach   *b.* pumpkin   *c.* sweet potato

7. M.C. started building a wall because _____.
   a. he was angry with Lurhetta and had to keep busy
   b. he wanted to prove to Jones that he could do it
   c. he wanted something big between him and the spoil

8. M.C. told Jones that next summer he wouldn't be able to baby-sit his brothers and sisters because _____.
   a. he was moving to town
   b. he was running away
   c. he was going to get a job

9. M.C. came to realize that his family will never _____ Sarah's Mountain.
   a. own   *b.* move away from   *c.* farm

10. This book won the _____ .
    a. Library Association Award   *b.* Newbery Medal   *c.* Caldecott Medal

M.C. HIGGINS, THE GREAT

I. *Directions:* Read the statements below. Put an *F* in front of those that state a fact and an *O* in front of those that express an opinion.

_____ *1.* Mayo Cornelius Higgins was thirteen years old.

_____ *2.* M.C. Higgins, the Great loved his nickname.

_____ *3.* M.C.'s friend Ben had six fingers on each hand.

_____ *4.* Ben and his family were witchy.

_____ *5.* M.C. and his family lived on Sarah's Mountain.

_____ *6.* M.C. thought living in the mountains was boring.

_____ *7.* M.C. regretted not having a TV.

_____ *8.* Ben was M.C.'s friend.

_____ *9.* M.C. won his pole by swimming the Ohio River.

_____ *10.* James K. Lewis thought M.C.'s mother had a wonderful voice.

II. *Directions:* Write your answers to the following questions. Use a separate sheet of paper.

1. M.C. was afraid the pile of rubble might break loose and bury his home and family. Do you think building a wall was the best solution to this problem? Why or why not?

2. What do you predict M.C.'s life will be like when he is ten years older?

3. Ben and his family live on a small flat area in the mountains. Now they are able to grow enough food for the entire family, but what do you think will happen when the family doubles in size in a few years?

4. What if Ben was the new kid at your school? You and your classmates notice that he has six fingers on each hand. How does this make you feel? How will you treat Ben? What questions will you ask him? If you had to change places with Ben, how would you want others to treat you? Would you have surgery so you would look like the others?

_____

Illustration based on a popular hoop toy from the 1870s. If you found this Rabbit-in-Hoop toy in good condition today, you could sell it for a great deal of money. It is considered to be a rare toy.

PROJECTS FOR *M.C. HIGGINS, THE GREAT*

Directions: Choose one of the following projects or design your own. If you design your own project, fill out the form below and submit it to your teacher for approval.

1. Reread the description in Chapter 12 of what Lurhetta described as being the biggest cobweb she ever saw. Use string to recreate what you think this web looked like. Use wooden blocks for the houses and attach your string web to these houses. Place the houses and web in a shallow cardboard box filled with tamped-down dirt. Add Play-Doh® shaped like vegetables. Then, add plastic figures to represent the children picking vegetables from the web.

2. What if a terrible rainstorm occurred when M.C. was almost finished building the wall? Write what you think would have happened to M.C. and his family if the pile of rubble broke loose.

3. There are no illustrations in the book. Pick your favorite scene and illustrate it. Add a caption describing the scene.

4. Write a report telling about the environmental effects of strip mining. Explain why the water in the stream was yellow, the vegetables smaller, the deer and rabbits scarcer.

5. Mountain folklore abounds with riddles. Make up a riddle that M.C. could have written. Read it to your class to see if anyone can solve it.

PROJECT PROPOSAL

Name _____ Beginning Date _____ Completion Date _____

Describe the project in detail: _____

_____

Why do you want to do this project? _____

_____

What will the final product be? _____

_____

How will you share your final product? _____

_____

Comments: _____

_____

Section 3

FAVORITE BOOKS
FOR
NOVEMBER

The following books are on "November Book List B" in *Ready-to-Use Reading Activities Through the Year.*

Activity Sheets	Book Title	Reading Level	Award
3-1 to 3-5	*The Great Gilly Hopkins*	5	Newbery Medal
3-6 to 3-10	*How to Eat Fried Worms*	4.4	
3-11 to 3-15	*Sarah, Plain and Tall*	3.5	Newbery Medal
3-16 to 3-20	*Tales of a Fourth Grade Nothing*	4.9	

The Great Gilly Hopkins by Katherine Paterson.
New York: Dell, 1978. 148 pages.

Galadriel Hopkins keeps getting shuffled from one foster home to another because she is so unmanageable and rebellious. When Gilly moves in with Mrs. Maime Trotter, she feels the protective shell she has built around herself starting to crack. She comes to love Trotter and William Ernest, Trotter's other foster child. Just when Gilly begins putting down roots, she is uprooted yet one more time to go live with her lonely grandmother. When Gilly finally meets her mother, who abandoned her at birth, Gilly discovers that the way she always imagined her was just a fairy tale. Gilly calls Trotter and asks to come home, but Trotter tells her she *is* home.

How to Eat Fried Worms by Thomas Rockwell.
New York: Dell, 1973. 127 pages.

When Alan says he'll bet Billy fifty dollars that he can't eat fifteen worms in fifteen days, Billy laughs it off. Then, he thinks about the minibike he wants to buy. He takes Alan's bet. At first, just the thought of actually eating a worm grosses him out. After the first few, however, it gets easier. Alan begins worrying that Billy might win. He starts trying to cheat. Family, friends, neighbors, and the family doctor get drawn into the boys' hilarious antics. When the contest is finally over, guess what Billy is hooked on!

Sarah, Plain and Tall by Patricia MacLachlan.
New York: Harper, 1985. 58 pages.

Jacob and his children Anna and Caleb have been terribly lonely since his wife and their mother died. Jacob's friend encourages him to place an advertisement for a wife in a newspaper. Sarah, a spinster from Maine, answers the ad and comes for a month's visit "just to see." Sarah brings warmth, laughter, and singing back into their lives. Near the end of her visit, Sarah drives the wagon into town alone. Jacob, Anna, and Caleb spend the day wondering if Sarah, who misses the sea and the people she left behind, will buy a train ticket home or return to them to share their life on the prairie. The reader shares Jacob's, Anna's, and Caleb's joy when Sarah returns and explains that no matter how much she misses all she left behind, she'd miss *them* more if she didn't stay.

Tales of a Fourth Grade Nothing by Judy Blume.
New York: Dell, 1972. 124 pages.

Peter's biggest problem comes in a small package. The problem answers to the name of Fudge. Fudge has a knack for making Peter's life miserable. He flies off the jungle gym while Peter is baby-sitting, he embarrasses Peter in public, he ruins a school project, and he eats Peter's pet turtle. As if these weren't bad enough, Fudge is such a cute two-and-a-half-year-old that he not only gets all the attention, but also gets hired to make the TV commercial that Peter was hoping to get. It's all too much for Peter. He ends up feeling like a real nothing.

THE GREAT GILLY HOPKINS
Comprehension Test A

Directions: Read each question carefully. Circle the letter of the choice that best answers each question.

1. Who wrote this book?

    a. Judy Blume   *b.* Katherine Paterson   *c.* Paula Danziger

2. Why had Gilly been in three foster homes in less than three years?

    a. She kept running away.

    b. Her foster mothers kept having nervous breakdowns.

    c. She was too hard to manage.

3. How many boys did Gilly beat up when they were trying to get their basketball back?

    a. six   *b.* four   *c.* eight

4. Gilly found two five-dollar bills _____.

    a. in William Ernest's toy box

    b. in Mr. Randolph's encyclopedia

    c. in Mrs. Trotter's cookie jar

5. Mr. Randolph wanted to shock his son by wearing a tie with _____.

    a. neon-colored stripes and squiggles

    b. goldfish in an aquamarine pool

    c. fat ballet dancers in purple tutus

6. How did Trotter know Gilly was at the bus station?

    a. The police phoned her.

    b. The clerk who sold Gilly a ticket called her.

    c. Trotter followed her in a taxi.

7. Why did Mr. Randolph move into Trotter's house right before Thanksgiving?

    a. He got the flu.

    b. He was hiding from his lawyer son.

    c. He was evicted from his house.

8. When Gilly wrote to her mother saying her situation was desperate, _____.

    a. her mother arranged for Gilly to go live with her grandmother

    b. her mother ignored her

    c. her mother called the social worker and complained about Trotter

9. Gilly discovered that her mother's brother _____.

    a. had been killed in Vietnam

    b. had also run away from home

    c. was coming for a visit at Christmas

10. Gilly thought her mother looked like a _____.

    a. fairy princess   *b.* flower child gone to seed   *c.* Hollywood glamour queen

THE GREAT GILLY HOPKINS
Comprehension Test B

Directions: Read each question carefully. Circle the letter of the choice that best answers each question.

1. What was Gilly's real name?

    a. Galanna Hinton   *b.* Galadriel Hopkins   *c.* Galinda Hunter

2. When Gilly moved in with Mrs. Trotter, who was the foster child already living in the house?

    a. William Ernest   *b.* Everett Scott   *c.* Nevil Desmond

3. Mrs. Trotter got angry when she thought Gilly _____.

    a. made fun of Mr. Randolph

    b. called William Ernest retarded

    c. stole money at school

4. Gilly's plan to find more money could be summed up in one word: _____.

    a. Agnes   *b.* gum   *c.* dust

5. Gilly stole over a hundred dollars from _____.

    a. the church collection plate

    b. Mrs. Trotter's purse

    c. Mr. Randolph's checking account

6. Why didn't Trotter want Miss Ellis to take Gilly away?

    a. She didn't want to lose the monthly check.

    b. She needed a baby sitter for William Ernest.

    c. Trotter needed Gilly.

7. Who came to visit on Thanksgiving Day?

    a. Mr. Randolph's lawyer son

    b. Miss Ellis, the social worker

    c. Gilly's grandmother

8. Gilly called her grandmother _____.

    a. Nanny   *b.* Grams   *c.* Nonnie

9. When William Ernest came home from school with a bloody nose, Trotter said _____.

    a. it made her prouder than a punch-drunk pickle

    b. it made her madder than a hissing polecat

    c. it made her sadder than a weeping willow

10. Gilly's mother came home for Christmas because _____.

    a. Gilly's grandmother sent her the money

    b. Trotter threatened to take her to court in a custody battle

    c. she wanted to take Gilly back to California to live with her

THE GREAT GILLY HOPKINS
Comprehension Test C

Directions: Read each question carefully. Circle the letter of the choice that best answers each question.

1. Who was Gilly's social worker?

   a. Mrs. Dixon   *b.* Ms. Richmond   *c.* Miss Ellis

2. Mrs. Trotter said Mr. Randolph could flatter the stripe off a _____.

   a. zebra   *b.* barber pole   *c.* polecat

3. Why did Gilly make a card for Miss Harris that called her a bad name?

   a. She was bigoted.

   b. Agnes dared her to do it.

   c. Miss Harris treated her like everyone else.

4. Gilly made William Ernest a _____.

   a. paper airplane

   b. batch of chocolate chip cookies

   c. kite

5. Gilly tried to buy a bus ticket to go visit her real mother in _____.

   a. San Francisco, California

   b. Miami, Florida

   c. Phoenix, Arizona

6. Trotter kissed Gilly on the forehead when Gilly said she was going to _____.

   a. clean the house without expecting to be paid

   b. teach William Ernest to defend himself

   c. stop getting into trouble at school and raise her grades

7. When did Gilly realize that she wanted to stay with Trotter and William Ernest?

   a. when Trotter said she could go if she wanted

   b. when her grandmother said she's get her out of there soon

   c. when Miss Ellis told Gilly she'd found a nice home for her

8. Gilly couldn't move into her mother's old room because everything was _____.

   a. old and out of style   *b.* pink and perfect   *c.* dirty

9. Gilly first met her mother _____.

   a. in the airport   *b.* at Nonnie's house   *c.* at the bus station

10. Gilly phoned Trotter and told her she wanted to come home, but Trotter said _____.

    a. she was already home

    b. a new kid had her old room

    c. they didn't want her back

THE GREAT GILLY HOPKINS

I. *Directions:* Put the events in the correct order. The numeral *1* has been placed next to the event that happened first. Continue numbering the events.

__1__ Gilly's foster mother Mrs. Richmond enters the hospital with a bad case of nerves.

_____ Gilly writes a card to Miss Harris calling her a bad name.

_____ Gilly bribes Agnes to keep her mouth shut.

_____ Gilly reads poetry to Mr. Randolph.

_____ Gilly meets her mother for the first time.

_____ Gilly's grandmother arrives to take her to live in Jackson, Virginia.

_____ Mrs. Trotter faints and pins Gilly to the floor.

_____ William Ernest gets a bloody nose at school.

_____ Gilly realizes that she wants to stay with Trotter.

_____ Gilly writes a letter to her mother saying she is in desperate need of being rescued from a religious fanatic and a retarded boy.

II. *Directions:* Write your answers to the following questions. Use a separate sheet of paper.

1. When Gilly was wondering what would happen to Agnes, she thought, "Would she stomp herself angrily into the floor, or would someone's kiss turn her magically into a princess? Alas, Agnes, the world is woefully short of frog smoochers." What do you think this last sentence means?

_____

_____

2. When Miss Ellis came to tell Gilly she was going to live with her grandmother, her voice was "bright and fake like a laxative commercial." Why do you think Miss Ellis was talking this way? How do you think Gilly felt when she heard this fake voice?

_____

_____

3. How do you think Gilly will act now that Trotter has told her that her home is with her grandmother?

_____

_____

ART 7

PROJECTS FOR *THE GREAT GILLY HOPKINS*

Directions: Choose one of the following projects or design your own. If you design your own project, fill out the form below and submit it to your teacher for approval.

1. Gilly chose a gaudy tie for Mr. Randolph to wear in order to shock his lawyer son. The tie had 4-inch-high fat ballet dancers in purple tutus pirouetting on a greenish background. Design another gaudy tie for Mr. Randolph.

2. Gilly loved bubble gum. Pretend you are Gilly and write a poem titled "Ode to Gum." (An ode is a poem, rhymed or unrhymed, addressed to a person or thing and dignified in style.)

3. Gilly made William Ernest a paper airplane that soared higher and further than any others she had ever made. Design a paper airplane that can fly "as high as a housetop." If you need help with the design, read *The Paper Airplane Book* by Seymour Simon (New York: Viking Press, 1971).

4. Illustrate the following:
   a. Gilly's mother
   b. Trotter, when she fainted and fell on top of Gilly
   c. Trotter, William Ernest, and Mr. Randolph all looking like three-day-old death

---

PROJECT PROPOSAL

Name _____ Beginning Date _____ Completion Date _____

Describe the project in detail: _____

_____

Why do you want to do this project? _____

_____

What will the final product be? _____

_____

How will you share your final product? _____

_____

Comments: _____

_____

HOW TO EAT FRIED WORMS
Comprehension Test A

Directions: Read each question carefully. Circle the letter of the choice that best answers each question.

1. Who wrote this book?
   - *a.* Wilson Rawls
   - *b.* Thomas Rockwell
   - *c.* Matt Christopher

2. The bet was for _____ dollars.
   - *a.* 100
   - *b.* 50
   - *c.* 25

3. Where did the boys dig up the first worm?
   - *a.* by the creek
   - *b.* from under a big rock
   - *c.* in a manure pile

4. How was the first worm cooked?
   - *a.* fried
   - *b.* fricasseed
   - *c.* boiled

5. Where was the first worm eaten?
   - *a.* in the garage
   - *b.* in the barn
   - *c.* in the basement

6. What did Billy's father eat when he was in college?
   - *a.* a live crayfish
   - *b.* a live snake
   - *c.* fifty live goldfish

7. One rule stated that the worms could not be _____.
   - *a.* left whole
   - *b.* chopped up
   - *c.* glued together

8. The eleventh worm was made into _____.
   - *a.* Whizbang Worm Delight
   - *b.* Baked Alaskan Worm Dessert
   - *c.* Mississippi Mud Worm Pie

9. The thirteenth worm was eaten _____.
   - *a.* raw
   - *b.* boiled
   - *c.* grilled

10. Alan tried to trick Billy into giving up by sending a fake _____.
    - *a.* note from the school nurse
    - *b.* telegram from the coroner
    - *c.* letter from the family doctor

HOW TO EAT FRIED WORMS
Comprehension Test B

Directions. Read each question carefully. Circle the letter of the choice that best answers each question.

1. Tom got sent to bed because he wouldn't _____.
   a. eat salmon casserole for supper
   b. clean his room
   c. take out the trash

2. According to the bet, the person eating the worms had to eat one once a _____.
   a. month   b. day   c. week

3. Why did the boys choose a huge night crawler?
   a. so Billy couldn't gulp it down
   b. so it had to be cut into bites
   c. both of the above

4. What was put on the first worm so the first few bites would go down easier?
   a. mayo, honey, salt, and pepper
   b. mustard, ketchup, horseradish, and lemon
   c. chocolate, sugar, cinnamon, and maple syrup

5. What was the word Tom whispered in Billy's ear so he would eat a worm?
   a. minibike   b. bicycle   c. skateboard

6. Who did Billy's father call at 3:30 A.M.?
   a. 911   b. Poison Control   c. Dr. McGrath

7. What did Mrs. Forrester agree to do when Alan and Joe had to go out of town?
   a. make sure Billy ate a worm a day
   b. eat the worms herself
   c. tell Billy the bet was off

8. Who kept gnawing his thumbnail?
   a. Tom   b. Joe   c. Alan

9. Why did Tom use a siren to wake up the neighborhood?
   a. so they would get mad at Alan and Joe
   b. so they could witness Billy eating the thirteenth worm
   c. so they would demand that the bet be called off

10. What did Alan try to substitute for worm fifteen?
    a. beans   b. spaghetti   c. salami

HOW TO EAT FRIED WORMS
Comprehension Test C

Directions: Read each question carefully. Circle the letter of the choice that best answers each question.

1. Alan bet _____ that he couldn't eat fifteen worms.

    a. Joe   *b.* Billy   *c.* Tom

2. Which two boys were going to provide the worms?

    a. Alan and Joe   *b.* Tom and Billy   *c.* Alan and Tom

3. Why did Billy do push-ups, knee bends, and jumping jacks before the start of the contest?

    a. He was preparing himself to eat a worm.
    b. He was trying to make himself throw up.
    c. He was getting ready to run away.

4. Joe said crazy people are like dogs—if they see you're afraid, they'll _____.

    a. drool on you   *b.* role over and play dead   *c.* attack

5. Why did Alan call Joe O'Hara in the middle of the night?

    a. He just thought of a sneaky trick to play on Billy.
    b. He needed to be reassured that he wouldn't lose the bet.
    c. He wanted to ask Joe for money.

6. On the day of the ninth worm, what trick did Alan and Joe try to play on Billy?

    a. They substituted a rubber worm.
    b. They substituted a snake.
    c. They glued two worms together.

7. The tenth worm was made into _____.

    a. spaghetti with wormballs
    b. wormloaf with mushroom sauce
    c. Alsatian smothered worm

8. The twelfth worm was made into a _____.

    a. peanut butter jelly-and-worm sandwich
    b. toasted-cheese-and-worm sandwich
    c. bacon-lettuce-tomato-and-worm sandwich

9. When Billy, Tom, Alan, and Joe were fighting, who got hit over the eye with a rock?

    a. Alan   *b.* Tom   *c.* Billy

10. How did Billy figure out that something had been substituted for worm fifteen?

    a. He burped beans.
    b. He belched red peppers.
    c. He threw up piccalilli.

HOW TO EAT FRIED WORMS

Directions: Some words from the story are hidden in the puzzle. Find the hidden words and circle them. You may go across and down.

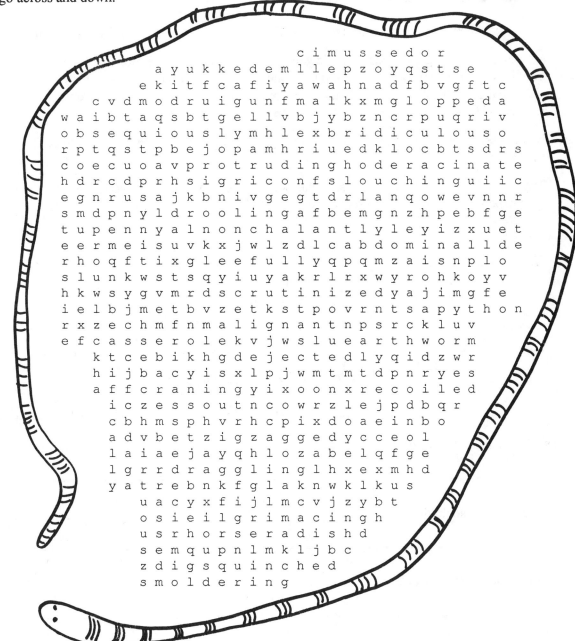

grimacing	fricasseed	treacle	protruding	drooling
slouching	craning	cistern	mealybugs	deracinate
obsequiously	embarrassed	autopsy	gleefully	clambering
recoiled	smoldering	fulmar	slunk	glopped
beatifically	cavorting	worchestershire	python	tupenny
disdainfully	secrete	piccalilli	dejectedly	zigzagged
yukked	anxious	maraschino	horseradish	malignant
casserole	igloo	earthworm	dribbled	paralysis
furtively	mussed	squinched	nonchalantly	abdominal
draggling	geez	scrutinized	ridiculous	virtuous

PROJECTS FOR *HOW TO EAT FRIED WORMS*

Directions: Choose one of the following projects or design your own. If you design your own project, fill out the form below and submit it to your teacher for approval.

1. Write a cookbook featuring at least twenty different worm dishes. Illustrate your cookbook.

2. Answer the following questions. What do you think is a really revolting thing to eat? How much money would it take to get you to eat it? What if someone was actually willing to make a bet with you? Would you take the bet? Tell why or why not. If you would take the bet, write diary entries telling about your actions and thoughts while the bet is on. Include the recipes you used during the bet.

3. Put on a skit reenacting a scene from the book. (You may substitute spaghetti or licorice for the night crawlers.)

4. Prepare a television commercial to "sell" this book to others. You have 60 seconds for the commercial. Videotape your commercial and show it to your class.

5. Create a worm word search.

6. Create a worm maze.

PROJECT PROPOSAL

Name _____ Beginning Date _____ Completion Date _____

Describe the project in detail: _____
_____

Why do you want to do this project? _____
_____

What will the final product be? _____
_____

How will you share your final product? _____
_____

Comments: _____
_____

SARAH, PLAIN AND TALL
Comprehension Test A

Directions: Read each question carefully. Circle the letter of the choice that best answers each question.

1. Who wrote this book?
    - a. Patricia MacLachlan
    - b. Cynthia Voight
    - c. Lila Perl

2. Mama died shortly after _____.
    - a. Anna was born
    - b. Caleb was born
    - c. they moved to the prairie

3. Sarah Wheaton from Maine answered the ad, saying she had always loved _____.
    - a. to live by the sea
    - b. to be single and independent
    - c. working hard and traveling

4. Sarah asked Jacob Witting if he had opinions on _____.
    - a. independent females
    - b. cats
    - c. mild-mannered females

5. Sarah's cat was named _____.
    - a. Seal
    - b. Porpoise
    - c. Fog

6. Who loved Sarah first?
    - a. Anna and Caleb
    - b. Lottie and Nick
    - c. Jacob and Jack

7. Sarah and William used to slide down a dune into the _____.
    - a. sea
    - b. pond
    - c. lake

8. Maggie told Sarah that no matter where you are _____.
    - a. there are always things to miss
    - b. you can make new friends
    - c. you can feel at home

9. Why did Anna, Caleb, Sarah, and Jacob sleep in the barn with all the animals?
    - a. because of the tornado
    - b. because of the squall
    - c. because of the hurricane

10. When Sarah went to town, she told Caleb and Anna to take care of _____.
    - a. each other
    - b. her chickens
    - c. Seal

SARAH, PLAIN AND TALL
Comprehension Test B

Directions: Read each question carefully. Circle the letter of the choice that best answers each question.

1. The family's two dogs were named _____.
    a. Rick and Nettie
    b. Mick and Lettie
    c. Nick and Lottie

2. Jack was Papa's _____.
    a. horse that he'd raised from a colt
    b. mule that he'd bought for $1
    c. best friend that he'd known since they were kids

3. Papa placed an ad in the newspaper for a _____.
    a. housekeeper   b. governess   c. wife

4. Anna wanted Papa to write Sarah and ask if she _____.
    a. cooks   b. sings   c. sews

5. Sarah agreed to visit the Wittings for one _____ to see how things went.
    a. week   b. month   c. year

6. What did Sarah hang from the ceiling to dry?
    a. flowers   b. wet clothes   c. herbs

7. Sarah's brother was a _____.
    a. carpenter   b. farmer   c. fisherman

8. Maggie gave Sarah _____.
    a. sheep and herbs
    b. chickens and plants
    c. a cat and a quilt

9. Sarah wanted to learn how to _____.
    a. ride a horse
    b. drive a wagon
    c. ride a horse *and* drive a wagon

10. Caleb told Sarah the thing missing from her drawing of the fields was _____.
    a. flowers
    b. the colors of the sea
    c. the animals and the birds

SARAH, PLAIN AND TALL
Comprehension Test C

Directions: Read each question carefully. Circle the letter of the choice that best answers each question.

1. Anna told Caleb she would have named him _____.
   a. Mettlesome   b. Troublesome   c. Pesky

2. Papa said he didn't sing the old songs anymore because _____.
   a. Caleb and Anna couldn't carry a tune
   b. the piano was out of tune
   c. he'd forgotten them

3. Why did Anna seem to have a grudge against her brother?
   a. He asked too many questions.
   b. He was a pest and got into everything.
   c. Their mother died right after he was born.

4. Sarah's favorite colors were _____.
   a. blue, gray, and green   b. green, gold, and blue   c. red, white, and blue

5. Sarah brought Anna and Caleb gifts _____.
   a. she made herself   b. from a department store   c. from the sea

6. Sarah said her brother William was _____.
   a. handsome and medium height
   b. short and fat
   c. plain and tall

7. Sarah taught Anna and Caleb to swim in the _____.
   a. creek   b. cow pond   c. river

8. Sarah told Papa she could help repair the roof because _____.
   a. she was not afraid of heights
   b. she loved an excuse to wear overalls
   c. she was a good carpenter

9. When Sarah went to town, Papa cautioned her _____.
   a. not to pick up any strangers
   b. to be home before dark
   c. to drive slowly

10. Sarah said although she'd always miss her own home, she wouldn't leave because _____.
    a. she'd miss Papa, Anna, and Caleb more
    b. she couldn't get along with her brother's new wife
    c. she didn't have enough money to buy a train ticket home

SARAH, PLAIN AND TALL

I. *Directions:* Below are sentences taken from the story. Read each sentence carefully. One word in each sentence is underlined. There are three words below each sentence. One of these words is a synonym for the underlined word. A synonym is a word that has almost the same meaning as the underlined word. Write the letter of the synonym on the blank before each sentence.

_____ 1. It was <u>dusk</u> and the dogs lay before him on the warm hearthstone.
   a. morning   *b.* noon   *c.* evening

_____ 2. I had gone to bed thinking how <u>wretched</u> he looked.
   a. pitiful   *b.* appealing   *c.* handsome

_____ 3. "I am good at <u>sums</u> and writing," said Sarah.
   a. division   *b.* addition   *c.* subtraction

_____ 4. "I am <u>sly</u> too," said Sarah stubbornly.
   a. stubborn   *b.* determined   *c.* tricky

_____ 5. I shook my head, <u>weary</u> with Caleb's questions.
   a. tired   *b.* entertained   *c.* puzzled

II. *Directions:* Write a letter to Sarah. Tell her about yourself. Ask her questions you would like answered. Use a separate sheet of paper.

III. *Directions:* Write your answers to each of the following questions.

1. How are Sarah and Jacob different?

_____

_____

2. How are Sarah and Jacob alike?

_____

_____

3. Do you think Sarah and Jacob will have a happy marriage? Why or why not?

_____

_____

_____

PROJECTS FOR *SARAH, PLAIN AND TALL*

Directions: Choose one of the following projects or design your own. If you design your own project, fill out the form below and submit it to your teacher for approval.

1. Write the advertisement that Jacob placed in the newspaper.

2. The author "paints" a story of loneliness, longing, and warmth using few words. Her spare prose is like a watercolor picture with soft, blurred images inviting us to fill in the details with our imagination. Choose a scene from the story and write it in the form of a play. Fill in the details with dialogue and narration.

3. Write about the wedding scene using the same spare writing style as the author.

4. Sarah hung flowers from the ceiling to dry. Look in gardening books to find out which flowers retain their color when dried in this manner. Pick some of these flowers and hang them to dry. Then, make a small bouquet that Anna and Caleb might have given Sarah.

5. Since spices were often expensive and hard to find, cooks often used herbs to flavor dishes. List several herbs Sarah would probably have had in her kitchen herb garden. Tell how she could preserve the herbs for use in the winter. Give recipes for two dishes that Sarah would likely have made.

PROJECT PROPOSAL

Name _____ Beginning Date _____ Completion Date _____

Describe the project in detail: _____

_____

Why do you want to do this project? _____

_____

What will the final product be? _____

_____

How will you share your final product? _____

_____

Comments: _____

_____

TALES OF A FOURTH GRADE NOTHING
Comprehension Test A

Directions: Read each question carefully. Circle the letter of the choice that best answers each question.

1. Who wrote this book?
   a. Patricia Reilly Giff   *b.* Judy Blume   *c.* Beverly Cleary

2. Peter's biggest problem was _____.
   a. his mother   *b.* his brother   *c.* his father

3. Mr. and Mrs. Yarby seemed to think Fudge and Peter were lacking _____.
   a. enough toys   *b.* books   *c.* good manners

4. Warren Hatcher lost the Juicy-O account because _____.
   a. the Yarbys didn't think he was doing a good job
   b. he couldn't stand the Yarbys
   c. the Yarbys didn't like Peter and Fudge

5. Peter's mother said Sheila was going to be a real beauty, but Peter thought she looked like a _____.
   a. dog   *b.* pig   *c.* monkey

6. Jennie's mother said she couldn't do a thing with her, especially since she's started _____.
   a. biting
   b. holding her breath
   c. throwing temper tantrums

7. What did Fudge smear on the wall of Hamburger Heaven?
   a. mashed potatoes   *b.* peas   *c.* chocolate cake

8. What did Mr. Hatcher cook for supper when Mrs. Hatcher was out of town?
   a. lamb chops and fries
   b. beans and franks
   c. mushroom omelet

9. When they went to the movies, why did Father stuff paper towels up Fudge's pants legs?
   a. so the wet pants wouldn't touch his legs
   b. so he wouldn't make so much noise when he kicked the seat in front of him
   c. so it wouldn't hurt when Fudge kicked people

10. How did Fudge get to the hospital?
    a. in a taxi
    b. in an ambulance
    c. Mr. Hatcher carried him

TALES OF A FOURTH GRADE NOTHING
Comprehension Test B

Directions: Read each question carefully. Circle the letter of the choice that best answers each question.

1. What did Peter Warren Hatcher win at Jimmy Fargo's birthday party?

   a. a goldfish　　　　　*b.* a gerbil　　　　　*c.* a turtle

2. What was Fudge's real name?

   a. Warren Drexel　　　*b.* Farley Henry　　　*c.* Farley Drexel

3. What did Fudge stick all over Mr. Yarby's suitcase?

   a. green stamps　　　　*b.* gum　　　　　　*c.* lollipops

4. When Father had enough of Fudge refusing to eat, he said, _____

   a. "Let him starve."

   b. "Eat it or wear it!"

   c. "Give him a dose of castor oil."

5. What happened to Fudge's two front teeth?

   a. They were knocked out when he tried to fly like a bird.

   b. The dentist pulled them out.

   c. Fudge pulled them out so he could get money from the Tooth Fairy.

6. During the birthday party, who made a puddle in the middle of the floor?

   a. Sam　　　　　　　*b.* Ralph　　　　　　*c.* Jennie

7. Fudge ruined the Flying Train Committee's _____.

   a. booklet　　　　　　*b.* poster　　　　　　*c.* notes

8. Peter decided he was a fourth grade nothing when Fudge _____.

   a. got a part in a movie

   b. got a part in a TV commercial

   c. got his name in the newspaper

9. Why did Fudge run off in the middle of the movie?

   a. He wanted to touch the bears on the screen.

   b. He wanted Peter to play hide-and-seek with him.

   c. He wanted some more popcorn and candy.

10. Why did Mrs. Hatcher get upset with people at the hospital?

    a. They wouldn't treat Fudge because the Hatchers didn't have insurance.

    b. They were very slow and kept the Hatchers waiting.

    c. They kept laughing at Fudge.

TALES OF A FOURTH GRADE NOTHING
Comprehension Test C

Directions: Read each question carefully. Circle the letter of the choice that best answers each question.

1. Who was Henry Bevelheimer?
   a. Peter's fourth grade teacher
   b. the elevator operator
   c. the family doctor

2. Where did Mrs. Hatcher find part of her missing flowers?
   a. in Fudge   b. in the garbage   c. in Dribble's bowl

3. When Fudge thought he'd made someone so mad they were about ready to kill him, _____.
   a. he patted their face and laughed
   b. he smiled and showed his dimples
   c. he kissed them and looked lovable

4. Why don't the leaves in New York City turn red, yellow, and orange in the fall?
   a. There's too much air pollution.
   b. They don't get enough sunlight.
   c. It's too far north.

5. After Fudge lost his teeth, Peter started calling him _____.
   a. Dracula   b. Fang   c. Vampire

6. Who did Fudge kick in the face?
   a. the dentist   b. Peter   c. the shoe salesman

7. What did Fudge do with Peter's sharp scissors?
   a. cut up all of Peter's socks
   b. cut his hair
   c. cut up Peter's books

8. Janet tried to bribe Fudge into cooperating by offering him _____.
   a. crackers   b. money   c. Oreo® cookies

9. Why was Friday, May 10, the most important day of Peter's life?
   a. Fudge ate Dribble.
   b. Dribble had baby turtles.
   c. Peter got a dog.

10. Peter named his new dog _____.
    a. Turtle   b. Dribble   c. Pal

TALES OF A FOURTH GRADE NOTHING

I. *Directions:* Below are sentences taken from the story. First, read each sentence. Next, decide whether the underlined verb is in the present or past tense. Then, write present or past on the blank before each item. The first one is done for you.

past 1. Fudge <u>liked</u> it a lot.

_____ 2. Being nine <u>has</u> its advantages.

_____ 3. Fudge <u>is</u> always in my way.

_____ 4. My mother <u>made</u> a face.

_____ 5. I <u>went</u> into my bedroom.

_____ 6. He <u>knows</u> everybody in the building.

_____ 7. I <u>learned</u> to stand on my head in gym class.

_____ 8. <u>Eat</u> your cereal.

_____ 9. I <u>mopped</u> some blood off Fudge's face.

_____10. My mother <u>dashed</u> in from the kitchen.

II. *Directions:* Draw Dribble crawling from the glass bowl.

III. *Directions:* Below are sentences taken from the story. If the verb is in the present tense, rewrite the sentence in the past tense. If the sentence is in the past tense, rewrite the sentence in the present tense.

1. My mother put her arm around me.

_____

2. The teachers were at a special meeting.

_____

3. I live at 25 West 68th Street.

_____

4. He knows everybody in the building.

_____

5. He spends a lot of time watching commercials on TV.

_____

PROJECTS FOR *TALES OF A FOURTH GRADE NOTHING*

Directions: Choose one of the following projects or design your own. If you design your own project, fill out the form below and submit it to your teacher for approval.

1. Draw an X-ray of Fudge showing Dribble in his tummy.

2. Rewrite the scene when Fudge swallows Dribble from Dribble's point of view.

3. Write another adventure for Fudge.

4. Peter, Jimmy, and Sheila had a bad experience while baby-sitting Fudge. Have you ever had a bad, funny, or unusual experience while baby-sitting? Write an anecdote about your experience. Interview others about their baby-sitting experiences. Write down these experiences and compile them into a book.

5. Make a poster giving baby-sitting tips. If you need help, read *Baby-Sitting for Fun and Profit* by Rubie Saunders (New York: Pocket Books, 1984).

6. Read about Judy Blume. Write a bio-poem about this popular author.

7. Make a crossword puzzle about Judy Blume's books.

PROJECT PROPOSAL

Name _____ Beginning Date _____ Completion Date _____

Describe the project in detail: _____

_____

Why do you want to do this project? _____

_____

What will the final product be? _____

_____

How will you share your final product? _____

_____

Comments: _____

_____

Section 4

FAVORITE BOOKS
FOR
DECEMBER

The following books are on "December Book List B" in *Ready-to-Use Reading Activities Through the Year*.

Activity Sheets	Book Title	Reading Level	Award
4-1 to 4-5	*Anne Frank: Diary of a Young Girl*	8	
4-6 to 4-10	*The Best Christmas Pageant Ever*	3	
4-11 to 4-15	*Johnny Tremain*	5.5	Newbery Medal
4-16 to 4-20	*Racso and the Rats of NIMH*	4	

Anne Frank: Diary of a Young Girl by Anne Frank.
New York: Pocket Books, 1952. 258 pages.

Anne Frank was only thirteen years old when she and her family went into hiding in 1942. They hid in a secret attic in an office building. Some of the people who worked in the building brought them food. The Frank family and four others hid in this secret attic for just over two years before they were found by the Nazis and sent to concentration camps. No one except Mr. Frank survived. Although Anne did not survive, her diary did. Through this diary we see Anne's life set against a background of unbelievably horrific world events. Her daily struggle to survive in the "Secret Annexe" under almost unbearable conditions leads each reader to question if he or she would have had Anne's courage, her determination, and her continued belief in the basic goodness of people.

***The Best Christmas Pageant Ever* by Barbara Robinson.**
New York: Harper, 1972. 80 pages.

The Herdmans are the town terrors. They lie, cheat, steal, set fires, and terrorize kids and adults alike. For years, the library and the church have been safe places to go to be free of the Herdmans. Then, the Herdmans hear a rumor that there is free cake and cookies at church every Sunday. The invasion is on! Not only do they start attending church (some say just so they can steal money from the collection plate), but they take over all the major roles in the Christmas pageant. Next, they invade the library to find out more about the people in the Christmas story. Because of their interpretation of this story, the Christmas pageant is definitely different than in past years. Some say the change is for the better. Others are still in shock and haven't yet regained the power of speech.

***Johnny Tremain* by Esther Forbes.**
New York: Dell, 1943. 269 pages.

Johnny Tremain is a teenage apprentice silversmith in Boston in 1773. When he meets Paul Revere, John Hancock, Sam Adams, and other patriots he becomes caught up in tne events leading to the Revolutionary War. Johnny Tremain lives in dangerous, but highly exciting times. As we follow him on his daring adventures, we gain rare insight into this period of history.

***Racso and the Rats of NIMH* by Jane Leslie Conly.**
New York: Harper, 1986. 278 pages.

Racso runs away from his city home and sets out to find the rats of NIMH. He has heard about this famous community from his father Jenner, who was a former member. Racso wants to find NIMH so he can get an education and become a hero. When he arrives, he quickly learns that his street-smart way of acting and talking does not impress the others. When the community discovers that a dam is being built that will flood their home, they all work together to save not only their home, but the entire valley as well. Racso comes up with the idea to sabotage the computer that will run the dam. The rats take on this dangerous task. They come close to failing, but are helped by an unexpected ally—Jenner. Racso learns what being a hero really means.

ANNE FRANK: DIARY OF A YOUNG GIRL
Comprehension Test A

Directions: Read each question carefully. Circle the letter of the choice that best answers each question.

1. Who wrote this book?
   a. Rita Mickish   *b.* Cynthia Voight   *c.* Anne Frank

2. What name did Anne give her diary?
   a. Buddy   *b.* Kitty   *c.* Pal

3. What caused Anne's family to decide it was time to go into hiding?
   a. The Germans sent a call-up for Anne's father.
   b. The Germans sent a call-up for Anne.
   c. The Germans sent a call-up for Margot.

4. Anne said you only get to know people when you've _____.
   a. had a jolly good row with them
   b. lived under the same roof with them
   c. gone on vacation with them

5. The eighth person to go into hiding with the Franks and Van Daans was _____.
   a. a widowed doctor
   b. a dentist whose wife was out of the country
   c. Harry Goldberg

6. Anne accused Dussel of being small-minded and pedantic. *Pedantic* means _____.
   a. a person who has great learning, but no common sense
   b. a person who is overly concerned with trifling points
   c. both of the above

7. What did Anne do every day to ward off worry and depression?
   a. took Valerian pills   *b.* read a joke book   *c.* exercised

8. Anne was thankful that she had a talent for _____.
   a. writing   *b.* painting   *c.* singing

9. On D-Day, June 6, 1944, the "Secret Annexers" heard General Dwight D. Eisenhower announce that _____.
   a. the Germans had surrendered
   b. Winston Churchill had arrived in Berlin
   c. the invasion had begun

10. On August 4, 1944, the Grüne Polizei raided the "Secret Annexe" and _____.
    a. put all the occupants in prison
    b. sent the occupants to concentration camps
    c. shot all the occupants

ANNE FRANK: DIARY OF A YOUNG GIRL
Comprehension Test B

Directions: Read each question carefully. Circle the letter of the choice that best answers each question.

1. Why was June 12, 1942 special to Anne?
   a. She had a birthday party.
   b. She became a teenager.
   c. Her boyfriend gave her a ring.

2. What type of transportation is *shank's mare?*
   a. one's own legs
   b. riding a horse
   c. riding in a horse-drawn cart

3. Where was the hiding place of the Frank family?
   a. in an abandoned train station
   b. in the attic of Anne's school
   c. in Mr. Frank's office building

4. This story took place in _____.
   a. Berlin, Germany   b. Warsaw, Poland   c. Amsterdam, Holland

5. Anne wrote that she was the first adolescent to become madly interested in _____.
   a. mythology   b. economics   c. world politics

6. Anne's first wish for when she was allowed to go outside again was for _____.
   a. school   b. a long hot bubble bath   c. a big tray of cream cakes

7. Margot said Peter could never be her boyfriend because she wanted her boyfriend to be _____.
   a. rich and powerful
   b. tall and handsome
   c. her intellectual superior

8. April 15, 1944 was an important date to Anne because _____.
   a. the radio announced that England had invaded Holland
   b. Elli and Miep gave Anne her first pair of high heels
   c. Peter kissed her for the first time

9. How many of her own birthdays did Anne celebrate in the "Secret Annexe"?
   a. one   b. two   c. three

10. Hitler declared that _____ were the master race.
    a. Slavs   b. Jews   c. Germans

ANNE FRANK: DIARY OF A YOUNG GIRL
Comprehension Test C

Directions: Read each question carefully. Circle the letter of the choice that best answers each question.

1. As punishment for talking in class, the math teacher made Anne write _____.

   a. 100 sentences stating that she would no longer talk during class

   b. 101 reasons why talking in class was rude

   c. a composition called "The Chatterbox"

2. Harry Goldberg's grandmother did not want him to date Anne because _____.

   a. her family was from the wrong side of the tracks

   b. he was three years older

   c. she didn't think Anne was bright enough

3. What most frightened Anne in the evenings and at night?

   a. the dark   *b.* the silence   *c.* the strange sounds

4. Anne thought her parents _____.

   a. favored Margot over her

   b. were the best parents in the world

   c. were behind the times

5. In June of 1943 all students who wanted to continue school had to _____.

   a. pay a bribe to school officials

   b. pay fees that had tripled since last term

   c. sign a paper saying they were in sympathy with Germany

6. The big disadvantage to keeping cats in the "Secret Annexe" was the _____.

   a. litter box smell

   b. horrible fights they got into

   c. fleas

7. In April of 1944, Anne wrote that it was difficult to get _____ in Holland and the rest of Europe.

   a. shoes   *b.* food   *c.* coffee

8. Anne read fifty pages of *The Emperor Charles V* in five days. It took _____ days to finish the 598-page book.

   a. approximately 40 days   *b.* approximately 60 days   *c.* approximately 80 days

9. Anne's one golden rule was to laugh about everything and to _____.

   a. not bother about the others

   b. not take anything too seriously

   c. keep your troubles to yourself

10. Hitler's "final solution" to the "Jewish question" was _____.

   a. extermination   *b.* deportation   *c.* relocation

ANNE FRANK: DIARY OF A YOUNG GIRL

Directions: Anne Frank said her hobbies and interests were writing, genealogy, history, mythology, reading, art history, and film stars. She longed to be able to visit the library to learn more about each of these interests. Anne couldn't visit the library but you can. Use an almanac, atlas, encyclopedia, and unabridged dictionary to answer the following questions. Write your answers on the lines.

 1. In 1942, who won an Academy Award as best actor? _____

 2. In 1942, who won an Academy Award as best actress? _____

 3. Worldwide depression caused widespread unemployment. How many million people were jobless in Germany in 1932? _____

 4. Anne was born on June 12. This means that her sun sign is _____.

 5. Who won the Nobel Prize for literature in 1942? _____

 6. Who was the father of Queen Elizabeth I of England? _____

 7. When was Johann Wolfgang von Goethe, the German poet, scientist, and novelist, born? _____

 8. The correct spelling of cold cream of potato soup is _____.
     (vichyssoise   vichissoize   vesheswaz)

 9. These twin brothers were nursed by a wolf and grew up to become the founders of Rome. _____

 10. The Greek god of fire and patron of metalworkers was _____.

 11. The common European species of strawberry is _____.

 12. Amsterdam and Rotterdam are both industrial cities. In which direction would you travel if you went from Amsterdam to Rotterdam? _____

 13. Who was the leader of India who was holding a fast in February of 1943? _____

 14. By what name was Casablanca known in medieval times? _____

 15. What does cum laude mean? _____

 16. What was the middle name of American poet Emily Dickinson? _____

 17. What is the name of the one-piece garment worn by citizens of ancient Rome? _____

 18. Which Greek sun god was the patron of prophecy, music, and medicine? _____

 19. Who was the Roman god of agriculture? _____

 20. What was the name of the English monarch who lost the battle of Runnymede and was forced to sign the Magna Carta? _____

PROJECTS FOR *ANNE FRANK: DIARY OF A YOUNG GIRL*

Directions: Choose one of the following projects or design your own. If you design your own project, fill out the form below and submit it to your teacher for approval.

1. On Monday, September 28, 1942, Anne wrote that after arguing with Mrs. Frank, Mrs. Van Daan looked like a coarse red-faced fishwife. Anne wished she could draw her like this. Make the drawing for Anne.

2. What if Anne had been able to hide when the raid on the "Secret Annexe" occurred? Continue her diary from this point until the country is liberated two months later.

3. Take an event in the story and rewrite it in the form of a play. Assign parts, bring in appropriate props, paint scenery, select costumes, and perform the play.

4. Anne was a Gemini. Read about the personality traits of a person born under the astrological sign of Gemini. List those traits displayed by Anne.

5. Make a list of things you would miss if you had to go into hiding like Anne. Make a list of things you would take with you if you were allowed to fill one large school bag and one large shopping bag.

PROJECT PROPOSAL

Name _____ Beginning Date _____ Completion Date _____

Describe the project in detail: _____

_____

Why do you want to do this project? _____

_____

What will the final product be? _____

_____

How will you share your final product? _____

_____

Comments: _____

_____

THE BEST CHRISTMAS PAGEANT EVER
Comprehension Test A

Directions: Read each question carefully. Circle the letter of the choice that best answers each question.

1. Who wrote this book?
   a. Judy Blume   *b.* Judith Viorst   *c.* Barbara Robinson

2. How many Herdman kids were there?
   a. six   *b.* five   *c.* four

3. What was Imogene Herdman really good at?
   a. doing her lessons   *b.* finding out secrets   *c.* softball

4. The angel choir looked good, but they couldn't _____.
   a. get along   *b.* act   *c.* sing

5. Why did the Herdmans start coming to Sunday school in the first place?
   a. They were bored at home.
   b. They needed to supplement their allowance by stealing from the collection plate.
   c. They thought there was free cake, candy, and popcorn balls.

6. While in her hospital bed, Mrs. Armstrong told a group of ladies _____.
   a. the Herdmans wouldn't be in the pageant if she'd still been in charge
   b. the Herdmans should be run out of town
   c. nobody else had the ability to run the pageant

7. Why did the Herdmans want to go to the library for the first time?
   a. to trash it
   b. to look up Herod the king
   c. to drive the librarian nuts

8. For the pageant, Imogene offered to steal _____.
   a. a baby to be Jesus
   b. costumes for the angel choir
   c. candy to give to all the kids

9. Why did the whole congregation show up for the pageant this year?
   a. The Rev. Hopkins threatened to resign if they didn't.
   b. They wanted to see what the Herdmans would do.
   c. Mrs. Armstrong told them to stay home.

10. How did Imogene get a black eye?
    a. Alice finally got up the nerve to hit her.
    b. Mrs. Armstrong hit her with her crutch.
    c. She walked into the corner of the choir-robe cabinet.

THE BEST CHRISTMAS PAGEANT EVER
Comprehension Test B

Directions: Read each question carefully. Circle the letter of the choice that best answers each question.

1. How did the Herdmans set fire to Fred Shoemaker's toolhouse?
   a. They were playing with matches.
   b. They were making fire bombs.
   c. They were playing with a chemistry set.

2. What did Claude Herdman bring to first grade for Show-and-Tell?
   a. their one-eyed cat   *b.* Leroy Herdman's chemistry set   *c.* the fire chief's hat and boots

3. Mrs. Armstrong was the head of anything she belonged to because she _____.
   a. was so good at getting contributions
   b. was so good at giving orders
   c. was so good at organizing things

4. Why wasn't Alberta Bottles asked to whistle "What Child Is This?" for this year's pageant?
   a. Last year, she fainted in the middle of the third verse.
   b. Last year, she threw up in the manger.
   c. Last year, she spit on the minister's son, who was playing Joseph.

5. Who always got to be Mary in the pageant?
   a. Lucille Golden   *b.* Wanda Pierce   *c.* Alice Wendleken

6. What did Gladys and Ollie do while Imogene was snitching money from the collection plate?
   a. stood guard
   b. acted as lookouts
   c. drew mustaches on the disciples in the *Illustrated Bible*

7. The librarian said she'd heard everything there was to hear when _____.
   a. Imogene asked for a library card
   b. Imogene asked about Jesus
   c. Imogene asked where the poetry books were kept

8. On the night of the dress rehearsal, _____.
   a. the ladies let the applesauce cake burn up
   b. someone called the fire department because of smoke in the ladies' room
   c. both of the above

9. What did the Herdman Wise Men bring Jesus?
   a. bath salts and baby oil   *b.* ham   *c.* gold, frankincense, and myrrh

10. What did the Herdmans ask for after the pageant?
   a. ham, candy, and small testaments
   b. a poinsettia plant
   c. a set of Bible-story pictures

THE BEST CHRISTMAS PAGEANT EVER
Comprehension Test C

Directions: Read each question carefully. Circle the letter of the choice that best answers each question.

1. What lesson did the Herdmans learn from the fire?
    a. Don't play with matches and gasoline.
    b. Where there's a fire there are free doughnuts.
    c. Don't admit anything.

2. Why did teachers keep promoting the Herdmans although they never learned anything?
    a. The school never kept anyone back.
    b. Mrs. Herdman went to the School Board.
    c. No teacher wanted two Herdmans in a room the same year.

3. Why couldn't Mrs. Armstrong run the Christmas pageant this year?
    a. She fell and broke her leg.
    b. She knew the Herdman kids wanted to be in it.
    c. She had to break in a new husband.

4. What did Charlie like best about Sunday school?
    a. He learned new songs about Jesus.
    b. There were no Herdmans there.
    c. It gave him a good feeling.

5. Gladys Herdman told Alice Wendleken not to volunteer to be Mary, or _____.
    a. she'd stick beans up her nose
    b. she'd stick a pussy willow down her ear
    c. she'd sic the one-eyed cat on her

6. At the first rehearsal for the pageant, what did the Herdmans hear for the first time?
    a. they were being taken away by Child Welfare
    b. they were welcome to be there
    c. the Christmas story

7. The air in the girls' bathroom was all blue because _____.
    a. Imogene was in there smoking cigars
    b. the ladies sneaked in there to smoke
    c. Imogene was in there smoking cigarettes

8. Why did Mrs. Hopkins get mad at Rev. Hopkins?
    a. He ran out into the street in his pajamas and bathrobe.
    b. He tried to cancel the pageant.
    c. He said the applesauce cake was dry.

9. What did Imogene do during the pageant?
    a. bossed everyone around   *b.* kicked Alice   *c.* cried

10. What was the narrator's name?
    a. Barbara   *b.* Mary   *c.* the story doesn't say

THE BEST CHRISTMAS PAGEANT EVER

I. *Directions:* Hey! Unto you directions are given! Each of the following sentences from the story has spelling, capitalization, and punctuation errors. Rewrite each sentence correctly.

1. the herdman's smoked cigors, and kused there teachers

_____

_____

2. the cat shoot strate up in The air and tore up the rume?

_____

_____

3. Alberta passed out whil whisteling whut child is this!

_____

_____

4. every time you go in the girls rume the air is blu

_____

_____

5. christmas came over imogene all at ounce like a case of chils!

_____

_____

ART 12

II | *Directions:* Write your answers to each of the following questions. Use a separate sheet of paper if necessary.

1. Do you think the Herdmans' lives have been changed because of their participation in the Christmas pageant? Why or why not?

_____

_____

2. Who do you think will run next year's pageant? Why?

_____

_____

PROJECTS FOR *THE BEST CHRISTMAS PAGEANT EVER*

Directions: Choose one of the following projects or design your own. If you design your own project, fill out the form below and submit it to your teacher for approval.

1. Create a puppet show depicting an event in the story. This means you'll have to make the puppets, backdrop, and scenery in addition to writing and performing the skit.

2. Write a new adventure for the Herdman kids.

3. Design a poster for the Christmas pageant starring the Herdman kids.

4. Write a bio-poem about Imogene Herdman.

5. Bake an applesauce cake to share with your class, but don't burn it as the ladies on the pot-luck committee did.

6. Make an "Attack Cat" sign that the Herdmans could put in their weed-covered front yard. Be sure to draw the Herdmans' cat on the sign.

7. What if the Herdmans decided to work together to design their own Christmas card? What do you think it would look like? Make this card.

8. The teacher made a new rule for Show-and-Tell after the Herdmans' cat paid a visit. Make a poster giving at least five rules for Show-and-Tell.

PROJECT PROPOSAL

Name _____ Beginning Date _____ Completion Date _____

Describe the project in detail: _____

_____

Why do you want to do this project? _____

_____

What will the final product be? _____

_____

How will you share your final product? _____

_____

Comments: _____

_____

JOHNNY TREMAIN
Comprehension Test A

Directions: Read each question carefully. Circle the letter of the choice that best answers each question.

1. Who wrote this book?

   a. Esther Forbes   *b.* Scott O'Dell   *c.* Elizabeth George Speare

2. Mr. Lapham's daughter-in-law and her _____ girls lived with him.

   a. seven   *b.* two   *c.* four

3. How did Johnny hurt his hand?

   a. He caught it in the bellows.

   b. The poor quality charcoal caused the fire to flare up.

   c. His hand touched melted silver.

4. Johnny's heart broke and he cried bitterly when _____.

   a. he learned that Mr. Tweedie was to marry Cilla

   b. Isannah screamed and told him she didn't want him to touch her

   c. Mr. Lapham told him to find work elsewhere

5. Johnny got a job _____.

   a. baby-sitting   *b.* setting type   *c.* delivering papers

6. Boston's citizens met at Old South Church to demand that _____.

   a. the English king refund their taxes

   b. the Sons of Liberty be hanged for treason

   c. the ships laden with tea return to England

7. The English Parliament voted to close the port of Boston _____.

   a. until the tea had been paid for

   b. forever

   c. for six months in order to teach the Colonists a lesson

8. When the British caught a Yankee farmer selling their muskets, they _____.

   a. flogged him

   b. tarred and feathered him

   c. put him in the stocks

9. Why did so many British regulars desert?

   a. They were yellow.

   b. They were Whigs.

   c. They wanted to go home.

10. How did Johnny find out the British were moving out for a campaign?

    a. Dove told him.   *b.* Sandy told him.   *c.* Pumpkin told him.

JOHNNY TREMAIN
Comprehension Test B

Directions: Read each question carefully. Circle the letter of the choice that best answers each question.

1. Apprentices were little more than slaves until they had served their masters for _____ years.
   a. seven   *b.* six   *c.* five

2. What did Johnny possess that would prove he was kin to rich Mr. Lyte?
   a. a birth certificate *b.* a letter from his mother *c.* an engraved silver cup

3. Johnny was finally able to talk about his accident to Rab, who _____.
   a. worked for the *Boston Observer*
   b. worked for a shipbuilder
   c. worked for a butcher

4. Which political party believed that taxation without representation was tyranny?
   a. Whigs   *b.* Tories   *c.* Democrats

5. Johnny started learning to use his crippled hand because _____.
   a. he started taking physical therapy
   b. he had to use both hands to control Goblin
   c. he wanted to be a silversmith again

6. When Adams said, "This meeting can do nothing more to save the country," Johnny _____.
   a. blew on the silver whistle
   b. gave a loud war whoop
   c. jumped for joy

7. Why was Johnny jealous of Rab?
   a. Rab had two good hands.
   b. Rab was taller and better built.
   c. Rab and Cilla liked each other.

8. Cilla told Johnny she couldn't marry Rab because _____.
   a. she loved Johnny
   b. Rab didn't treat women well
   c. Cilla Silsbee sounded silly

9. Why were women all over New England letting their pewter be melted?
   a. It could be made into bullets for the minutemen.
   b. Pewter was out of style.
   c. They needed the money it brought.

10. Who was Billy Dawes?
    a. a British officer who led the advance on Lexington
    b. the man who rode with Paul Revere
    c. a deserter who was shot before a firing squad

JOHNNY TREMAIN
Comprehension Test C

Directions: Read each question carefully. Circle the letter of the choice that best answers each question.

1. What famous patriot asked Mr. Lapham to make a sugar basin?
    a. Paul Revere   *b.* John Hancock   *c.* Samuel Adams

2. What master silversmith offered to buy the remainder of Johnny's apprenticeship?
    a. John Coney   *b.* Paul Revere   *c.* John Adams

3. When Johnny applied to John Hancock for work, he was _____.
    a. hired on the spot
    b. sent away
    c. told they would call him if anything came up

4. Which witnesses convinced the judge that Johnny was no thief?
    a. Lavinia Lyte and Rab
    b. Rab and Cilla
    c. Cilla and Isannah

5. What did the Sons of Liberty plan for the night of December 6, 1773?
    a. the Boston Massacre
    b. the midnight ride of Paul Revere
    c. the Boston Tea Party

6. Who rode to New York and Philadelphia with the news of the Boston Tea Party?
    a. Johnny Tremain   *b.* Sam Adams   *c.* Paul Revere

7. Who called Madge a toothsome, plump, suet pudding?
    a. Mr. Tweedie   *b.* Frizel, Junior   *c.* Sergeant Gale

8. James Otis said we would go to war with England so that _____.
    a. a man could stand up
    b. we would no longer suffer English tyranny
    c. we would no longer pay taxes

9. King George was angry because General _____ had not seized Yankee military supplies.
    a. Gale   *b.* Howe   *c.* Burgoyne

10. Where did Aunt Jennifer hide Uncle Lorne when the British came for him?
    a. in a wine barrel
    b. in a feather bed
    c. in the wood pile

JOHNNY TREMAIN

Directions: Below are sentences taken directly from the story. One word in each sentence has been left out. The missing words are in the bowl. First, use a dictionary to learn the definition of each word. Then, write each word on the correct line.

1. Mr. Lyte opened his jeweled snuffbox, took _____, sneezed and blew his nose.

2. He thinks they are white _____ big enough to carry horses off in their talons.

3. But all enjoyed themselves, although Isannah drank herself sick and silly on _____.

4. This money was divided between the owner of the horse and the rider, and Johnny bought himself spurs, boots, and a fur-lined _____, all secondhand.

5. Although too badly injured ever to be skillful again, it was no longer in danger of _____ —as it had been in Johnny's pocket.

6. The five little squabs, three of each kind of pastry, a wreath of jellied eels (because she said it was a specialty of the house), a _____—white bread tied into little knots, buttered and baked.

7. When either cold or excited, his _____ increased.

8. I know it's Lord's Day, but there's a _____ I must have printed and posted secretly tonight.

9. The crowd made way for a _____.

10. . . . Boston was thrown into a _____ of anger and despair.

11. They were planning to put down _____ all right.

12. Ma _____ him.

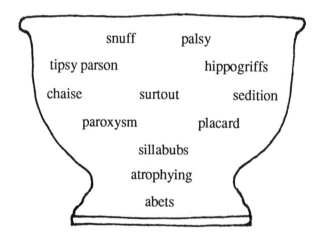

snuff   palsy

tipsy parson   hippogriffs

chaise   surtout   sedition

paroxysm   placard

sillabubs

atrophying

abets

_____

Illustration based on bowl designed by Paul Revere.

PROJECTS FOR *JOHNNY TREMAIN*

Directions: Choose one of the following projects or design your own. If you design your own project, fill out the form below and submit it to your teacher for approval.

1. When Johnny wanted to buy Cilla a picture book to help her learn to read, he chose one on dying martyrs. Was this typical of children's books in 1773? Write a report on the history of children's books.

2. When Lydia tells Johnny that she has scraps of a torn-up letter in her pocket, Johnny says, "Lydia, give me your pocket." Lydia unpins her calico pocket from her waistband and gives it to Johnny. When you read this, did you wonder how she could hand him her pocket? Did you know that pockets were not sewn into clothing until the 1840s? Prepare a report, including illustrations, on how pockets were made and worn before the 1840s. One excellent source is *The Needle Arts* (Alexandria, VA: Time-Life Books).

3. Read the nursery rhyme that begins "Lucy Locket lost her pocket." Copy this nursery rhyme onto a sheet of paper. Next, write another verse for the rhyme. You may find this nursery rhyme in a book such as *Anthology of Children's Literature* by Edna Johnson, Evelyn Sickels, and Frances Sayers (Boston: Houghton Mifflin, 1959).

4. Make a patchwork or embroidered pocket that Lydia or Lucy might have worn.

PROJECT PROPOSAL

Name _____ Beginning Date _____ Completion Date _____

Describe the project in detail: _____

_____

Why do you want to do this project? _____

_____

What will the final product be? _____

_____

How will you share your final product? _____

_____

Comments: _____

_____

RACSO AND THE RATS OF NIMH
Comprehension Test A

Directions: Read each question carefully. Circle the letter of the choice that best answers each question.

1. Who wrote this story?

   a. E.B. White   *b.* Jane Leslie Conly   *c.* Robert C. O'Brien

2. Timothy wanted to become _____.

   a. an engineer   *b.* a teacher   *c.* a doctor

3. When Racso was dragging Timothy on the sling, who found them?

   a. Mrs. Frisby   *b.* the owl   *c.* the rats from Thorn Valley

4. Nolan returned from the river to spread the word that _____.

   a. fish were dying from pollution

   b. Racso was a very good swimmer

   c. Thorn Valley would be under water by Christmas

5. When Racso was paralyzed with fear, Elvira revived him with _____.

   a. horseradish broth   *b.* a slap in the face   *c.* smelling salts

6. Racso's real name was _____.

   a. Otto   *b.* Oliver   *c.* Oscar

7. What did Racso and Isabella cook for Christopher when he was ill?

   a. chicken soup   *b.* mint candy   *c.* herb tea with honey

8. What did the rats erase while they were in the control room at the damsite?

   a. their previous notes

   b. computer disks

   c. all traces that they had been there

9. Who died after causing the power to go out by biting through the rubber on the cable?

   a. Jenner   *b.* Nolan   *c.* Jeremy

10. Lindsey Scott wrote an article hinting that the damage to the dam was caused by _____.

    a. careless workmen

    b. farmers

    c. rats

RACSO AND THE RATS OF NIMH
Comprehension Test B

Directions: Read each question carefully. Circle the letter of the choice that best answers each question.

1. Jeremy couldn't fly Timothy to Thorn Valley because _____.
   a. he was attacked by a cat and couldn't fly for a month
   b. they had a bad argument and were no longer speaking
   c. his mother broke her wing and he had to take care of her

2. Timothy's father, as well as Racso's father, had _____.
   a. run away from home
   b. escaped from a laboratory named NIMH
   c. died in a fire

3. Nicodemus was the founder of the rat community and Hermoine was the _____.
   a. Presiding Rat   b. Queen   c. President

4. Why did Christopher and Racso pick all of Berta's peppermint?
   a. They couldn't read her instructions.
   b. They wanted to make herb tea.
   c. They were mad at her and wanted to get even.

5. Representative Jones had a cousin who _____.
   a. was a newspaper reporter
   b. owned a construction company that was working on the dam
   c. was a weatherman on TV

6. Racso and his partner _____ set out to make a map of the south side of the creek.
   a. Elvira   b. Isabella   c. Martha

7. How did Arthur get copies of the computer manual?
   a. They tore out the necessary pages.
   b. Beatrice helped Arthur take notes from the manual.
   c. Racso taught them to use the photocopier.

8. Who entered the computer room and set the explosive charge?
   a. Nicodemus   b. Timothy   c. Arthur

9. Which rat was sent back to the Fitzgibbon farm with news of the dam?
   a. Timothy   b. Sally   c. Justin

10. What kind of event did the rats hold on September 10 at 10:00 A.M.?
    a. a graduation ceremony for Timothy's class
    b. a memorial service for Jenner
    c. a wedding ceremony for Justine and his bride

RACSO AND THE RATS OF NIMH
Comprehension Test C

Directions: Read each question carefully. Circle the letter of the choice that best answers each question.

1. On the journey to school, Timothy saved _____.
   a. Racso from drowning
   b. acorns for the winter
   c. bits of chocolate bar wrappers

2. When _____ tried to swoop down and spear Racso with its talons, Timothy saved him.
   a. a crow   b. a hawk   c. an owl

3. The head of Rat Security was _____.
   a. Isabella   b. Justin   c. Brendan

4. What were Racso and Christopher going to make with the peppermint?
   a. tea   b. candy   c. potpourri

5. Racso's plan to ruin the dam was to _____.
   a. program the computer to destroy it
   b. drill holes in it
   c. blow it up

6. Why did Lindsey and Jack come to Thorn Valley?
   a. They were covering the dam story.
   b. They were camping.
   c. They were looking for land to buy.

7. How did Racso save Beatrice when the two men trapped her in a trash can?
   a. He wrote a note that said "STOP."
   b. He bit the men.
   c. He made the men chase him around the room.

8. When the power went out at the damsite, what did the workmen shout?
   a. "Run for your lives!"
   b. "Sabotage!"
   c. "Fire! Fire!"

9. Justin announced that he was going to marry _____.
   a. Beatrice   b. Isabella   c. Elvira

10. How did Mrs. Frisby get to and from the ceremony honoring a rat hero?
    a. She walked with a shrew, a mole, and two chipmunks.
    b. She rode in a wagon pulled by a cat.
    c. She flew on Jeremy's back.

RACSO AND THE RATS OF NIMH

I. Directions: Racso loved using backward language. Backward language was a kind of word puzzle. It was easy to figure out if you knew the code, but difficult otherwise. Racso would probably love the following puzzle. In the puzzle we'll give you the consonants R, S, T, L, N, and the vowel E. You have to fill in the missing letters. To help you, each word has been assigned to a category. You guessed it! The categories are in backward language. You have to figure out the categories and then fill in the puzzle. All of the words in the puzzle are from the story.

1. (nosrep) | S | | | E | N | T | | S | T | S |

2. (ecalp) | | N | | E | R | – | | L | | | | | | S | E |

3. (gniht) | | E | | | E | R | | | N | T |

4. (ecalp) | S | T | R | E | | | | E | |

5. (gniht) | | | | L | L | | | E | N |

6. (nosrep) | L | | | R | | T | | R | | | | | R | | E | R |

7. (gniht) | | R | N | – | | | S | | S |

8. (ecalp) | | L | | | R | | N | |

9. (nosrep) | T | E | | | | E | R | S |

10. (gniht) | | | | | | | L | | T | E |

11. (nosrep) | | | | | T | | R |

12. (gniht) | | | | T | | N | | R | |

II. Directions: Make a similar puzzle of ten items on a separate sheet of paper. Don't forget to put the categories in backward language. Exchange your puzzle with a friend.

PROJECTS FOR *RACSO AND THE RATS OF NIMH*

Directions: Choose one of the following projects or design your own. If you design your own project, fill out the form below and submit it to your teacher for approval.

1. Reread the description of the sling that Racso made for Timothy. Make a similar one. You may enlarge the scale.

2. Make the playground equipment the children of NIMH would have used.

3. Make a wicker basket like the one that Isabella tied onto her back as a knapsack.

4. Racso is Oscar spelled backwards. Racso liked using this backward language. He learned it from his father and taught it to Timothy and others at school. Write a letter from Racso to his father in the backward language they liked so much.

5. Make a mobile featuring several of the characters in the story. Hang it from the ceiling of your classroom or the library.

6. Make some peppermint candy to bring to class to share.

7. Make a crossword puzzle about the characters and events in the story.

8. Make a one-minute television commercial about this book. Try to sell others on the idea of reading the book. Videotape your commercial.

PROJECT PROPOSAL

Name _____ Beginning Date _____ Completion Date _____

Describe the project in detail: _____

_____

Why do you want to do this project? _____

_____

What will the final product be? _____

_____

How will you share your final product? _____

_____

Comments: _____

_____

Section 5

FAVORITE BOOKS
FOR
JANUARY

The following books are on "January Book List B" in *Ready-to-Use Reading Activities Through the Year*.

Activity Sheet	Book Title	Reading Level	Award
5-1 to 5-5	*Across Five Aprils*	6	Newbery Honor
5-6 to 5-10	*From the Mixed-Up Files of Mrs. Basil E. Frankweiler*	5.6	Newbery Medal
5-11 to 5-15	*In the Year of the Boar and Jackie Robinson*	5	
5-16 to 5-20	*The Slave Dancer*	5.9	Newbery Medal

Across Five Aprils **by Irene Hunt.**
New York: Berkley Books, 1965. 190 pages.

Jethro Creighton is nine years old in April 1861 when news of the outbreak of the Civil War reaches his family's backwoods farm in southern Illinois. Jethro's family is torn apart as his brothers, cousin, and a beloved family friend leave to join the great cause. The family's grief is deepened when one brother decides to fight for the Confederacy. Jethro has to grow up quickly and accept the responsibilities of a man as he cares for two family farms. He eagerly pores over newspapers and the few letters that get through in an effort to understand the tragedy that is tearing the country apart and costing hundreds of thousands of lives. After four long, hard, desperate years, news reaches them that General Robert E. Lee has surrendered. Their jubilation turns to grief as they learn of the assassination of President Lincoln. Jethro and others had pinned their hopes on Mr. Lincoln's powers to heal old scars and hatreds and to help rebuild a country that had been torn asunder. The future appears frightening and uncertain. The one bright spot in this hour of darkness is that all but one loved one will be coming home to rebuild a future together.

From the Mixed-Up Files of Mrs. Basil E. Frankweiler by E.L. Konisburg. New York: Dell, 1987. 159 pages.

Claudia Kincaid feels that she is being discriminated against. She wonders where it is written that older sisters have to be responsible for younger brothers. She begins thinking of running away in order to teach her parents a lesson. They won't have Claudia to boss around anymore. Thinking of running away progresses into making actual plans. There is one hitch in Claudia's plan, however. Everything costs money and she doesn't have much. When Claudia looks for ways to get money, her eyes light upon her brother Jamie, who is always loaded. She lures him into her plan to run away to The Metropolitan Museum of Art. They put the plan into action and discover that living in the museum is exciting. During the day, they join school groups and take tours so they can learn a little about a lot of things. On one of these tours, they see a little statue of an angel. They learn of the great controversy surrounding this beautiful statue. Did Michelangelo create it or not? Claudia and Jamie set out to discover the true answer to this mystery. A clue leads them to the home of Mrs. Basil E. Frankweiler, who owned the stature before the museum bought it. Mrs. Frankweiler gives them one hour to search through her seventeen file cabinets to see if they can discover the truth. Claudia feels that she must learn the truth because this will allow her to go home feeling different inside. If she can't go home feeling different, she'll always think that running away was just a waste of time. As the clock slowly ticks away the minutes, Claudia becomes more and more driven. Will she discover the answer in time?

In the Year of the Boar and Jackie Robinson by Bette B'ao Lord. New York: Harper and Row, 1984. 169 pages.

Sixth Cousin, a.k.a. Bandit, a.k.a. Shirley Temple Wong, arrives in America in the Year of the Dog. Her mother and father speak English, but Shirley knows only two words. These two words don't help her when she gets lost the very first time she leaves their new apartment or on her first day of school. These two words also don't help her make friends. Shirley's classmates in fifth grade pretty much ignore her, and she has to cope with desperate loneliness. Oh, how she misses her many cousins in China! One day as she is leaving school totally absorbed in thought about how hard it is to be accepted by her classmates, she accidentally collides with Mabel, the biggest, meanest, scariest girl in fifth grade. Mess with Mabel and you get trouble. Shirley's trouble arrives in the form of two fists in her eyes. Shirley's parents get in a flap over her two black eyes and drag her off to the police station so she can tell who attacked her. Shirley sees Mabel following them and refuses to squeal. An amazing thing happens! The next time they meet, Mabel offers friendship rather than fisticuffs. Mabel invites Shirley to play stickball over the protests of their classmates. The protests quiet down after Mabel has a few words with each in turn. Shirley and the rest of the team get caught up in the excitement of the 1947 World Series. They live, eat, breathe, and sleep baseball. They rejoice when Jackie Robinson and the Brooklyn Dodgers win a game and deeply mourn each loss. Even though "de Bums" lose the World Series, Jackie Robinson remains their hero. Imagine their excitement when they learn that their hero is actually going to visit their school! When Shirley hands him the key to P.S. 8, she is filled with pride. Jackie Robinson challenges each student to excel in the future. Shirley thinks that 1947, the Year of the Boar, is also the year when her dreams come true.

The Slave Dancer by Paula Fox.
New York: Dell, 1973. 127 pages.

Jesse Bollier lives with his sister and widowed mother in a poor area of New Orleans. One evening as he is returning home from an errand, he is pressganged and taken aboard a slave ship. He wonders what his kidnappers want with him and why they made sure he brought his fife along. Jesse quickly loses his innocence as the crew introduces him to greed, cruelty, and evil. Each day is torture. Will he ever see his family again? Is there no one on board he can trust? How will he survive this horrible ordeal? Things go from bad to worse when the slaves are brought on board. Over 100 men, women, and children are packed into the hold of the ship like sardines. When Jesse learns how the Captain wants him to use his fife, he is sickened and horrified. How can he possibly play while the slaves are forced to dance? He notices a boy about his own age and wishes they could become friends. Jesse gets his wish. A violent storm hits and the ship goes down. The only two survivors are Jesse and his new friend Ras. The two boys help one another to shore. They are discovered by an old runaway slave. He nurses the boys back to health, arranges for Ras to escape to the North, and shows Jesse the way home. As Jesse grows into manhood, the horrific adventure fades into memory. Only one thing brings back the memories that are almost too painful to bear—Jesse can't stand hearing music.

ACROSS FIVE APRILS
Comprehension Test A

Directions: Read each question carefully. Circle the letter of the choice that best answers each question.

1. Who wrote this book?
   - *a.* Scott O'Dell
   - *b.* Irene Hunt
   - *c.* John Steinbeck

2. Shadrach Yale was a _____.
   - *a.* schoolmaster
   - *b.* doctor
   - *c.* general

3. Bill Creighton and Wilse Graham both thought war would be fought mostly because of _____.
   - *a.* greed
   - *b.* slavery
   - *c.* ignorance

4. Which Creighton brother fought on the Confederate side?
   - *a.* Eb
   - *b.* John
   - *c.* Bill

5. People said that General Grant's initials stood for _____.
   - *a.* Uncle Sam
   - *b.* United States
   - *c.* Unconditional Surrender

6. Why did someone burn the Creightons' barn and put coal oil in their well?
   - *a.* because Matt wouldn't pay a gambling debt
   - *b.* because their son was a Johnny Reb
   - *c.* because everyone hated the Creighton family

7. After learning that her brother had been killed, Jenny lost _____.
   - *a.* her childish ways
   - *b.* her dreams of the future
   - *c.* her hope of getting away from the farm

8. What began pouring into Illinois during the winter of 1862?
   - *a.* refugees
   - *b.* deserters
   - *c.* renegades

9. Why did the newspaper editor escort Jenny to Washington, D.C.?
   - *a.* to meet the President
   - *b.* to speak before a congressional committee
   - *c.* to see Shadrach

10. William Tecumsah Sherman wired Lincoln, "_____ is ours and fairly won."
    - *a.* Atlanta
    - *b.* Mobile
    - *c.* Nashville

ACROSS FIVE APRILS
Comprehension Test B

Directions: Read each question carefully. Circle the letter of the choice that best answers each question.

1. In 1852, three of Ellen Creighton's children died of a disease called _____.

  a. paralysis   *b.* bubonic plague   *c.* typhoid

2. Who was Jethro's favorite brother?

  a. Eb   *b.* Bill   *c.* Tom

3. How did the Confederates start the war?

  a. by firing on the White House

  b. by firing on the Capitol

  c. by firing on Fort Sumter

4. Tom wrote that many froze to death because they _____.

  a. had never received winter gear

  b. threw away their blanket rolls and heavy coats

  c. ran out of wood for the fire

5. Jethro had to become the man of the family when he was only _____.

  a. ten   *b.* nine   *c.* eleven

6. Tom Creighton was killed at _____.

  a. Bull Run on December 25

  b. Fort Sumter on November 11

  c. Pittsburgh Landing on April 6

7. Why did Sam Gardiner shoot Guy Wortman in the behind with buckshot?

  a. He broke into Sam's store to vandalize it.

  b. He stole Sam's best horse.

  c. He tried to elope with Sam's daughter.

8. How much did Hig Phillips pay someone to go to war for him?

  a. $3,000   *b.* $300   *c.* $30,000

9. Where did John meet up with Bill?

  a. across enemy lines

  b. in a prisoner-of-war camp

  c. in the deserters' campground

10. Which state was the first to ratify the thirteenth amendment?

  a. Missouri

  b. Pennsylvania

  c. Illinois

ACROSS FIVE APRILS
Comprehension Test C

Directions: Read each question carefully. Circle the letter of the choice that best answers each question.

1. Jethro was _____ years old when the Civil War began.

   a. nine   *b.* ten   *c.* eleven

2. At Bull Run, the first battle of the war, _____.

   a. there was a standoff

   b. Confederate troops had Union troops scurrying to safety

   c. the North took the South "by the britches"

3. Ellen was addicted to _____.

   a. the caffeine in coffee

   b. chewing tobacco

   c. sweets

4. Why did the men in the general store give Jethro a bad time?

   a. because he knocked over their checkers

   b. because they hated all kids

   c. because they knew his brother was fighting with the Rebs

5. Why did ruffians throw a bundle of switches into the Creightons' yard?

   a. to try to set the house on fire

   b. to challenge Jethro to fight

   c. as a sign of punishment to come

6. What did Dave Burdow send Jethro on the day of the barn-raising?

   a. two carpenters   *b.* a team and wagon   *c.* a load of logs

7. Shadrach thought General McClellan was _____.

   a. afraid of something

   b. the best general in the Union Army

   c. the equal of Robert E. Lee

8. Why did representatives of the Federal Registrars come to the Creighton farm?

   a. to take supplies for the army

   b. to draft Jethro

   c. to look for Eb Carron, who had deserted

9. When Jethro needed help to decide what to do about Eb, he wrote to _____.

   a. Ulysses S. Grant   *b.* Abraham Lincoln   *c.* Robert E. Lee

10. Who was "Mr. Big" with Ol' Abe?

    a. Grant   *b.* Sherman   *c.* McClellan

ACROSS FIVE APRILS

I. *Directions:* Column A contains words from the story. Match each word to its correct meaning in Column B.

Column A

_____ 1. comeuppance
_____ 2. delinquent
_____ 3. prophetic
_____ 4. perplexities
_____ 5. gangrene
_____ 6. feint
_____ 7. parry
_____ 8. denounced
_____ 9. nullification
_____ 10. jubilantly
_____ 11. gimcracks
_____ 12. ne'er-do-well
_____ 13. terrain
_____ 14. pandemonium
_____ 15. degradation
_____ 16. amnesty
_____ 17. vicious
_____ 18. invective
_____ 19. paeans
_____ 20. permeate

Column B

a. to accuse or blame
b. savage, malicious, spiteful
c. a showy object that is cheap or useless
d. a false attack or blow
e. a violent or wild uproar
f. a foretelling of future events
g. a person who violates the law
h. a song of praise or thanksgiving
i. a lazy or worthless person
j. abusive language or speech
k. to be reduced in honor or quality
l. pardon granted to a person or group
m. something that confuses or bewilders
n. to penetrate or seep through
o. to deflect a blow or weapon
p. a penalty or rebuke that is deserved
q. having great joy
r. a plot of ground
s. infection causing part of the body to rot
t. to deprive of legal force

II. *Directions:* If you had been a twenty-year-old male at the outbreak of the Civil War, would you have fought for the North or the South? Explain your answer on a separate sheet of paper.

III. *Directions:* Write a newspaper headline about an important event in April 1861 or April 1865.

PROJECTS FOR *ACROSS FIVE APRILS*

Directions: Choose one of the following projects or design your own. If you design your own project, fill out the form below and submit it to your teacher for approval.

1. Shadrach taught Jethro about Copernicus and his revolutionary theory that Earth revolves around the sun. Write a report explaining how scientists and others reacted to this theory.

2. What if Jethro had drawn a time line about the Civil War to help his two young cousins understand it better? Make a time line beginning in April 1861, when the Creighton family learned that the war had started, and ending in April 1865 when the war was over.

3. Reread the description of Shadrach's room that had been added onto the school. Make a model of this room and use miniatures to decorate it correctly.

4. Make a model of the jail in Newton.

5. Make a word search using the names of generals and battle sites of the Civil War.

6. The Creighton family was accused of being Copperheads. Write a report about how this term came about and to whom it applied.

PROJECT PROPOSAL

Name _____ Beginning Date _____ Completion Date _____

Describe the project in detail: _____

_____

Why do you want to do this project? _____

_____

What will the final product be? _____

_____

How will you share your final product? _____

_____

Comments: _____

_____

FROM THE MIXED-UP FILES OF MRS. BASIL E. FRANKWEILER
Comprehension Test A

Directions: Read each question carefully. Circle the letter of the choice that best answers each question.

1. Who wrote this book?
   a. Judy Blume   *b.* E.L. Konisburg   *c.* Paula Danziger

2. How did Claudia and her brother get from the train station to The Metropolitan Museum of Art?
   a. by train   *b.* on foot   *c.* by taxi

3. When Jamie found a chocolate bar on the ground, Claudia told him not to eat it because _____.
   a. there might be drugs in it
   b. it was dirty
   c. it might have pins in it

4. Where did the museum's director of public relations send a letter to Claudia and Jamie?
   a. to Mrs. Frankweiler's home
   b. to their post office box
   c. to their home

5. What was the name of Mrs. Frankweiler's butler?
   a. Jeeves   *b.* Parks   *c.* James

6. What was *nouilles et fromage en casserole?*
   a. macaroni and cheese   *b.* chili mac   *c.* cheeseburgers

7. Why didn't Mrs. Frankweiler tell the museum the truth about Michelangelo's sculpture of Angel?
   a. She would rather have the secret.
   b. She was holding out for more money.
   c. Her husband made her promise not to tell.

8. Claudia and Jamie rode home in a _____.
   a. Mercedes   *b.* Rolls Royce   *c.* Jaguar

9. Mrs. Frankweiler regretted not ever _____.
   a. having children
   b. learning how to keep a secret
   c. being able to have fun

10. Sheldon was Mrs. Frankweiler's _____.
    a. lawyer   *b.* accountant   *c.* chauffeur

FROM THE MIXED-UP FILES OF MRS. BASIL E. FRANKWEILER
Comprehension Test B

Directions: Read each question carefully. Circle the letter of the choice that best answers each question.

1. Who was Mrs. Basil E. Frankweiler's lawyer?
   a. Brandenberg   *b.* Lindbergh   *c.* Saxonberg

2. What special item was on display in the Italian Renaissance section of the museum?
   a. a statue of an angel
   b. a sarcophagus
   c. a painting

3. Where did Claudia and Jamie take a bath?
   a. in the men's restroom
   b. in the fountain
   c. in the women's restroom

4. What was Jamie's favorite expression?
   a. "Oh, boloney!"   *b.* "Oh, heck!"   *c.* "Oh, darn!"

5. Mrs. Frankweiler lived in a house that looked like a _____.
   a. museum   *b.* church   *c.* school

6. How did Mrs. Frankweiler get the proof that Michelangelo really did make the statue of Angel?
   a. She stole it.
   b. She won it in a poker game.
   c. She bought it.

7. How old was Mrs. Basil E. Frankweiler?
   a. 92   *b.* 85   *c.* 82

8. The children lived in _____.
   a. Connecticut   *b.* New York   *c.* New Jersey

9. Jamie and Claudia decided to adopt Mrs. Frankweiler as their _____.
   a. mother   *b.* grandmother   *c.* aunt

10. Why was the museum going to increase security?
    a. Someone stole Angel.
    b. Someone robbed the restaurant in the museum.
    c. Someone found a violin case in a sarcophagus.

FROM THE MIXED-UP FILES OF MRS. BASIL E. FRANKWEILER
Comprehension Test C

Directions: Read each question carefully. Circle the letter of the choice that best answers each question.

1. Where did Claudia go when she ran away from home?
   a. The Metropolitan Museum of Art
   b. The New York Public Library
   c. The Smithsonian Institution

2. The $225 statue would be worth millions if it could be proved that it was by _____.
   a. Michelangelo   b. Franz Josef II   c. Leonardo da Vinci

3. What happened to their clothes when Claudia and Jamie did the laundry?
   a. They were stolen.
   b. They shrunk so much they didn't fit any longer.
   c. They turned gray.

4. How did Jamie spend the last of their money?
   a. for a train ticket
   b. for a good meal in a restaurant
   c. for a taxi

5. What fascinated Claudia the most in Mrs. Frankweiler's home?
   a. the black marble bathtub
   b. the antique furniture
   c. the seventeen filing cabinets

6. Mrs. Frankweiler admired Claudia's _____.
   a. lack of emotion   b. hair   c. spirit

7. Mrs. Frankweiler traded Jamie and Claudia information about Angel for _____.
   a. a hug
   b. information about their crazy caper
   c. money

8. Claudia thought Mrs. Frankweiler sold the statue of Angel for the _____.
   a. money   b. publicity   c. excitement

9. Saxonberg was Claudia and Jamie's _____.
   a. godfather   b. grandfather   c. uncle

10. What did the security guards once find on an Etruscan chariot?
    a. a glass eye
    b. a set of false teeth
    c. a hearing aid

FROM THE MIXED-UP FILES OF MRS. BASIL E. FRANKWEILER

I. *Directions:* The author uses many compound words in the story. There are fifty-five compound words hidden in the sarcophagus. Circle the hidden words. You may go across and down.

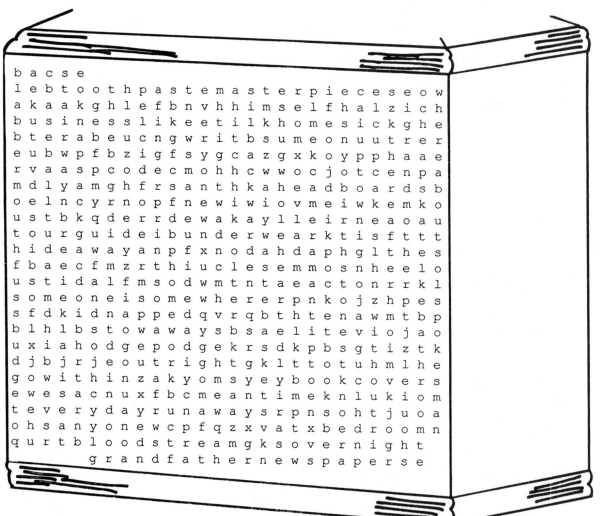

II. *Directions:* Claudia hid her violin case in an ancient Roman sarcophagus. Find an illustration of such a sarcophagus. Draw an appropriate design on the side of the sarcophagus above.

III. *Directions:* Claudia thought of "hushed and quiet words" such as *glide, fur, banana,* and *peace.* On a separate sheet of paper, make two columns. Label the left column "Hushed and Quiet Words" and the right column "Stressful and Loud Words." Write as many words as you can in each column.

PROJECTS FOR *FROM THE MIXED-UP FILES OF MRS. BASIL E. FRANKWEILER*

Directions: Choose one of the following projects or design your own. If you design your own project, fill out the form below and submit it to your teacher for approval.

1. Make a pamphlet featuring your favorite museum.

2. Reread the description of Jamie when Claudia said he looked like a Neanderthal man. Research Neanderthal man. Write a report and draw an illustration of Neanderthal man. Draw Jamie looking like one.

3. When Jamie used a compass, Claudia said no one had done that since Henry Hudson. Write a report about why Henry Hudson's name is connected with Manhattan.

4. Claudia and Jamie researched the life of Michelangelo. Do research of your own and write a report on this famous man.

5. Make a clay model of an ancient Roman sarcophagus. Paint it to look like carved marble.

6. You are a TV newscaster. Interview Claudia and Jamie upon their return home.

7. The story tells us a lot about Claudia and Jamie. Write a bio-poem about one of these characters. Illustrate your poem.

PROJECT PROPOSAL

Name _____ Beginning Date _____ Completion Date _____

Describe the project in detail: _____

_____

Why do you want to do this project? _____

_____

What will the final product be? _____

_____

How will you share your final product? _____

_____

Comments: _____

_____

IN THE YEAR OF THE BOAR AND JACKIE ROBINSON
Comprehension Test A

Directions: Read each question carefully. Circle the letter of the choice that best answers each question.

1. Who wrote this book?
   - *a.* Bette B'ao Lord
   - *b.* S.E. Hinton
   - *c.* Jean Craighead George

2. Sixth Cousin chose the American name _____.
   - *a.* Evelyn Rudi
   - *b.* Deanna Durbin
   - *c.* Shirley Temple

3. Mrs. Rappaport used the long pole behind her desk to _____.
   - *a.* point to places on the large map
   - *b.* open windows
   - *c.* threaten students who misbehaved

4. Shirley became best friends with _____.
   - *a.* Joseph
   - *b.* Mabel
   - *c.* Maria

5. The other kids called Shirley "Apple Shiner" or "Teacher's _____."
   - *a.* Pet
   - *b.* Shadow
   - *c.* Dog

6. Shirley slept in _____.
   - *a.* a closet
   - *b.* her own bedroom
   - *c.* the bathtub

7. Shirley's first job was _____.
   - *a.* bagging groceries at Mr. P's
   - *b.* baby-sitting Sean, Seamus, and Stephen
   - *c.* walking Toscanini every day

8. What part did Shirley have in the school play?
   - *a.* She was an Indian.
   - *b.* She was a turkey.
   - *c.* She was a Pilgrim.

9. Why couldn't Shirley be elected president of the U.S.?
   - *a.* She was a female.
   - *b.* She was not native born.
   - *c.* Her English wasn't good enough.

10. Shirley wanted a _____.
    - *a.* baby brother
    - *b.* perm so her hair looked like Emily's hair
    - *c.* telephone of her own

IN THE YEAR OF THE BOAR AND JACKIE ROBINSON
Comprehension Test B

Directions: Read each question carefully. Circle the letter of the choice that best answers each question.

1. Sixth Cousin was otherwise known as _____.
   a. Precious Coins   *b.* Bandit   *c.* Precious Moments

2. The principal with blue hair assigned Shirley to the _____ grade.
   a. third   *b.* fourth   *c.* fifth

3. Toscanini was a _____.
   a. parrot   *b.* parakeet   *c.* canary

4. Mrs. Rappaport explained that Jackie Robinson was the first African-American to play _____.
   a. basketball   *b.* football   *c.* baseball

5. In order to win the pennant, "de Bums" had to beat the _____.
   a. Cardinals   *b.* Mets   *c.* Yankees

6. Why was a savings account opened for Shirley?
   a. so she could save for a new bike
   b. so she could save for college
   c. so she could save for a trip to China

7. Shirley was going to replace the buttons in the piggy bank with coins by _____.
   a. getting another baby-sitting job
   b. hocking her baseball glove
   c. sharing Emily's lunch so she could keep her own lunch money

8. Shirley and her friends listened to the World Series at _____.
   a. school   *b.* Mabel's house   *c.* Mr. P's

9. Who was elected to represent the sixth grade?
   a. Mabel   *b.* Emily   *c.* Shirley

10. Who illustrated *In the Year of the Boar and Jackie Robinson*?
    a. Maurice Sendack
    b. Marc Simont
    c. Tomie de Paola

IN THE YEAR OF THE BOAR AND JACKIE ROBINSON
Comprehension Test C

Directions: Read each question carefully. Circle the letter of the choice that best answers each question.

1. The house of Wong was in _____.
   a. Chungking   *b.* Peking   *c.* Shanghai

2. Shirley and her mother traveled for a month by boat and landed in _____.
   a. Miami   *b.* Brooklyn   *c.* San Francisco

3. Who was the strongest and scariest girl in all of fifth grade?
   a. Molly   *b.* Mabel   *c.* Maude

4. Jackie Robinson played for the _____.
   a. New York Yankees
   b. New York Giants
   c. Brooklyn Dodgers

5. Why did Shirley put buttons instead of coins in her piggy bank?
   a. to buy candy for the Terrible Threesome
   b. to buy a ticket to a ball game
   c. to bribe Mabel to protect her

6. In order to win the World Series, "de Bums" had to beat the _____.
   a. Cardinals   *b.* Giants   *c.* Yankees

7. Gionfriddo robbed DeMaggio of _____.
   a. a sure home run
   b. his new car
   c. his money and his watch

8. When Mother told Shirley that she was with expectant happiness, this meant that Shirley was _____.
   a. returning home to visit her clan
   b. going to have a new brother or sister
   c. chosen to present the key of P.S. 8 to Jackie Robinson

9. Jackie Robinson challenged the students to _____.
   a. break down barriers
   b. excel
   c. change stereotypes

10. The Year of the Boar was _____.
    a. 1947   *b.* 1941   *c.* 1951

IN THE YEAR OF THE BOAR AND JACKIE ROBINSON

Directions: Shirley, Mable, Tommy, Maria, Joseph, and Irvie loved baseball, especially the Brooklyn Dodgers. They could have answered the following questions. Can you? You may use an encyclopedia, almanac, or other reference material. Write your answers on the lines.

1. Who is said to have invented the game of baseball in Cooperstown, New York? _____

2. When was the first night game played? _____

3. In what year was the first World Series officially held? _____

4. Which New York Yankee was named the Most Valuable Player of the Year in 1947? _____

5. While in college, Jackie Robinson excelled in three sports other than baseball. What were the sports? _____

6. In what year did Jackie Robinson become the first African-American to play on a major league team? _____

7. What was Robinson's batting average from 1947 to 1956? _____

8. When was Robinson elected to the Baseball Hall of Fame? _____

9. In what year was Robinson named MVP? _____

10. How many years after he was inducted into the Baseball Hall of Fame did Robinson pass away? _____

11. Who was the first pitcher to throw a curve? _____

12. When was the first catcher's mask worn? _____

13. When was the National League organized? _____

14. When was the first chest protector worn? _____

15. Where is the Baseball Hall of Fame located? _____

16. Which player is in the record books for Most Runs, Most Runs Batted In, Most Home Runs, Most Bases on Balls, and Most Strikeouts during a World Series (through 1988)? _____

17. Which two men were the National League home run champions in 1947?
_____ and _____

18. Who was the National League batting champion in 1947? _____

19. Which team was the American League pennant winner in 1947? _____

20. Exactly how far is it from home plate to the pitcher's mound? _____

PROJECTS FOR *IN THE YEAR OF THE BOAR AND JACKIE ROBINSON*

Directions: Choose one of the following projects or design your own. If you design your own project, fill out the form below and submit it to your teacher for approval.

1. Write a report about the Chinese practice of binding women's feet. Why did they do this? When did the practice begin? Is it still being done today? When did a girl have her feet bound? What happened to her ability to walk? What is your opinion of this practice?

2. Irvie loved to ask questions about spiders. How many eyes do spiders have? Do spiders eat three meals a day? Where are a spider's ears located? Add at least twelve more questions to this list. Use this list to play a trivia quiz with your classmates.

3. List at least six books about spiders. Include both fiction and nonfiction books on this list.

4. You are a reporter for *The Sporting News*. Your assignment is to write a feature article about the 1947 World Series.

5. Prepare a radio commercial advertising this book.

6. Draw a large baseball glove on a sheet of paper. Make a word search inside the glove.

7. Make a Chinese food dish to bring to class to share.

PROJECT PROPOSAL

Name _____ Beginning Date _____ Completion Date _____

Describe the project in detail: _____

_____

Why do you want to do this project? _____

_____

What will the final product be? _____

_____

How will you share your final product? _____

_____

Comments: _____

_____

THE SLAVE DANCER
Comprehension Test A

Directions: Read each question carefully. Circle the letter of the choice that best answers each question.

1. Who wrote this book?

    a. Esther Forbes   *b.* Emily Cheney Neville   *c.* Paula Fox

2. In the story, pressganged means _____.

    a. kidnapped   *b.* ironed   *c.* flattened

3. How did Captain Cawthorne mark Jesse?

    a. He bit his ear and left a scar.

    b. He cut his cheek.

    c. He flogged him.

4. Why did the captain have Purvis flogged?

    a. for hitting him

    b. for stealing an egg

    c. for leading a mutiny

5. A black person too old to work or who had a physical defect was called a _____.

    a. cabociero   *b.* barracoon   *c.* macaroon

6. Why did the captain have Nicholas Spark thrown overboard?

    a. He incited a riot.

    b. He pointed his pistol at the captain.

    c. He shot a slave.

7. The shackles were removed from the slaves when the ship neared the coast of _____.

    a. Cuba   *b.* Louisiana   *c.* Bermuda

8. Jesse and Ras threw _____ into the water to help keep them afloat.

    a. the lifeboat   *b.* the boom   *c.* a sea chest

9. Arrangements were made to transport Ras _____.

    a. back to Africa

    b. to the North

    c. to Jamaica

10. Jesse would always remember the last fateful voyage of _____.

    a. *The Sharkey*

    b. *The Sundance*

    c. *The Moonlight*

THE SLAVE DANCER
Comprehension Test B

Directions: Read each question carefully. Circle the letter of the choice that best answers each question.

1. Where did Jesse, Betty, and their mother live?
   a. New Orleans   *b.* St. Louis   *c.* Savannah

2. Who tried to make friends with Jesse right after he was brought aboard the ship?
   a. Curry   *b.* Benjamin Stout   *c.* Nick Spark

3. Who did Jesse come to trust?
   a. Curry   *b.* Ned   *c.* Purvis

4. The African chiefs held their captives in a confined place called a _____.
   a. cabociero   *b.* barracoon   *c.* macaroon

5. Why was Jesse forced to play his fife every other morning?
   a. to make the slaves dance
   b. to amuse the captain
   c. to entertain the crew

6. Why did Stout make Jesse go down into the hold?
   a. to spy on the slaves
   b. to look for his fife
   c. as punishment for offending him

7. Why did Captain Cawthorne order the slaves thrown overboard?
   a. He went mad.
   b. He was drunk.
   c. An American ship spotted them.

8. Jesse and Ras were washed up on the beach in _____.
   a. Mississippi   *b.* Cuba   *c.* Louisiana

9. Daniel was _____.
   a. the ship's doctor
   b. a Spanish nobleman
   c. a runaway slave

10. Jesse became apprenticed to _____.
    a. a chandler
    b. an apothecary
    c. a banker

THE SLAVE DANCER
Comprehension Test C

Directions: Read each question carefully. Circle the letter of the choice that best answers each question.

1. Jesse was kidnapped while he was returning home from _____.
   a. school
   b. his job sweeping out the general store
   c. visiting Aunt Agatha

2. The African chiefs sold their people cheaply so they could get _____.
   a. trade goods   b. gold   c. silver

3. Cawthorne filled the hold with nearly _____ slaves.
   a. 50   b. 100   c. 200

4. After leaving Africa, the ship headed for the Portuguese-held island São Tomé to _____.
   a. take on more crew
   b. take on more slaves
   c. take on food and water

5. Why was Jesse flogged?
   a. He stole a loaf of bread.
   b. He refused to play his fife.
   c. He drank an extra ration of water.

6. When Jesse first saw sharks, he said they looked like great white _____.
   a. worms   b. whales   c. maggots

7. An old man named _____ cared for Jesse and Ras after the shipwreck.
   a. Daniel   b. David   c. Dwight

8. As soon as Jesse finished his apprenticeship, he moved to _____.
   a. Africa   b. Rhode Island   c. Cuba

9. In the War Between the States, Jesse _____.
   a. fought on the Confederate side
   b. fought on the Union side
   c. refused to fight

10. After his horrible experience on the ship, Jesse could not _____.
    a. sleep in a bed
    b. stop having nightmares
    c. listen to music

THE SLAVE DANCER

I. *Directions:* Words from the story are hidden in the puffs of smoke. Write the words on the correct lines. You probably remember what each word means from the way it was used in the story, but you may use a dictionary if necessary.

becalmed
cabociero

apothecary
blockade

chandler
mizzenmast

carronade
turbulence
spyglass
jettison
davits

impertinent
envisage
taffrail

keening
impale
dirge

mortify
lament

holystone
revivified
zenith

1. _____ soft sandstone used to scrub a ship's deck
2. _____ motionless due to lack of wind
3. _____ to fix on a sharp stake
4. _____ the mast aft of the mainmast
5. _____ small telescope
6. _____ to prevent entrance or exit
7. _____ to humiliate
8. _____ rail around ship's stern
9. _____ a short, light cannon on a ship's upper deck
10. _____ to throw overboard to lighten the ship
11. _____ a broker
12. _____ violence or disturbance
13. _____ to wail or mourn aloud
14. _____ pair of small cranes used to raise and lower a boat
15. _____ uttering a loud wailing cry
16. _____ restored or revived
17. _____ the highest point
18. _____ druggist
19. _____ merchant who supplies ship's provisions
20. _____ to get a mental picture
21. _____ slow, mournful music
22. _____ rude, saucy

II. *Directions:* In Jesse's day, newspapers ran letters to the editor expressing opinions both for and against slavery. Write a letter to the editor expressing your personal opinion on this issue.

PROJECTS FOR *THE SLAVE DANCER*

Directions: Choose one of the following projects or design your own. If you design your own project, fill out the form below and submit it to your teacher for approval.

1. Write a report on the slave trade.

2. What if Jesse had kept a journal? Write this journal from the time he began the terrible journey until its long-awaited end.

3. Create the front page of a newspaper from the time period of the book.

4. What if Jesse had been interviewed by a reporter as soon as he returned home? Simulate this interview with another class member.

5. Create a newspaper ad for a crew member aboard a slave ship.

6. Dress as Jesse or Ras and tell the story from their point of view.

7. Make a map showing *The Moonlight*'s route from New Orleans to journey's end.

8. Choose a scene from the story to illustrate.

9. Play a tune on a fife. Be sure the tune is appropriate to the time period of the story.

PROJECT PROPOSAL

Name _____ Beginning Date _____ Completion Date _____

Describe the project in detail: _____

_____

Why do you want to do this project? _____

_____

What will the final product be? _____

_____

How will you share your final product? _____

_____

Comments: _____

_____

Section 6

FAVORITE BOOKS
FOR
FEBRUARY

The following books are on "February Book List B" in *Ready-to-Use Reading Activities Through the Year.*

Activity Sheets	Book Title	Reading Level	Award
6-1 to 6-5	*Roll of Thunder, Hear My Cry*	4	Newbery Medal
6-6 to 6-10	*Sounder*	5.2	Newbery Medal
6-11 to 6-15	*To Be a Slave*	5	Newbery Honor
6-16 to 6-20	*With You and Without You*	6	

Roll of Thunder, Hear My Cry **by Mildred D. Taylor.**
New York: Bantam, 1976. 210 pages.

Cassie Logan's great-grandparents were slaves. Her grandparents became land owners, so now she and her family have more independence and security than their sharecropping neighbors. Cassie makes it to fourth grade without learning that she is considered inferior by the white people in the area. When she first encounters unfair treatment, her natural instinct is to fight. When the lynchings, burnings, and killings in her neighborhood escalate, Cassie learns that there are things that have to be borne in order to survive in the South in the 1930s. She learns this lesson well, but her sense of independence and security are changed forever.

Sounder by William H. Armstrong.
New York: Harper and Row, 1969. 116 pages.

Sounder is a coon dog who lives with a poor African-American family. Sounder loves the mother, three young children, and oldest boy, but he belongs heart and soul to the father of the family. When hunting is bad and his family is hungry, the father steals a ham. When the sheriff comes to arrest the father, Sounder tries to protect his beloved master. The family watches in horror as the sheriff shoots Sounder and takes the father away in chains. Hope flares briefly when Sounder gets up from where he has fallen, but then they see how horribly he has been wounded. Sounder disappears into the woods. Now the family is alone. The mother and oldest son eke out a meager living. When the son isn't working in the fields, he goes from work camp to work camp searching for his father. On his journeys, he meets a teacher who befriends him. The strength that his mother instills in him and the new knowledge the teacher imparts to him, help the boy deal with the return of his father and Sounder, who are both heartbreakingly changed. The boy learns to accept the changes.

To Be a Slave by Julius Lester.
New York: Dial, 1968. 156 pages.

The book chronicles the story of slavery using the narratives of former slaves. The reader will be left with a better understanding of slavery from its beginnings until the end of the Civil War and beyond. The thoughts and feelings of former slaves shed the light of truth on this dark period of our country's history.

With You and Without You by Ann M. Martin.
New York: Scholastic, 1986. 179 pages.

When Liza's family learns that Dad has only a few months to live, they vow to make their last Christmas together the best one ever. Dad dies a few months later. Even though the family has had time to prepare for this devastating event, Liza has trouble getting on with her own life. She feels that since Dad isn't around to have any more happy times, no one else should either. She feels guilty for even thinking of doing something that's fun. Her family and friends try to help, but she continues to be racked with guilt. When Marc Radley asks her out the first Christmas after Dad's death, Liza turns him down at first. Slowly she comes to terms with the fact that Dad may be gone physically, but his spirit will be with her and the rest of the family forever. Finally, she learns to have fun and laugh again.

ROLL OF THUNDER, HEAR MY CRY
Comprehension Test A

Directions: Read each question carefully. Circle the letter of the choice that best answers each question.

1. Who wrote this book?

   a. Eve Bunting   *b.* Mildred D. Taylor   *c.* Betty Ren Wright

2. The Logan children attended the _____.

   a. Jefferson Davis County School

   b. Robert E. Lee School

   c. Great Faith Elementary and Secondary School

3. Moe Turner had to walk a total of _____ hours to and from school.

   a. three   *b.* seven   *c.* five

4. Big Mama ironed with _____.

   a. an iron heated in the fireplace

   b. an electric iron

   c. an iron with hot coals placed in the bottom

5. Stacey was whipped for cheating on a test, but the guilty person was _____.

   a. Moe   *b.* T.J.   *c.* Little Willie

6. T.J. tricked Stacey out of _____.

   a. a new pair of pants

   b. his allowance for a whole month

   c. a new wool coat

7. Who shot Papa?

   a. the Wallaces   *b.* Mr. Granger   *c.* T.J. Avery

8. How did Hammer get money to lend to his brother?

   a. He sold drugs.

   b. He sold his car.

   c. He robbed a bank.

9. Why did Mr. Granger order the group of men to go to the Logan place?

   a. to hang Mr. Logan and Mr. Morrison

   b. to burn them out

   c. to fight the fire

10. Who did T.J. bring to the revival?

    a. his girlfriend

    b. Jeremy

    c. Melvin and R.W.

ROLL OF THUNDER, HEAR MY CRY
Comprehension Test B

Directions: Read each question carefully. Circle the letter of the choice that best answers each question.

1. Who preferred to remain on good terms with everyone?
   - *a.* Christopher-John
   - *b.* Cassie
   - *c.* Stacey

2. Which Logan children did Miss Crocker whip with a hickory stick?
   - *a.* Cassie and Stacey
   - *b.* Stacey and Clayton Chester
   - *c.* Cassie and Clayton Chester

3. Papa swung a mean _____.
   - *a.* left hook
   - *b.* switch
   - *c.* belt

4. Uncle Hammer bought a _____ just like the one Mr. Granger had.
   - *a.* house
   - *b.* fur-lined coat
   - *c.* car

5. Mama told Cassie that slaves were taught religion so they _____.
   - *a.* could sing and dance on Sunday
   - *b.* would be obedient to their masters
   - *c.* could be saved

6. What was Mrs. Logan teaching when members of the school board showed up?
   - *a.* Darwin's theory of evolution
   - *b.* the history of slavery
   - *c.* astrology

7. Why did three men shoot Mr. Logan?
   - *a.* He smart-mouthed them.
   - *b.* He got in a fight with them.
   - *c.* He was continuing the boycott.

8. When Kaleb Wallace blocked the road with his truck, Mr. Morrison _____.
   - *a.* picked it up and moved it aside
   - *b.* rammed it off the road with the farm wagon
   - *c.* threw him through the windshield

9. How did Hammer get money to David?
   - *a.* He sent it by a trusted friend.
   - *b.* He brought it in person.
   - *c.* He mailed it.

10. After Mr. Barnett died, T.J. was _____.
    - *a.* lynched
    - *b.* put in jail
    - *c.* tarred and feathered

ROLL OF THUNDER, HEAR MY CRY
Comprehension Test C

Directions: Read each question carefully. Circle the letter of the choice that best answers each question.

1. Who was going to be in Mama's class?
   - *a.* Little Man
   - *b.* Christopher-John
   - *c.* Stacey

2. L.T. Morrison lived with the Logans and worked as a _____.
   - *a.* teacher
   - *b.* hired man
   - *c.* preacher

3. When men in cars arrived in the middle of the night, the family's dog _____.
   - *a.* attacked the first man he came to
   - *b.* hid under the porch
   - *c.* barked and ran around the house

4. In town, Cassie got in trouble with Mr. Barnett and _____.
   - *a.* Mr. Jamison
   - *b.* Miss Crocker
   - *c.* Lillian Jean Simms

5. The Logan family organized _____.
   - *a.* a new political party
   - *b.* a new parent-teacher organization
   - *c.* a boycott

6. Who was instrumental in getting Mrs. Logan fired?
   - *a.* T.J.
   - *b.* Claude
   - *c.* Little Willie

7. When the bank called in his loan, Papa got the money _____.
   - *a.* by selling a few acres
   - *b.* by selling his horse and mule
   - *c.* from his brother

8. Why did Stacey help T.J. home after he was badly beaten?
   - *a.* out of friendship
   - *b.* out of fear
   - *c.* out of stupidity

9. Who saved T.J. when the mob came for him?
   - *a.* Mr. Jamison
   - *b.* Mr. Morrison
   - *c.* Mr. Avery

10. How did the fire start?
    - *a.* Lightning hit a fence post.
    - *b.* T.J.'s former friends set it.
    - *c.* Mr. Logan set it.

ROLL OF THUNDER, HEAR MY CRY

I. *Directions:* Complete each sentence with a word from the butter churn.

1. Christopher-John's whistling was _____ and nervously shrill.

2. He was moody and _____ quiet.

3. No matter how angry Stacey got, T.J. remained _____.

4. T.J. tried to remain on _____ terms with Stacey.

5. When Stacey refused to believe T.J., he eyed him _____ and continued his tale.

6. Cassie thought the Great Faith Elementary and Secondary School was a _____ end to an hour's journey.

7. The children could no longer _____ the frozen road to school.

8. The gong of the school bell _____ across the compound.

9. The covers of the books were a _____ red.

10. Cassie's joy in having her own book _____ to a sinking disappointment.

11. Little Man had a _____ for cleanliness.

12. Miss Crocker's voice droned on _____.

13. Little Man's voice _____.

14. Miss Crocker was appalled at Little Man's _____.

15. His brow _____.

II. *Directions:* Cassie was given the chore of churning butter. On a separate sheet of paper, explain how Cassie's family made butter. Include an illustration of each step in the butter-making process.

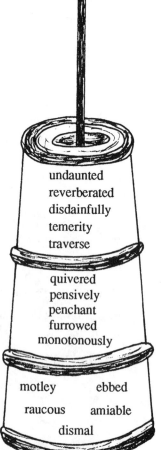

undaunted
reverberated
disdainfully
temerity
traverse

quivered
pensively
penchant
furrowed
monotonously

motley   ebbed

raucous   amiable

dismal

PROJECTS FOR *ROLL OF THUNDER, HEAR MY CRY*

Directions: Choose one of the following projects or design your own. If you design your own project, fill out the form below and submit it to your teacher for approval.

1. Illustrate several events in the story. Use your illustrations to present a brief summary of the story to your class.

2. Write a report about how African-Americans were treated in the South during the period from immediately after the Civil War until the beginning of the civil rights movement.

3. Prepare a mural depicting the events in Cassie Logan's life during the year covered in the story.

4. Cassie's great-grandfather knew how to use herbs as medicines. Give a demonstration and report on the use of herbal medicine.

5. What if T.J. wrote a letter to Stacey while he was in jail? Write this letter for T.J.

6. Create a board game based on African-American history from the end of the Civil War until the civil rights movement of the mid-twentieth century.

7. Dress as one of the characters and give a brief summary of the book from this person's point of view.

PROJECT PROPOSAL

Name _____ Beginning Date _____ Completion Date _____

Describe the project in detail: _____

_____

Why do you want to do this project? _____

_____

What will the final product be? _____

_____

How will you share your final product? _____

_____

Comments: _____

_____

SOUNDER
Comprehension Test A

Directions: Read each question carefully. Circle the letter of the choice that best answers each question.

1. Who wrote this book?
  a. William H. Armstrong   *b.* Wilson Rawls   *c.* Scott O'Dell

2. To earn extra money, the boy's mother _____.
  a. raised coon dogs
  b. shelled walnuts
  c. sewed clothes

3. The boy's mother said he had to learn how to _____.
  a. coon hunt   *b.* read   *c.* lose

4. The boy disliked curtains on windows because he _____.
  a. was afraid there were eyes looking out at him
  b. thought they would catch on fire
  c. thought they were only for rich people

5. One day, the boy found a big book in the trash, but _____.
  a. he had to put it back
  b. someone took it away from him
  c. he couldn't understand it

6. After he was shot, Sounder never barked until _____.
  a. the vet operated on him
  b. the boy took him hunting again
  c. his master returned home

7. The boy put Sounder's _____ under his pillow to wish on.
  a. ear   *b.* picture   *c.* leather leash

8. When he wasn't needed to work the fields, the boy _____.
  a. tried to find his father
  b. would read by the light from the wood stove
  c. hunt coons

9. Who showed the boy compassion and understanding?
  a. the judge   *b.* the teacher   *c.* the sheriff

10. The boy's mother believed in _____.
  a. astrology   *b.* nothing   *c.* signs

SOUNDER
Comprehension Test B

Directions: Read each question carefully. Circle the letter of the choice that best answers each question.

1. Sounder was _____.
   a. a purebred redbone
   b. part redbone and part bulldog
   c. a golden retriever

2. Who took the boy's father away in chains?
   a. the sheriff   b. the Ku Klux Klan   c. the warden

3. After his father was arrested, the boy's mother took the ham and _____.
   a. buried it   b. returned it   c. burned it

4. The boy and his father sold bittersweet and _____ at Christmas.
   a. holly   b. mistletoe   c. ivy

5. The boy went through trash barrels to find _____.
   a. clothes to take home
   b. food to barter
   c. newspapers to practice his reading

6. Who helped the boy when he injured his hand?
   a. the preacher   b. the teacher   c. a lawyer

7. The boy's father was crippled from a _____.
   a. beating   b. wagon wreck   c. dynamite blast

8. When men were mean to the boy, he would _____.
   a. cry and run away
   b. think about how to get revenge
   c. strike them

9. In the face of adversity, the family _____.
   a. gave up   b. broke up   c. carried on

10. Father was gone for _____ years.
    a. six   b. two   c. four

SOUNDER
Comprehension Test C

Directions: Read each question carefully. Circle the letter of the choice that best answers each question.

1. The boy's father was arrested for stealing _____.
   a. a horse　　　　　*b.* money　　　　　*c.* a ham

2. What kind of leaves have strong acid that can be used to toughen the skin?
   a. elm　　　　　*b.* oak　　　　　*c.* maple

3. What did the boy take to his father at the jail?
   a. a cake　　　　　*b.* a Christmas present　　　　　*c.* a file

4. There were _____ children in the family.
   a. two　　　　　*b.* three　　　　　*c.* four

5. The boy went to live with _____.
   a. a teacher
   b. his grandparents
   c. the people in the big house

6. Sounder was _____.
   a. shot
   b. run over by a wagon
   c. caught in a steel trap

7. Sounder completely lost _____.
   a. an eye　　　　　*b.* his tail　　　　　*c.* both ears

8. Sounder's beloved master was the _____.
   a. mother　　　　　*b.* father　　　　　*c.* boy

9. The boy's mother did _____ for the people in the big house.
   a. laundry
   b. baby-sitting
   c. field work

10. Father died _____.
    a. in jail
    b. on the cabin's porch
    c. in the woods

SOUNDER

Directions: The boy in the story loved books and learning. He could have answered the following questions about African-American history. Can you? You may use an encyclopedia for extra help. Write your answers on the lines. The names are in the ham.

1. Who invented Aunt Jemima's® Pancake Flour? _____

2. Who invented the egg beater? _____

3. Who was the first African-American to serve on the United States Supreme Court?

   _____

4. Who sang at the Lincoln Memorial after the Daughters of the American Revolution (DAR) refused to let her sing at Constitution Hall? _____

5. Who wrote the "Maple Leaf Rag" and was known as the king of ragtime?

6. Who won four medals in the 1936 Olympic Games held in Berlin, Germany?

   _____

7. Who helped over 300 slaves escape on the Underground Railroad? _____

8. Who was the surveyor who helped plan Washington, D.C.? _____

9. Who was one of the first rebels shot by British Troops in the Boston Massacre? _____

10. Who was the first African-American to have her poetry published? _____

11. Who is known as the mother of the modern civil rights movement? _____

12. Who was the first African-American to enter professional baseball? _____

13. Who is remembered for creating synthetic products from peanuts? _____

14. Who won the Nobel Prize for Peace in 1964? _____

Benjamin Banneker
Crispus Attucks
Martin Luther King, Jr.
Mme. Jenkins   Marian Anderson
George Washington Carver   W. Johnson
Thurgood Marshall   Jackie Robinson
Scott Joplin   Rosa Lee Parks
Harriet Tubman   Jesse Owens
Phillis Wheatley

PROJECTS FOR *SOUNDER*

Directions: Choose one of the following projects or design your own. If you design your own project, fill out the form below and submit it to your teacher for approval.

1. Write a journal entry giving your opinion about each of the following questions. Do you think six years of hard labor was a fair sentence for stealing a ham? Do you think the father would have been treated the same if he had been white? What are some lessons on life that the boy learned from his family's ordeal? This story took place a long time ago in the South; how have things changed for African-Americans since that time?

2. Make a crossword puzzle about this story.

3. Write at least six diary entries for the boy as he traveled around looking for his father.

4. Make a diorama showing the home of the boy's family, the teacher's house, or the schoolhouse.

5. Write a letter recommending this book to one of your friends or relatives who lives in another city.

6. Make a clay model of Sounder.

PROJECT PROPOSAL

Name _____ Beginning Date _____ Completion Date _____

Describe the project in detail: _____

_____

Why do you want to do this project? _____

_____

What will the final product be? _____

_____

How will you share your final product? _____

_____

Comments: _____

_____

TO BE A SLAVE
Comprehension Test A

Directions: Read each question carefully. Circle the letter of the choice that best answers each question.

1. Who wrote this book?
   a. Scott O'Dell   *b.* Julius Lester   *c.* Wilson Rawls

2. A slave who helped the overseer on a plantation was known as a _____.
   a. driver   *b.* turncoat   *c.* traitor

3. A *slave coffle* was a _____.
   a. box to bury slaves in
   b. handbill advertising the slave's best qualities
   c. group of slaves chained together

4. _____ of the South's white population did not own slaves.
   a. One-half   *b.* Three-fourths   *c.* Two-thirds

5. White preachers told slaves that they _____.
   a. would be free in the next life
   b. should obey their masters
   c. couldn't go to the white man's heaven

6. The behavior the overseers called "rascality" was actually _____.
   a. a disease
   b. a result of stupidity
   c. sabotage

7. Many insurrections never went past the talking stage because slaves lacked the necessary _____.
   a. weapons   *b.* brains   *c.* courage

8. During the Civil War, most African-Americans _____.
   a. fought on the side of the Union
   b. fought on the side of the Confederacy
   c. remained on the plantations

9. When it seemed like the South might lose the war, some slave owners _____.
   a. moved their slaves to Texas
   b. killed all their slaves
   c. sold all their slaves

10. The Union Army left the South in _____.
    a. 1866
    b. 1876
    c. 1886

TO BE A SLAVE
Comprehension Test B

Directions: Read each question carefully. Circle the letter of the choice that best answers each question.

1. When twenty slaves were brought to the Jamestown colony in 1619, the African slave trade _____.
   a. was already 100 years old
   b. first began
   c. was unprofitable

2. Confederate general Nathan Bedford Forrest was _____ in the 1850s.
   a. an abolitionist   b. a slave trader   c. a suffragist

3. Slaves were allowed to grow their own vegetables in a small plot called a _____.
   a. kitchen garden   b. conservatory   c. truck patch

4. *Uncle Tom's Cabin* was written by _____.
   a. Harriet Beecher Stowe
   b. Henry Ward Beecher
   c. Margaret Mitchell

5. *Paddyrollers* were men who _____.
   a. rounded up slaves to sell at auction
   b. caught slaves who were sneaking off to a gathering
   c. stole slaves from plantation owners

6. The _____ began in April of 1861.
   a. Mexican War   b. Revolutionary War   c. Civil War

7. The Emancipation Proclamation of 1863 freed _____.
   a. all slaves
   b. slaves in areas of the South that were under Union control
   c. slaves in the Deep South only

8. African-Americans were at Appomatox to watch General _____ surrender to General Grant.
   a. Lee   b. Davis   c. Sherman

9. The Ku Klux Klan was organized in 1866 by former Confederate general _____.
   a. Robert E. Lee
   b. Ulysses S. Grant
   c. Nathan Bedford Forrest

10. Abraham Lincoln wanted to send former slaves _____.
    a. out west
    b. to Canada
    c. back to Africa

TO BE A SLAVE
Comprehension Test C

Directions: Read each question carefully. Circle the letter of the choice that best answers each question.

1. African chiefs sold people into slavery in exchange for _____.
   a. cold hard cash
   b. stocks and bonds
   c. liquor, tobacco, guns, and ammunition

2. The election of _____ in 1860 sparked the sale of thousands of slaves.
   a. Abraham Lincoln
   b. Martin Van Buren
   c. Ulysses S. Grant

3. Slaves took their baskets of cotton to be weighed in the _____.
   a. smokehouse   b. ginhouse   c. cottonhouse

4. Slaves known as "Uncle Toms" usually worked in the _____.
   a. master's house   b. barn   c. fields

5. When slaves *set the flo'*, they were _____.
   a. dancing   b. working   c. running away

6. Slaves called members of the Union Army _____.
   a. turncoats   b. bluecoats   c. scapegoats

7. At the outbreak of the Civil War, African-Americans were used by the Union Army as _____.
   a. slaves   b. paid laborers   c. infantrymen

8. Freedom for all slaves came in _____.
   a. 1861   b. 1863   c. 1865

9. In 1876, the South passed laws that insured _____.
   a. segregation
   b. equality
   c. civil rights

10. This book was a _____ book.
   a. Newbery Honor
   b. Caldecott Medal
   c. Edgar Award

TO BE A SLAVE

I. Directions: All of the clues in the puzzle are from the book. Read the clues and fill in the puzzle.

ACROSS

1. African tribal chiefs sold their own people for tobacco, liquor, guns, and ___.
2. Many slaves lived on ___.
5. Before using slaves, English colonists tried to use ___ laborers.
8. There were 30 Africans with ___ when he discovered the Pacific Ocean.
9. Religion was one way of resisting the ___ effects of slavery.
10. Many Africans committed ___ rather than become a slave.
11. Slaves were sold on the auction ___.
12. Poor white prisoners and debtors came to the New World as ___ laborers.
13. Twenty slaves were brought to ___ colony in 1619.

DOWN

1. Africans were tightly wedged into space on the ship during the trip from Africa to ___.
3. President Lincoln wanted to relocate former slaves to ___ in the West.
4. Africans went with ___ to Peru.
6. *Massa* means ___.
7. The Emancipation Proclamation freed slaves in the parts of the South under ___ control.
9. The first American-built slave ship was called the ___.

II. Directions: Explain the primary difference between an indentured servant and a slave.

PROJECTS FOR *TO BE A SLAVE*

Directions: Choose one of the following projects or design your own. If you design your own project, fill out the form below and submit it to your teacher for approval.

1. Make a bibliography of at least twelve books for Black History Month. Write the book titles and authors' names on a large poster. Draw a box in front of each title. For each book that you have read, write a number in the box indicating how you would rate it on a scale of 1 to 10 (with 10 being the highest rating). Ask other class members to rate books that you have not read.

2. Prepare a television commercial to "sell" this book to others. You have 60 seconds for the commercial. Videotape your commercial and show it to your class.

3. Make a model of a typical slave cabin.

4. Create the front page of a newspaper dated the day after President Lincoln signed the Emancipation Proclamation.

5. Create a skit based on an event in the book. Perform the skit for your class.

6. Imagine you are a slave who has just learned that you are free. Write a journal entry about how you feel and what you do after receiving this joyous news.

PROJECT PROPOSAL

Name _____ Beginning Date _____ Completion Date _____

Describe the project in detail: _____

_____

Why do you want to do this project? _____

_____

What will the final product be? _____

_____

How will you share your final product? _____

_____

Comments: _____

_____

WITH YOU AND WITHOUT YOU
Comprehension Test A

Directions: Read each question carefully. Circle the letter of the choice that best answers each question.

1. Who wrote this book?
   a. Ann M. Martin   *b.* Betty Ren Wright   *c.* Nancy K. Robinson

2. Fifi was a _____.
   a. poodle   *b.* Persian cat   *c.* golden retriever

3. When Dad first went into the hospital, Mom said the doctors thought he had _____.
   a. AIDS   *b.* cancer   *c.* heart disease

4. Liza's role in the Christmas pageant was _____.
   a. the Spirit of the Future
   b. Tiny Tim
   c. Scrooge

5. On Christmas Eve, Liza fell asleep reading a book by _____.
   a. Sir Arthur Conan Doyle
   b. Agatha Christie
   c. Dorothy Sayers

6. Dad died _____.
   a. on Christmas Eve
   b. at the beginning of June
   c. on Hope's birthday

7. After Dad died, Mom had to sell _____.
   a. the house   *b.* both cars   *c.* all of her jewelry

8. When Marc first started asking Liza out, she was reluctant to go because _____.
   a. she didn't like him
   b. she didn't have anything to wear
   c. she felt guilty about having fun after Dad's death

9. Brent won a full scholarship to
   a. Harvard   *b.* Princeton   *c.* Yale

10. Hope taught herself to _____.
    a. read   *b.* play the piano   *c.* ride a bike

WITH YOU AND WITHOUT YOU
Comprehension Test B

Directions: Read each question carefully. Circle the letter of the choice that best answers each question.

1. All the O'Hara kids except _____ were latchkey kids.

   a. Carrie　　　　　　　　*b.* Brent　　　　　　　　*c.* Hope

2. When Liza had to make an oral report in social studies class, she _____.

   a. fainted
   b. played sick and stayed home
   c. barfed all over the teacher's desk

3. Dad said they were all lucky because _____.

   a. they had time to prepare for death
   b. they had a lot of friends
   c. they were wealthy

4. The O'Hara family always had _____ for dinner on Christmas Eve.

   a. roast goose　　　　　　*b.* clam chowder　　　　　*c.* pizza

5. Brent got a _____ for Christmas.

   a. motorcycle　　　　　　*b.* bike　　　　　　　　*c.* car

6. Liza's father died when she was in _____ grade.

   a. fifth　　　　　　　　*b.* eighth　　　　　　　*c.* seventh

7. How did Liza find out that Marc liked her?

   a. Denise said Cathryn said Marc told Justin.
   b. He asked her out.
   c. He sent her a note.

8. Hope's teacher sent a note home saying that Hope had _____.

   a. withdrawn from all activities
   b. cried all day
   c. taken a tool kit

9. Liza's Christmas present to Marc was _____.

   a. a print　　　　　　　*b.* a book　　　　　　　*c.* an album

10. Liza was the last one in the family to be able to _____.

    a. visit Dad's grave
    b. learn to live on a tight budget
    c. stop feeling sorry for herself

WITH YOU AND WITHOUT YOU
Comprehension Test C

Directions: Read each question carefully. Circle the letter of the choice that best answers each question.

1. Mr. O'Hara was _____.
   a. head of the English department
   b. an account executive
   c. a neurosurgeon

2. Charlie died because he _____.
   a. was attacked by a dog
   b. got a virus
   c. was hit by a car

3. Liza's best friend was _____.
   a. Margie   b. Denise   c. Marc

4. After Liza's role in the Christmas pageant, Dad gave her a _____.
   a. red rose   b. gold locket   c. ruby ring

5. Which of Liza's classmates had also lost his or her father?
   a. Margie   b. Denise   c. Marc

6. Brent wanted to win a scholarship to go to _____.
   a. Harvard   b. Princeton   c. Yale

7. Why was the new kitten named Dr. J.?
   a. He liked to leap through the air.
   b. He like to play with a ball.
   c. He acted like someone special.

8. Liza got upset at the Christmas party when everyone _____.
   a. started drinking
   b. kidded her about having a boyfriend
   c. sang Christmas carols

9. Marc's Christmas present to Liza was a _____.
   a. ring   b. bracelet   c. pair of earrings

10. Liza and Marc agreed to _____.
    a. see each other over the summer
    b. just be friends
    c. break up

WITH YOU AND WITHOUT YOU

Directions: Below are sentences about things that happened in the story. One word in each sentence has been left out. The missing words are in the bracelet. First, use a dictionary to learn the definition of each word. Then, write each word on the correct line.

1. Liza and her sister and brother were _____ kids.

2. Brent enjoyed teasing Carrie because she was so _____.

3. Mr. O'Hara suffered from _____.

4. The _____ is the predicted outcome of a disease.

5. When Mom told the family that Dad was very ill, her voice was _____.

6. Denise was _____ toward Liza.

7. Denise's father died of an _____.

8. Hope was _____ when she thought Dad died and came back.

9. Liza overheard a private conversation between Mom and Dad even though she wasn't trying to _____.

10. Liza hated _____.

11. Dad requested no _____ be given.

12. Brent graduated as the class _____.

13. Carrie told Liza it was _____ to keep thinking about the day her father died.

14. Hope leaned close to Liza's ear and whispered _____.

15. Brent turned into a real _____.

16. Liza was accused of trying to _____ her ideas on everyone else.

17. The family grew tired of Liza's _____ sensitivity.

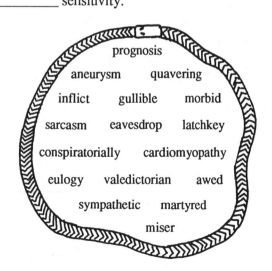

prognosis
aneurysm   quavering
inflict   gullible   morbid
sarcasm   eavesdrop   latchkey
conspiratorially   cardiomyopathy
eulogy   valedictorian   awed
sympathetic   martyred
miser

PROJECTS FOR *WITH YOU AND WITHOUT YOU*

Directions: Choose one of the following projects or design your own. If you design your own project, fill out the form below and submit it to your teacher for approval.

1. The O'Hara family didn't write an epitaph for Charlie. Write one for him. Did a pet of yours ever die? Write an epitaph for your pet.

2. Liza didn't keep a journal, but she "wrote" things in her head. What if she had decided to put her thoughts on paper for the following three events in her life: the Christmas when the family learned that Dad was going to die, the sad time in June when he died, and the following Christmas. Write these journal entries for Liza.

3. On the anniversary of Dad's birth, Liza wrote a poem about him. Write a poem about a family member or friend of yours who died.

4. The O'Hara family had special holiday traditions. Tell about the holiday traditions your family observes.

5. Hope made Christmas decorations at school. Bring to class at least three decorations that you made yourself. Include a sheet of step-by-step directions for each item so others can make similar decorations.

6. Make a bibliography of at least twelve other books that deal with the death of a loved one.

PROJECT PROPOSAL

Name _____ Beginning Date _____ Completion Date _____

Describe the project in detail: _____

_____

Why do you want to do this project? _____

_____

What will the final product be? _____

_____

How will you share your final product? _____

_____

Comments: _____

_____

Section 7

FAVORITE BOOKS
FOR
MARCH

The following books are on "March Book List B" in *Ready-to-Use Reading Activities Through the Year.*

Activity Sheets	Book Title	Reading Level	Award
7-1 to 7-5	*The Cat Ate My Gymsuit*	5.5	
7-6 to 7-10	*James and the Giant Peach*	4.5	
7-11 to 7-15	*Julie of the Wolves*	5	Newbery Medal
7-16 to 7-20	*One Fat Summer*	7	

The Cat Ate My Gymsuit by Paula Danziger.
New York: Dell, 1974. 119 pages.

Marcy Lewis feels like an unattractive, untalented, clumsy, blimp. Her father agrees with her and often tells her so. Her mild-mannered mother just keeps apologizing for everything. Her little brother prefers the company of his teddy bear to that of his family. Marcy begins to gain confidence in herself thanks to a remarkable teacher named Ms. Finney. When Ms. Finney is fired, Marcy and other classmates band together to try to help get her reinstated. Marcy's father is violently opposed to this, so Marcy has to face the consequences of standing up to him. Marcy learns to be true to herself no matter what the consequences.

James and the Giant Peach by Roald Dahl.
New York: Puffin Books, 1961. 119 pages.

When a hungry rhinoceros makes a meal of James Henry Trotter's parents, his life changes from one filled with love, laughter, and happiness to one blemished with hatred, tears, and loneliness. James is forced to live with his horrid relatives, Aunt Sponge and Aunt Spiker. They beat him and won't let him play with other children. He prays for escape. In his wildest dreams, he never imagines that the answer to his prayers will be a strange, little, old man who hands him a bag of magic green crystals. The man tells James to put the crystals in water and drink them so that he'll never be miserable again. As James runs toward the kitchen for water, he stumbles and drops the crystals under an old peach tree. Despair turns to disbelief as he watches the old tree produce a peach the size of a small house. His evil, greedy aunts sell tickets so villagers can see this strange apparition. While James is doing his chores, he notices an opening in the peach. He gathers his courage and goes in. He meets creatures as big as himself. They become friends and share a fantastical adventure as the peach rolls over the aunts and away to freedom. The friends help each other overcome attacks by sharks and Cloud-Men. Seagulls fly them across the Atlantic Ocean to New York City. The peach falls and lands on the spire of the Empire State Building. James and his friends become instant celebrities and happily bask in all the love and attention lavished on them.

Julie of the Wolves by Jean Craighead George.
New York: Harper and Row, 1972. 170 pages.

Julie Edwards Miyax Kapugen is caught between two different worlds. When she lives in town and adopts the customs of white men, she is Julie. When she lives in the wild and adopts the customs of her Eskimo ancestors, she is Miyax. Julie is unhappy when her aunt takes her away from her father so that she can live in town and attend school. Her unhappiness deepens when she is forced into an arranged marriage, so she runs away. She becomes hopelessly lost on the North Slope of Alaska. She learns the ways of wolves and is adopted by a pack who literally save her life. Although she is without human contact and faces winter on the tundra, Julie is peaceful and happy. It takes a heart-rending tragedy to show her that "the hour of the wolf and the Eskimo is over." She changes her mind about living alone on the tundra and heads toward the town.

One Fat Summer by Robert Lipsyte.
New York: Harper/Keypoint, 1977. 232 pages.

Bobby Marks hates summer because he can't hide his fat under layers of clothes. Each year, when Bobby's family leaves the city to spend the summer at their cabin on Rumson Lake, he's miserable. There's no way anyone is going to see him in shorts or a swimsuit. He misses out on a lot of activities because he won't go near the water. His father is on his case to go to summer camp to lose weight. In order to avoid this fate worse than death, Bobby gets a job taking care of Dr. Kahn's large lawn. Bobby has a few problems, though. The work is so hard that he suffers a heat stroke, gets blisters on top of blisters, and becomes so stiff and sore that he can hardly move. Since Willie, the local bully, wants Bobby's job, Bobby needs to be able to move fast to keep out of harm's way. Willie intends to get the job even if he has to hurt Bobby. Things come to a head when Willie goes for Bobby with a gun. They struggle and both end up in the lake. Weeks of yardwork have given Bobby muscles he never had before. He needs all of his strength to overcome the enraged Willie. With this battle won, Bobby begins looking forward to the last few weeks of summer. He's lost so much weight that he even begins looking forward to beginning a new school year.

THE CAT ATE MY GYMSUIT
Comprehension Test A

Directions: Read each question carefully. Circle the letter of the choice that best answers each question.

1. Who wrote this book?
   - *a.* Paula Danziger
   - *b.* Judith Viorst
   - *c.* Judy Blume

2. Smedley was a _____.
   - *a.* person
   - *b.* club
   - *c.* dog

3. Marcy was afraid that she suffered from a case of contagious terminal _____.
   - *a.* hepatitis
   - *b.* pimples
   - *c.* AIDS

4. Marcy's father told her she was a fat _____.
   - *a.* dummy
   - *b.* loser
   - *c.* klutz

5. Joel's father said that getting suspended could _____.
   - *a.* turn into a real learning experience
   - *b.* keep them out of good colleges
   - *c.* ruin their lives

6. Stuart liked peanut butter and _____ sandwiches.
   - *a.* avocado
   - *b.* pickle
   - *c.* ham

7. Why did Marcy drink beer at Nancy's party?
   - *a.* She wanted to be like the others.
   - *b.* She was an alcoholic.
   - *c.* She wanted to get attention.

8. Ms. Finney decided to get a doctorate in _____.
   - *a.* education
   - *b.* journalism
   - *c.* bibliotherapy

9. Agnes was _____.
   - *a.* a pimple
   - *b.* Joel's old girlfriend
   - *c.* Stuart's teacher

10. Marcy decided to see a _____.
    - *a.* new boyfriend
    - *b.* psychologist
    - *c.* different doctor

THE CAT ATE MY GYMSUIT
Comprehension Test B

Directions. Read each question carefully. Circle the letter of the choice that best answers each question.

1. Marcy Lewis was tracked with other _____ students.
   a. average *b.* smart *c.* retarded

2. Marcy's father was _____.
   a. an alcoholic *b.* dead *c.* cold and verbally abusive

3. Whose father was on the Board of Education?
   a. Marcy's father *b.* Joel's father *c.* Nancy's father

4. Marcy's mother _____.
   a. popped tranquilizers
   b. was an alcoholic
   c. used crack cocaine

5. Marcy bought a new _____ for her date with Joel.
   a. purple pants suit
   b. pair of jeans and a sweatshirt
   c. party dress

6. Joel gave Marcy a good-night kiss on the _____.
   a. lips *b.* forehead *c.* cheek

7. Mr. Lewis tried to keep Marcy and her mother from going to the hearing _____.
   a. by hiding all the sets of car keys
   b. by taking a part out of the engine
   c. by blocking the doorway with his body

8. Ms. Finney did not return to the classroom because _____.
   a. the school board did not reinstate her
   b. she joined the Peace Corps instead
   c. she resigned

9. Mrs. Lewis enrolled in _____.
   a. college classes *b.* cooking classes *c.* aerobics classes

10. Joel thought Ms. Finney left just like his _____ had.
    a. former girlfriend
    b. father
    c. mother

THE CAT ATE MY GYMSUIT
Comprehension Test C

Directions: Read each question carefully. Circle the letter of the choice that best answers each question.

1. Marcy wouldn't participate in gym class because she felt _____.

    a. fat   *b.* scared   *c.* clumsy

2. About the only thing at school that Marcy liked was _____.

    a. being a member of the school newspaper staff

    b. lunch

    c. Ms. Finney

3. Who stood up in class and told the principal to hire Ms. Finney back?

    a. Marcy   *b.* Joel   *c.* Nancy

4. Mr. Stone fired Ms. Finney partly because she wouldn't _____.

    a. follow the curriculum

    b. say the Pledge of Allegiance

    c. go out with him

5. Marcy thought her parents should claim _____ on their income tax.

    a. Fang   *b.* Bear   *c.* Wolf

6. Joel wanted to leave Nancy's party early because _____.

    a. he and Marcy weren't getting along

    b. things were getting out of hand

    c. Nancy said he was a real party-pooper

7. Joel chose _____ to give his mother for her birthday.

    a. an expensive necklace

    b. a hideously ugly pin

    c. a handmade quilt

8. Stuart refused to go to school unless _____ was enrolled, too.

    a. Marcy   *b.* Joel   *c.* Wolf

9. Bibliotherapy means _____.

    a. studying the Bible in depth

    b. counseling using books and writing

    c. reading books written by a psychologist

10. Joel and Marcy were having a _____.

    a. good friendship

    b. romance

    c. big fight

THE CAT ATE MY GYMSUIT

I. *Directions:* When Ms. Finney asked someone to define a simile, Joel said it is a comparison of two dissimilar things using *like* or *as*. Complete each sentence below using a simile.

1. Ms. Finney _____

   _____

2. Ms. Finney's students _____

   _____

3. Mr. Stone _____

   _____

4. Marcy's father _____

   _____

5. Stuart thought Wolf _____

   _____

6. When Marcy looked in a mirror, _____

   _____

II. *Directions:* When Robert was asked to give an example of a metaphor, he knew that a metaphor can be thought of as a strengthened simile. A simile says something is LIKE something else, but a metaphor says something IS something else. (Simile: That child acts like a monster. Metaphor: That child is a monster.) A writer can make a stronger statement by using a metaphor instead of a simile. Complete each sentence below using a metaphor.

1. Marcy's family _____

   _____

2. Marcy's purple pants suit _____

   _____

3. Teacher independence _____

   _____

4. Student protest _____

   _____

PROJECTS FOR *THE CAT ATE MY GYMSUIT*

Directions: Choose one of the following projects or design your own. If you design your own project, fill out the form below and submit it to your teacher for approval.

1. Write a report about bibliotherapy. Include a biography of at least twelve books appropriate for use in bibliotherapy. Explain the purpose for which each book could be used.

2. Write and illustrate a children's book. Donate your book to a local hospital or shelter.

3. Marcy was creative when it came to making up excuses for why she couldn't participate in gym class. Make a list of twenty unique reasons why you can't do your homework.

4. Marcy wanted to change things about her appearance, her personality, and her life. Many people share these feelings at one time or another. If you're one of those people, list at least ten changes you'd like to make about your appearance, personality, or life. Tell how your life will be different after these changes.

5. Create a game board based on this book.

6. Make a 60-second television commercial to sell this book to others. Videotape your commercial.

PROJECT PROPOSAL

Name _____ Beginning Date _____ Completion Date _____

Describe the project in detail: _____

_____

Why do you want to do this project? _____

_____

What will the final product be? _____

_____

How will you share your final product? _____

_____

Comments: _____

_____

JAMES AND THE GIANT PEACH
Comprehension Test A

Directions: Read each question carefully. Circle the letter of the choice that best answers each question.

1. Who wrote this book?

    a. Roald Dahl   *b.* Louis Sachar   *c.* Dr. Seuss

2. James longed to go to _____, but his aunts wouldn't let him.

    a. summer camp   *b.* a rock concert   *c.* the seaside

3. What happened to the tiny green things when they fell out of the bag?

    a. They landed in the pond.

    b. They fell underneath the old peach tree.

    c. They blew away in the wind.

4. James thought the peach felt like _____.

    a. a fur coat

    b. the skin of a baby mouse

    c. the mold on old cheese

5. How did the peach get loose from the tree?

    a. The aunts cut it loose.

    b. The grasshopper shoved it free.

    c. The centipede nibbled the stem.

6. What came swimming up to the giant peach?

    a. sharks

    b. Aunt Sponge and Aunt Spiker

    c. a group of boys and girls on a field trip

7. When the Centipede accused James of being dotty, he meant that James was _____.

    a. howlingly funny   *b.* off his head   *c.* scared stiff

8. Who was boastful of being a pest?

    a. the Centipede   *b.* the Spider   *c.* the Ladybug

9. Why did the Cloud-Men start bombarding the peach with hailstones?

    a. The Spider call them Blunderheads.

    b. The Centipede called them Nincompoops.

    c. James called them Half-wits.

10. The peach landed on top of _____.

    a. St. Paul's Cathedral

    b. the Leaning Tower of Pisa

    c. the Empire State Building

JAMES AND THE GIANT PEACH
Comprehension Test B

Directions: Read each question carefully. Circle the letter of the choice that best answers each question.

1. What happened to James Henry Trotter's parents when they went shopping in London?
   a. They were trampled by an elephant.
   b. They were eaten by a rhinoceros.
   c. They were swallowed by a boa constrictor.

2. The little old man told James the bag contained one thousand _____.
   a. crocodile tongues   b. lizard eyeballs   c. parrot beaks

3. Aunt Spiker wouldn't let Aunt Sponge eat the giant peach because _____.
   a. she wanted it all for herself
   b. she was spiteful
   c. there was money to be made on it

4. Who was waiting for James inside the peach stone?
   a. his aunts   b. creatures   c. the little old man

5. How did the two aunts get ironed out flat?
   a. The peach rolled over them.
   b. A helicopter landed on them.
   c. The television van ran over them.

6. How did everyone climb up to the hole in the ceiling?
   a. by standing on chairs, tables, and beds
   b. the Old-Green Grasshopper jumped them up there
   c. they used a rope woven by Miss Spider

7. Why did James want hundreds of yards of string?
   a. so seagulls could lift the peach out of the water
   b. to tie up Aunt Sponge and Aunt Spiker
   c. to hook the peach onto a skyhook

8. What did the Spider do with the web as she climbed up it?
   a. ate it   b. cut it off   c. tucked it into her body

9. A grasshopper's ears are on its _____.
   a. legs   b. tummy   c. head

10. New Yorkers thought the giant peach was the biggest _____ in the history of the world.
    a. stunt   b. practical joke   c. bomb

JAMES AND THE GIANT PEACH
Comprehension Test C

Directions: Read each question carefully. Circle the letter of the choice that best answers each question.

1. What did Aunt Sponge and Aunt Spiker do to James?

    a. starved him   *b.* beat him   *c.* locked him in his room

2. The old man told James to add water to the green things and drink it so _____.

    a. he'd win the lottery

    b. he'd grow handsome and become a famous movie star

    c. he'd never feel miserable again

3. How much did the greedy aunts charge to view the giant peach?

    a. one shilling   *b.* one pound   *c.* tuppence

4. When the peach was bobbing up and down, how did everyone get out?

    a. through the side door

    b. through the hole in the ceiling

    c. through a hole in the floor

5. Who was blind?

    a. Spider   *b.* Ladybug   *c.* Earthworm

6. What did everyone shout when they found out they weren't going to die of thirst?

    a. Good Golly Miss Molly

    b. Holy Cats

    c. Jumping Jehoshophat

7. How many seagulls did it take to raise the giant peach out of the water?

    a. 500   *b.* 501   *c.* 502

8. What were the Cloud-Men doing with pots of paint and big brushes?

    a. painting a rainbow

    b. painting the seagulls so they'd stiffen and couldn't fly

    c. throwing them at each other during a fight

9. How did Centipede get the purple paint off his body?

    a. His friends peeled him like a banana.

    b. His friends rubbed him with sandpaper.

    c. A deluge washed it off.

10. During the night, the giant peach crossed the _____ Ocean.

    a. Atlantic   *b.* Pacific   *c.* Indian

JAMES AND THE GIANT PEACH

Directions: Roald Dahl uses wonderfully vivid verbs to keep this story pulsating with excitement. Some of the vivid verbs in the story are shown in the peach. Use these verbs to write about what happens when James and his friends meet a Dragon, Wampus, Gorgon, Sea-serpent, Prock, Manticore, Snozzwanger, Whangdoodle, and Oinck. Begin your story below and finish on a separate sheet of paper. Illustrate your story.

_____

_____

_____

_____

_____

_____

_____

_____

_____

_____

_____

_____

_____

tether
roar
bounce   smash
slosh   swash   swirl
surge   ooze   chorus   disentangle
murmur   rush   deluge   wither
shriek   plunge   charge   clamber
jostle
thresh   infuriate   gurgle   gush
slither   seeth   hustle
stampede   bob   scatter
perish

PROJECTS FOR *JAMES AND THE GIANT PEACH*

Directions: Choose one of the following projects or design your own. If you design your own project, fill out the form below and submit it to your teacher for approval.

1. Reread the poem on pages 37 and 38. Make up two new verses.

2. Write a research report on the White Cliffs of Dover and some of the famous events in history that occurred there.

3. Prepare a bibliography of Roald Dahl's books.

4. Make a diorama of the giant peach with James and all the creatures being pulled through the sky by the seagulls while passing the clouds topped with the Cloud-Men.

5. Make a mobile featuring the giant peach, James, Aunt Sponge, Aunt Spiker, Old-Green Grasshopper, Centipede, Earthworm, Ladybug, Miss Spider, Silkworm, Glow-Worm, the Cloud-Men, some sharks, and several seagulls.

6. Make a mobile featuring a Wampus, Gorgon, Sea-serpent, Prock, Manticore, Dragon, Oinck, Cockatrice, giant Scorpula, Vermicious Knid, Snozzwanger, and Whangdoodle.

7. Write and perform a rap about your favorite foods. Feature at least six of your favorites.

PROJECT PROPOSAL

Name _____ Beginning Date _____ Completion Date _____

Describe the project in detail: _____

_____

Why do you want to do this project? _____

_____

What will the final product be? _____

_____

How will you share your final product? _____

_____

Comments: _____

_____

JULIE OF THE WOLVES
Comprehension Test A

Directions: Read each question carefully. Circle the letter of the choice that best answers each question.

1. Who wrote this book?
    a. Mildred D. Taylor
    b. Sheila Solomon Klass
    c. Jean Craighead George

2. Old Eskimo hunters thought the riches of life were fearlessness, love, and _____.
    a. money   b. intelligence   c. goods

3. An ulo is a _____.
    a. half-moon shaped knife   b. bird   c. type of moss

4. Which wolf ate cooked meat from Miyax's hand?
    a. Kapu   b. Nails   c. Silver

5. Julie's Aunt Martha took her away from her father _____.
    a. because he was declared unfit to raise a child
    b. so Julie could go to school
    c. because she was mean and vindictive

6. Why did the pack turn on Jello and kill him?
    a. He was sick and lame.
    b. He did not contribute to the pack.
    c. He threatened to harm the pups.

7. After being lost on the tundra, the first sign of civilization was _____.
    a. a low-flying plane
    b. human tracks
    c. an oil drum

8. The gussak term for *grizzly* was _____.
    a. brown bear   b. black bear   c. red bear

9. To say "stay back" to Amaroq, Miyax _____.
    a. shouted at him
    b. turned and glared
    c. shoved an antler club at his face

10. Why did the men kill Amaroq?
    a. for a bounty
    b. for turning on Julie
    c. for fun

JULIE OF THE WOLVES
Comprehension Test B

Directions: Read each question carefully. Circle the letter of the choice that best answers each question.

1. Miyax ran away from home _____.
   a. because her father beat her
   b. because she and her mother fought all the time
   c. to get away from her husband

2. Miyax became a member of the wolf pack when she _____.
   a. patted Amaroq   b. played with the puppies   c. showed fear

3. How did Miyax learn that the migration to the south had begun?
   a. Packs of foxes marched south.
   b. Game disappeared altogether.
   c. The Arctic terns were flying in a V-formation.

4. People from all over the world came to Barrow to study _____.
   a. the top of the world
   b. at the University of Alaska
   c. Eskimo ways

5. Who crashed into Miyax's house and stole her food?
   a. Daniel   b. Jello   c. Kapugen

6. How could Miyax travel on top of the snow?
   a. by crawling flat on her stomach
   b. with snowshoes that she made
   c. with skis

7. *Ursus arctos* is the scientific name for _____.
   a. wolf   b. polar bear   c. grizzly

8. Julie saw the horrors of civilization when she looked
   a. at the underside of the plane
   b. into the faces of the hunters
   c. at the filth around Point Barrow

9. How did Julie close Kapu's wound?
   a. She taped it.
   b. She stitched it together.
   c. She bandaged his whole chest.

10. Julie decided to live _____.
    a. by herself on the tundra   b. in San Francisco with Amy   c. with Kapugen in Kangik

JULIE OF THE WOLVES
Comprehension Test C

Directions: Read each question carefully. Circle the letter of the choice that best answers each question.

1. Miyax was trying to get to her pen pal's house in _____.

   a. Barrow   *b.* San Francisco   *c.* Seattle

2. After she became lost, how did Miyax get meat for her first stew?

   a. She killed a caribou.

   b. Silver brought it to her door.

   c. She got it from Jello's belly-basket.

3. "Candy" to an Eskimo was _____.

   a. the liver of an animal

   b. store-bought gumdrops

   c. whale blubber

4. Julie's mother died when Julie was _____ years old.

   a. four   *b.* six   *c.* two

5. Who stole Miyax's backpack?

   a. David   *b.* Jello   *c.* a wolverine

6. The wolf pack tried to protect Miyax from a _____.

   a. grizzly   *b.* wolverine   *c.* polar bear

7. Wolves lived in _____ of the lower forty-eight states.

   a. five   *b.* two   *c.* three

8. Tornait was a _____.

   a. wolf pup   *b.* person   *c.* plover

9. How did Julie stop Kapu's bleeding?

   a. She put a tourniquet on it.

   b. She held the vein together with her fingers.

   c. She seared it with a hot knife.

10. Why did fountains of green light rise from the Earth and shoot to the sky?

    a. The oil drum was burning.

    b. The people in town set off fireworks.

    c. The Northern Lights were dancing.

JULIE OF THE WOLVES

I. Directions: Read the statements below. Put an *F* in front of those that state a fact and *O* in front of those that state an opinion.

_____ 1. Miyax was lost for many sleeps on the North Slope of Alaska.

_____ 2. Miyax thought the tundra was beautiful.

_____ 3. Miyax called the leader of the wolf pack Amaroq.

_____ 4. Miyax built a house of sod.

_____ 5. The sod house was ugly.

_____ 6. Miyax could talk wolf.

_____ 7. Julie was ashamed of her gussak clothes.

_____ 8. Julie wanted to look less like an Eskimo and more like her gussak pen pal.

_____ 9. The warm liver of a recently killed animal was the "candy" of Eskimo people.

_____ 10. Seal camp was boring.

ART 23

II. Directions: Write your answers to the following questions on a separate sheet of paper.

1. What do you predict Julie's life will be like when she is ten years older?

2. If you were Julie and had to decide whether to live alone on the tundra or to return to town, what decision would you make? Why?

3. What did you like about this book? What did you dislike? What would you change? If a friend asked you to tell him or her about this book, how would you summarize the story?

III. Directions: Julie ends her adventure with a song. Reread this song. Write the next verse to this song below.

_____

_____

_____

_____

PROJECTS FOR *JULIE OF THE WOLVES*

Directions: Choose one of the following projects or design your own. If you design your own project, fill out the form below and submit it to your teacher for approval.

1. Make a map for this story. Show places such as Barrow, Kangik, the North Slope of Alaska, and San Francisco, California. Indicate Miyax's intended route and the one she actually took. Include a key showing miles. Estimate how many miles Julie would have traveled from the time she ran away from Daniel until she found her father if she had not become lost and walked in circles.

2. There are many differences between the way of life of the Eskimo and the gussak. Write a report about these differences. At the end of the story, Julie says the hour of the Eskimo is over. What does she mean by this? Explain this in your report.

3. Create a time line for the period of Julie's life covered in the story.

4. Julie carved Amaroq and the other members of the pack. Recreate this carving.

5. Make the outfit Miyax wore on the tundra and the coat she made for Tornait. Display these costumes in a diorama.

6. Julie says the hour of the wolf is over. Write a report explaining how the encroachment of civilization—with its inherent violence and pollution—contributed to this.

PROJECT PROPOSAL

Name _____ Beginning Date _____ Completion Date _____

Describe the project in detail: _____

_____

Why do you want to do this project? _____

_____

What will the final product be? _____

_____

How will you share your final product? _____

_____

Comments: _____

_____

ONE FAT SUMMER
Comprehension Test A

Directions: Read each question carefully. Circle the letter of the choice that best answers each question.

1. Who wrote this book?
   a. Robert Lipsyte　　　　*b.* John Bellairs　　　　*c.* Stanley Kiesel

2. The ad said the job paid one dollar an hour, but the man hired Bobby for _____.
   a. 75¢　　　　*b.* $1.25　　　　*c.* 50¢

3. On the second day, Bobby's pay was cut by _____ an hour.
   a. 10¢　　　　*b.* 15¢　　　　*c.* 25¢

4. Bobby knew if Joanie was there, she'd tell him that he _____.
   a. should ask for a raise
   b. was being taken advantage of
   c. should quit his miserable job

5. Bobby was taken to the island in the middle of Rumson Lake and _____.
   a. left there without any clothes
   b. beaten up
   c. hung from the flagpole by his suspenders

6. Pete called Bobby _____.
   a. the Blob　　　　*b.* Fats　　　　*c.* Big Fella

7. Bobby was shocked to discover that he'd lost at least _____ pounds in a month.
   a. 23　　　　*b.* 13　　　　*c.* 33

8. After Willie beat up a teacher, he was told to join the marines or _____.
   a. go to jail
   b. do 200 hours of community service
   c. enlist in the army

9. Pete Marino's father accused Michelle of _____.
   a. being a tramp
   b. stealing money from the cash register
   c. wrecking the truck

10. Willie Rumson came after Bobby at the snack bar with a _____.
    a. tire jack　　　　*b.* knife　　　　*c.* .22 rifle

ONE FAT SUMMER
Comprehension Test B

Directions: Read each question carefully. Circle the letter of the choice that best answers each question.

1. Joanie won _____.
   - *a.* a large black-and-white panda
   - *b.* an enormous pink teddy bear
   - *c.* a huge purple pig

2. Joanie never talked about Bobby's weight or her _____.
   - *a.* big nose
   - *b.* crooked teeth
   - *c.* crossed eyes

3. This story took place during the summer of _____.
   - *a.* 1942
   - *b.* 1952
   - *c.* 1962

4. Bobby's favorite singer was _____.
   - *a.* Frank Sinatra
   - *b.* Fabian
   - *c.* Eddie Fisher

5. Who threatened Bobby?
   - *a.* Willie Rumson
   - *b.* Pete Marino
   - *c.* the Smith boys

6. Who did Michelle have a crush on?
   - *a.* Willie Rumson
   - *b.* Pete Marino
   - *c.* Jim Smith

7. On the way to the city, Bobby's mother questioned him about _____.
   - *a.* Willie
   - *b.* Pete
   - *c.* Michelle

8. Mother found out about Bobby's job when _____.
   - *a.* Dr. Kahn called her
   - *b.* Michelle told her
   - *c.* Joanie told her

9. Who took the gun away from Willie?
   - *a.* Jim
   - *b.* Pete
   - *c.* Marty

10. When Bobby asked Dr. Kahn to double his pay, Dr. Kahn told him _____.
    - *a.* he was fired
    - *b.* he could have 25¢ more an hour
    - *c.* he could have it

ONE FAT SUMMER
Comprehension Test C

Directions: Read each question carefully. Circle the letter of the choice that best answers each question.

1. Kids teased Bobby by calling him _____.
   a. the Crisco® Kid   *b.* Lard Bottom   *c.* Hippo Hips

2. Bobby's boss confiscated his wages on the first day to _____.
   a. pay for all the food he ate
   b. pay for all the soda he drank
   c. replace the mower blade

3. Bobby's father pressured him to _____.
   a. go to summer camp
   b. get a decent job
   c. go to summer school

4. Bobby's boss docked his pay on the second day because he _____.
   a. was late
   b. had to redo his first day's work
   c. took too long for lunch and left early

5. Bobby's mother was studying to become _____.
   a. a stockbroker   *b.* an engineer   *c.* a teacher

6. Who found Bobby in the old cabin and rowed him across the lake?
   a. Jim Smith   *b.* Connie Marino   *c.* Pete Marino

7. Joanie accused Bobby of resenting her because she _____.
   a. was smarter
   b. was more popular
   c. changed her looks for the better

8. Bobby hated shopping in the department called _____.
   a. Chubbytown   *b.* Huskytown   *c.* Big Boys' Shop

9. Bobby's parents kept arguing about _____.
   a. her going to work
   b. money
   c. his long hours on the job

10. When Bobby and his parents drove back to the cabin a day early, they _____.
    a. found Willie Rumson vandalizing the place
    b. found Pete and Michelle and his father there
    c. saw that someone had painted graffiti on the front door

ONE FAT SUMMER

Directions: This story took place during the summer of 1952. Below are questions about 1952. Write your answers on the lines. You may use an almanac or encyclopedia for extra help.

1. Ghiorso discovered the chemical element Einsteinium. What is its symbol? _____

   What is its atomic number? _____ What is its atomic weight? _____

2. What college was founded in 1952 in Stevenson, Maryland? _____

3. What was the name of the Pennsylvanian who was appointed Attorney General in 1952?

   _____

4. Who was the Speaker of the House of Representatives? _____

5. Who was President in the summer of 1952? _____

6. Who was Director of the C.I.A. in the summer of 1952? _____

7. What are the names of the two Englishmen who won the Nobel Prize in Chemistry in 1952?

   _____

8. Which newspaper won the Pulitzer Prize in Journalism in 1952?

   _____

9. What is the name of the woman who won the Pulitzer Prize in American Poetry in 1952?

   _____

   What was the title of her work? _____

10. What was the name of the person who was awarded the Spingarn Medal by the N.A.A.C.P. in 1952?

    _____

11. Who was Miss America in 1952? _____

    Where was she from? _____

12. Which actor won an Academy Award for *High Noon*? _____

13. Which director won an Academy Award for *The Quiet Man*? _____

14. What did the President seize on April 8, 1952 in an effort to avoid a strike?

    _____

15. Who was the NBA scoring champion in 1952? _____

PROJECTS FOR *ONE FAT SUMMER*

Directions: Choose one of the following projects or design your own. If you design your own project, fill out the form below and submit it to your teacher for approval.

1. When Michelle was upset, she liked to stay in her room and listen to Johnny Ray sing "Little White Cloud That Cried." Bobby's favorite song was "Any Time" by Eddie Fisher. Dress in a 1950s outfit and lip sync these songs for your class.

2. Rewrite this story as a picture book.

3. Bobby is about to start a new school year. He is a lot thinner and has some sharp new clothes. Prepare five diary entries telling about the first week of school.

4. Choose a book that Michelle, Bobby, or Joanie might have read during the summer of 1952. Read this book and tell your class about it.

5. If you have been to the Disney-MGM Studios Theme Park at Walt Disney World, you may have eaten in the 50's Prime Time Café. Diners are seated in 1950s-style kitchenettes and view vintage TV sitcoms while eating hearty meals served on Fiesta™ Ware plates. Their placemats pose trivia questions about 1950s TV shows. Make a 1950s trivia quiz and share it with your classmates.

6. Make a diorama of a typical 1950s kitchenette.

PROJECT PROPOSAL

Name _____ Beginning Date _____ Completion Date _____

Describe the project in detail: _____

_____

Why do you want to do this project? _____

_____

What will the final product be? _____

_____

How will you share your final product? _____

_____

Comments: _____

_____

Section 8

FAVORITE BOOKS
FOR
APRIL

The following books are on "April Book List B" in *Ready-to-Use Reading Activities Through the Year*.

Activity Sheet	Book Title	Reading Level	Award
8-1 to 8-5	**Charlie and the Chocolate Factory**	5	
8-6 to 8-10	**Frankenstein**	8	
8-11 to 8-15	**My Brother Sam Is Dead**	5.8	Newbery Honor
8-16 to 8-20	**The War Between the Pitiful Teachers and the Splendid Kids**	7.6	

Charlie and the Chocolate Factory by Roald Dahl.
New York: Puffin, 1964. 164 pages.

Charlie Bucket, his parents, and both sets of grandparents are so desperately poor that they're literally starving to death. Imagine the exquisite torture of living practically next door to a factory that makes the world's best chocolate! Imagine constantly inhaling this scrumptious smell, but not being able to afford to buy any! When Willy Wonka, the owner of the chocolate factory, announces that five lucky children will win tickets to visit the factory and will receive a lifetime supply of chocolate, Charlie knows it will take a miracle for him to win. He gets his miracle! Unbeknownst to anyone, Mr. Wonka has devised a series of tantalizingly tempting tests to see if any of the children are worthy of inheriting his chocolate factory. Charlie rises above all the temptations and passes every test. Willy Wonka wafts Charlie's family to the factory in a special glass elevator so they can help run the factory while Charlie learns all Mr. Wonka has to teach him. Charlie and his family will never be hungry again.

Frankenstein by Mary Wollstonecraft Shelley. Mahwah, NJ: Watermill Press, 1980. 333 pages.

Most readers will be familiar with this story from watching a movie or reading a watered-down version of it. Neither of these can compare with the classic tale as penned in the author's own words. The tale shows the selfish, weak nature of Victor Frankenstein and how his weaknesses wreck havoc on those he loves. The tale also shows a surprisingly human side to the monster Frankenstein creates. This tale will elicit feelings of both compassion and loathing, but the reader may be surprised to discover toward whom these feelings are directed!

My Brother Sam Is Dead by James Lincoln Collier and Christopher Collier. New York: Scholastic, 1974. 216 pages.

Tim Meeker is a young boy at the outbreak of the American Revolution. He doesn't understand why there has to be a war at all. Sam, his older brother, rushes to join the Continental Army. Their father is adamantly opposed to this and calls it treason against England. He says there are some drawbacks to being under English control, but nothing justifies going to war. Tim's family is torn apart when Sam leaves. During the first couple of years of fighting, the war seems almost unreal to Tim. He reads about it in the newspapers and hears gossip, but he doesn't actually see it with his own eyes. Then, one horrible day, war comes to his doorstep. He sees neighbors slaughtered. Food and supplies become scarce. Hunger and want become facts of life. First, Tim loses his father when he is captured and sent to a prison ship where he dies of cholera. Next, Tim loses his brother Sam when Sam is falsely accused of stealing cattle and is executed. Fifty years after the end of the war, Tim still wonders if the same end couldn't have been achieved by other means.

The War Between the Pitiful Teachers and the Splendid Kids by Stanley Kiesel. New York: Avon, 1980. 207 pages.

Skinny Malinky hates teachers—and the feeling is mutual! He is passed from teacher to teacher. The teachers seem eager to get him admitted to Scratchland School, a student's last stop before reform school. When Skinny arrives at Scratchland, he continues to have confrontations with his teachers. One confrontation leads to another until Skinny declares war. The teachers accept his challenge. A tournament is arranged in order to decide the winner. Big Alice Eyesore, the hyena girl, is the champion for the kids. The champion for the teachers is hidden under a full suit of armor. Can any teacher defeat Big Alice, who has already devoured one teacher as a little snack? The crowd is stunned when Big Alice seems to freeze as she is about to overpower the teachers' champion. Why doesn't she move? Have the teachers won? Will all of the losers be rounded up and solidified as threatened? Will life after solidification be worth living? Is there no escape? Can no one help? Is the war really over or is there one last battle to wage?

CHARLIE AND THE CHOCOLATE FACTORY
Comprehension Test A

Directions: Read each question carefully. Circle the letter of the choice that best answers each question.

1. Who wrote this book?
    a. Roald Dahl   *b.* Robert McCloskey   *c.* Steven Kellogg

2. If you found a Golden Ticket, you got _____.
    a. a case of candy every month for twenty years
    b. your weight in candy
    c. to visit the chocolate factory

3. What did an Oompa-Loompa dream about all night and talk about all day?
    a. breadfruit   *b.* kiwi fruit   *c.* cacao beans

4. What special treat was Mr. Wonka making for kids who had little money?
    a. Never Ending Bubblebusters
    b. Everlasting Gobstoppers
    c. Forever Ready Tonguethumpers

5. What did Willy Wonka invent to replace kitchens and cooking?
    a. a robot   *b.* a pill   *c.* a stick of gum

6. Why did the Oompa-Loompas wear space suits in the Television Chocolate room?
    a. to protect themselves from radiation
    b. so they wouldn't be broken into a million pieces
    c. because female Oompa-Loompas like men in uniform

7. Mike Teavee ended up very thin and 10 feet tall, but Willy Wonka said _____.
    a. all the basketball teams would want him
    b. he'd make a million dollars going on talk shows
    c. he could join the circus

8. Four out of five children got in trouble in the chocolate factory because they _____.
    a. were very greedy
    b. didn't mind adults
    c. wanted to show off

9. The glass elevator could shoot through _____.
    a. a time zone   *b.* space   *c.* a roof

10. Charlie's family _____.
    a. refused to enter the chocolate factory
    b. were whisked away to the chocolate factory
    c. starved to death while he was gone

CHARLIE AND THE CHOCOLATE FACTORY
Comprehension Test B

Directions: Read each question carefully. Circle the letter of the choice that best answers each question.

1. Mr. Bucket worked as _____.
   a. an aspirin bottle-stuffer   *b.* a toothpaste cap-screwer   *c.* a hairspray can-topper

2. Where did Charlie get the money to buy the candy bar with the Golden Ticket?
   a. He found a dollar.
   b. He got it from Grandpa Joe.
   c. He shoveled snow to earn extra money.

3. Who fell into the chocolate river while lapping it up like a dog?
   a. Mike Teavee
   b. Violet Beauregarde
   c. Augustus Gloop

4. What made hair sprout on your head and face?
   a. Hair Toffee
   b. Moustachy Pistachy
   c. Hairy Berry

5. After drinking a Fizzy Lifting Drink and rising into the air, you _____.
   a. had to stay there until the bubbles burst
   b. could get down by sneezing
   c. could get down by burping

6. Oompa-Loompas painted faces on _____.
   a. Square Candies That Look Round
   b. Has Beans
   c. Goober Gloppers

7. When Violet Beauregarde blew up like a giant blueberry, they _____.
   a. stuck a pin in her
   b. put her through a wringer
   c. juiced her

8. Who got broken into pieces, sent through the TV, and shrunk?
   a. Augustus Gloop   *b.* Mike Teavee   *c.* Veruca Salt

9. The Wonka vitamin made your _____ and fingers the same length.
   a. nose   *b.* toes   *c.* lips

10. If you sucked on _____, you could spit in six different colors.
    a. Luminous Lollies   *b.* Fruity Gloppers   *c.* Rainbow Drops

CHARLIE AND THE CHOCOLATE FACTORY
Comprehension Test C

Directions: Read each question carefully. Circle the letter of the choice that best answers each question.

1. Charlie's family was so poor that they ate three _____ meals a day.
   - *a.* substantial
   - *b.* nutritional
   - *c.* meager

2. Which adult went with Charlie when he first entered the chocolate factory?
   - *a.* Mother
   - *b.* Father
   - *c.* Grandpa Joe

3. Willy Wonka's yacht was made out of _____.
   - *a.* a gigantic chocolate almond bar
   - *b.* a big pink boiled-sweet
   - *c.* an enormous cream-filled cupcake

4. When Mr. Wonka didn't want to answer a question, he _____.
   - *a.* pretended not to hear it
   - *b.* ignored it
   - *c.* walked away

5. The Oompa-Loompas got tiddly by drinking _____.
   - *a.* Butterscotch
   - *b.* Butterschnapps
   - *c.* Butterrum

6. Willy Wonka said the Oompa-Loompas were always _____.
   - *a.* laughing
   - *b.* whistling
   - *c.* singing

7. Why did the squirrels push Veruca's Mum and Dad down the garbage chute?
   - *a.* They were too greedy.
   - *b.* They spoiled Veruca.
   - *c.* They yelled at Willie Wonka.

8. Mr. Wonka picked the child he liked best to _____.
   - *a.* adopt
   - *b.* be his spokesperson
   - *c.* take over the factory

9. Who ended up with a permanently purple face?
   - *a.* Augustus Gloop
   - *b.* Violet Beauregarde
   - *c.* Veruca Salt

10. Who ended up thin as a straw?
    - *a.* Augustus Gloop
    - *b.* Violet Beauregarde
    - *c.* Veruca Salt

CHARLIE AND THE CHOCOLATE FACTORY

I. *Directions:* You have just invented the world's most fantastic, scrumptious, marvelous chocolate treat ever. Now you have to let people know about your wonderful new invention. Create a newspaper ad to help market this new product.

II. *Directions:* Write a jingle for your new product.

_____

_____

_____

_____

_____

_____

III. *Directions:* Use your jingle to make a 30- to 60-second radio commercial selling your new product.

PROJECTS FOR *CHARLIE AND THE CHOCOLATE FACTORY*

Directions: Choose one of the following projects or design your own. If you design your own project, fill out the form below and submit it to your teacher for approval.

1. Make a mobile featuring Oompa-Loompas, Hornswogglers, Snozzwangers, and Whangdoodles.

2. Collect chocolate recipes from faculty, family, and friends. Publish a chocolate lover's cookbook. Organize a bake sale using recipes from the cookbook. Sell both the baked goods and copies of the cookbook. Donate the proceeds to a favorite charity or use the funds to buy something for your classroom or the school.

3. Maybe you don't dream of being turned loose in a chocolate factory. Maybe you'd prefer a pizza, donut, pretzel, or some other scrumptious food factory. What if you got your wish, just as Charlie Bucket did? Prepare a comic book about your adventure.

4. Make models of a male, female, and child Oompa-Loompa. Dress them appropriately.

5. Write the next chapter in the book.

6. Roald Dahl is a very popular author. Prepare a bibliography of his books.

7. Dress as one of the characters and tell the story from this point of view.

PROJECT PROPOSAL

Name _____ Beginning Date _____ Completion Date _____

Describe the project in detail: _____

_____

Why do you want to do this project? _____

_____

What will the final product be? _____

_____

How will you share your final product? _____

_____

Comments: _____

_____

FRANKENSTEIN
Comprehension Test A

Directions: Read each question carefully. Circle the letter of the choice that best answers each question.

1. Who wrote this book?
   a. Percy Bysshe Shelley
   b. Mary Wollstonecraft Godwin
   c. Mary Wollstonecraft Shelley

2. Robert Walton related these events in a series of letters to his _____.
   a. publisher   b. sister   c. wife

3. Victor's mother died after nursing Elizabeth through a case of _____.
   a. scarlet fever   b. typhoid   c. cholera

4. After Victor Frankenstein recovered from his nervous fever, he learned that _____.
   a. William had been murdered
   b. Elizabeth had been murdered
   c. Ernest had been murdered

5. The monster demanded that Frankenstein _____.
   a. find a woman willing to marry him
   b. create a female companion for him
   c. perform plastic surgery so he'd look more attractive to women

6. Victor pieced together a female monster off the coast of _____.
   a. Scotland   b. England   c. Ireland

7. Victor had little difficulty following the fiend north because _____.
   a. the fiend was slowed down by lameness
   b. the villagers attacked the fiend at every opportunity
   c. the fiend left messages to mark his route

8. Victor started gaining on the fiend when he _____.
   a. hired a guide   b. got a sledge and dogs   c. got a horse and sleigh

9. After being icebound for days, Walton's crew demanded _____.
   a. that he head southward if the ice broke up
   b. to take over command
   c. to be allowed to help kill Frankenstein's monster

10. On his deathbed, Frankenstein said that he _____.
    a. was wrong to have created the monster
    b. wished he had made more monsters
    c. did not blame himself for creating the monster

FRANKENSTEIN
Comprehension Test B

Directions: Read each question carefully. Circle the letter of the choice that best answers each question.

1. The man who told his life story to Robert Walton said he had always _____.
   a. been drawn to the metaphysical
   b. been fascinated with the supernatural
   c. feared the unknown

2. Victor Frankenstein decided to create an 8-foot human being because _____.
   a. he wanted to get in the record books
   b. small parts slowed him down
   c. he wanted to astound the scientific world

3. Soon after bringing the monster to life, Victor Frankenstein _____.
   a. went insane and was committed to an asylum
   b. was expelled from college
   c. became critically ill for several months

4. Victor's dearest friend was _____.
   a. Robert Walton   b. Cornelius Agrippa   c. Henry Clerval

5. Frankenstein's monster burned the DeLacy's cottage because they _____.
   a. refused to help him find his creator
   b. refused to befriend him
   c. called the police when they saw him

6. Why did Victor tear the female monster apart?
   a. He was angry when the monster threatened him.
   b. He was dissatisfied with his work.
   c. He didn't want to unleash another monster on the world.

7. Villagers told Victor that the fiend was armed with a _____.
   a. club   b. gun and many pistols   c. crossbow

8. Victor pursued the fiend across _____.
   a. ice fields   b. Siberia   c. the Yukon

9. Victor begged Walton to _____.
   a. help him escape
   b. kill him so he could join Elizabeth
   c. kill the fiend upon sight

10. Frankenstein's monster compared himself to a _____.
    a. fallen angel   b. mad scientist   c. genius

FRANKENSTEIN
Comprehension Test C

Directions: Read each question carefully. Circle the letter of the choice that best answers each question.

1. After studying many dead bodies, Dr. Frankenstein discovered _____.
   a. that his past studies had been out of date
   b. the meaning of life
   c. how to bestow animation on lifeless matter

2. Frankenstein's monster had black lips and _____ eyes.
   a. black   b. yellow   c. red

3. When Victor Frankenstein was ill, he was nursed back to health by _____.
   a. Henry Clerval   b. Margaret Saville   c. Elizabeth Lavenza

4. Victor left Ingolstadt and returned home to _____.
   a. Berlin, Germany   b. Vienna, Austria   c. Geneva, Switzerland

5. Frankenstein's monster learned to speak and read by _____.
   a. listening as Felix instructed his wife
   b. listening outside the first-grade classroom
   c. spying on schoolchildren

6. The monster vowed eternal hatred and vengeance to all mankind when _____.
   a. the DeLacey family threw him out
   b. Victor refused to make a mate for him
   c. he was shot after rescuing a young girl

7. Why did the monster kill Henry Clerval?
   a. Clerval was in the wrong place at the wrong time.
   b. He wanted revenge.
   c. Clerval tried to shoot him.

8. What event finally made Victor seek to destroy the monster?
   a. the entreaties of the peasants
   b. the judge ordered him to do so
   c. he lost another family member

9. How did Victor lose his enemy?
   a. the ice broke up   b. his sled dogs died   c. his food ran out

10. Victor said he could fulfill his lot on earth by _____.
    a. publishing his memoirs
    b. killing the monster he created
    c. telling other scientists how to create man

FRANKENSTEIN

Directions: The puzzle below contains words from the story. Find these words and circle them. You may go across and down.

```
        d e t e s t a t i o n m s r h z
      b e m s a n g u i n a r y m a r t y r s
      r t d l n f u t u r i t y a s s i z e s l z
      e o k o q f a c i l e p i s k l s t w x h i o
      c m i t y r o s a z a u g m e n t e d d y n s
      a n n i h i l a t i o n x v n b e d e w e d a
      p i c m d g b h f d q u r g e o c i t a d e l
      i p a p i h i k b s l t h r r u n t r t e f u
      t o n r l t v c e p i t h e t s a p d b m a b
      u t t e a a e n n u i e l i z r d u k w o t r
      l e a c t t r t i h x r m l e r q e n s n i i
      a n t a o o d u g w k a b s t r u s e o i g o
      t t i t r r u s n l z b r v s p n k u t a a u
      i q o e i i r r i y a l l e v i a t e d c b s
      o p n g n n e o t b f e s a g a c i t y a l t
      n a s o e s p h y s i o g n o m y o n t l e r
      i r r e s o l u t i o n d e s p o n d e n c e
      x o w n s e n v i r o n s s a u e c l p q l x
      y x e d t o d e b i l i t a t e d i k r u q o
        y d u s y p r o g n o s t i c a t e d r b r
        s l e o t r d i s q u i s i t i o n s s c d
        m s d a c q u i e s c e d n u i s h o z h i
    k j h s e r l p r e c i p i t o u s m t p l m a u l a c
      i o a s s e v e r a t i o n s c v u b e d i m t
      h l b c o n v a l e s c e n c e o o k m m i o e
      a g c a d u h i w i n e x o r a b l e n a n b s
      c h i m e r a v e i m m u r e d d l v i a n d s
      p a n e g y r i c m a l i c i o u s u z c x u r
    d e b i l i t y a z p y f m v w k r a e a d o r h d
      p z i l y b c k e j i x h m w a g f t g r a
      e n o u n c e d d x h e l a v t a m i x a t
      d a r a u g u r i e s a n l u s i r o c b e
      a d a e x f a c m e g u b i t h l y n x l t
      n b t u h i g w e v d o c g s r t o n n e i
      t o e l i x i r n t e f p n q m y r i a d s
      r n t c j m u l t i f a r i o u s q p s t k
      y p m q k l m a c h i n a t i o n s y l y
          r i g n o m i n y s r
```

ignominy
alleviated
multifarious
ameliorate
omnipotent
abstruse
futurity
affright
facile
citadel
martyrs
endued
assizes
debility
impediment
pedantry
imprecate
epithets
panegyric
siroc

penury
precipitous
augmented
benignity
exordium
disquisitions
environs
malignity

acme
ennui
viands
bedim
verdure
elixir
chimera
myriads

sagacity
malicious
obdurate
auguries
prognosticated
solemnization
unutterable
acquiesced

demoniacal
sanguinary
bedewed
physiognomy
irresolution
convalescence
recapitulation
incantations
debilitated
detestation
inexorable
annihilation
indefatigable
salubrious
machinations
dilatoriness
asseverations
despondence
paroxysms
tyros
immured

PROJECTS FOR *FRANKENSTEIN*

Directions: Choose one of the following projects or design your own. If you design your own project, fill out the form below and submit it to your teacher for approval.

1. Make a model of Frankenstein's monster.

2. Make a model of the monster's bride.

3. Write a character profile of Victor Frankenstein. List his strengths and weaknesses. Tell how his weaknesses produced misery, death, and destruction from the hands of the monster he created. Could this have been prevented if Victor had been less cowardly and selfish? List several instances where decisive action on Victor's part could have averted a death.

4. At one time, laudanum was a popular and widely used drug. Victor says he used it. Write a report about this drug.

5. Prepare a skit based on an event in the book. Perform the skit for your class.

6. Tell this story in the form of a rap.

7. What if, after receiving this narrative from her brother, Mrs. Seville had invited her best friend to tea in order to talk about the strange events related in her brother's letters? Write and perform this scene.

PROJECT PROPOSAL

Name _____ Beginning Date _____ Completion Date _____

Describe the project in detail: _____
_____

Why do you want to do this project? _____
_____

What will the final product be? _____
_____

How will you share your final product? _____
_____

Comments: _____
_____

MY BROTHER SAM IS DEAD
Comprehension Test A

Directions: Read each question carefully. Circle the letter of the choice that best answers each question.

1. Who wrote this book?
   a. Scott O'Dell and Myra O'Dell
   b. Harry Allard and James Allard
   c. James Lincoln Collier and Christopher Collier

2. Why was Father sitting in the taproom crying?
   a. He was broke and about to lose everything.
   b. Sam told him he was going to war.
   c. He and Mother had a fight.

3. Why did a Rebel soldier cut Father's cheek?
   a. because he was a Tory
   b. so he would feed his troops for free
   c. to make him hand over his gun

4. When Sam joined the army he was _____ years old.
   a. 16   b. 18   c. 20

5. Mr. Heron tried to hire Timmy to deliver _____ to Fairfield.
   a. goods   b. "business letters"   c. weapons

6. What happened to Father on the way home?
   a. He was captured by the Lobsterbacks.
   b. He was captured by the cowboys.
   c. He was captured by a band of rebels.

7. Tim said he didn't feel much like being a Tory anymore after he saw _____.
   a. Redcoats burn the town to the ground
   b. Mr. Heron getting paid for spying on his neighbors
   c. Lobsterbacks cut off Ned's head

8. Why was it so important to slow down the Lobsterbacks as they left Redding?
   a. to give people time to flee
   b. so Continental troops could catch up with them
   c. so people could hide their money

9. Sam was arrested for _____.
   a. mutiny   b. stealing cattle   c. treason

10. Why did General Putnam execute Sam?
    a. He hated Sam's family.
    b. He needed to keep the troops in line.
    c. Sam's father had stolen his girl years ago.

MY BROTHER SAM IS DEAD
Comprehension Test B

Directions: Read each question carefully. Circle the letter of the choice that best answers each question.

1. What did Sam call the British troops?
   a. Redcoats   *b.* Lobsterbacks   *c.* Rednecks

2. Who sat in the balcony at church?
   a. the choir
   b. women and female children
   c. children, Indians, and black people

3. When did Timmy first realize the war could affect him too?
   a. when the Rebels came searching for weapons
   b. when he learned that Sam was dead
   c. when Sam left to join the Rebels

4. In school, Timmy was best at _____.
   a. memorizing psalms   *b.* ciphering   *c.* spelling

5. When Tim crossed from Connecticut into New York, he said _____.
   a. he was in a foreign country
   b. it looked a lot different
   c. it was enemy territory

6. What happened to make Timmy realize that he was a Tory?
   a. his arrest   *b.* Sam's death   *c.* Father's capture

7. Father died on a British prison ship during an outbreak of _____.
   a. typhoid fever   *b.* scurvy   *c.* cholera

8. Tim said that hunger was like going around all day with _____.
   a. a fire in your stomach
   b. a nail in your shoe
   c. a gnawing in your bones _____.

9. Tim became a _____.
   a. professor   *b.* surveyor   *c.* lawyer

10. Mr. William Heron was spying for the _____.
    a. British
    b. Americans
    c. Americans and the British

MY BROTHER SAM IS DEAD
Comprehension Test C

Directions: Read each question carefully. Circle the letter of the choice that best answers each question.

1. People who did not want a war with England were called _____.
   - *a.* Patriots
   - *b.* Whigs
   - *c.* Tories

2. Sam said that Timmy could help the war effort by _____.
   - *a.* listening to gossip in the tavern
   - *b.* recruiting for the militia
   - *c.* stealing guns

3. By January of 1776, food was a real problem because _____.
   - *a.* it was so scarce
   - *b.* it kept going up in price
   - *c.* the quality was so poor

4. Why didn't Betsy want Timmy to deliver Mr. Heron's letter?
   - *a.* she wanted to earn the shilling herself
   - *b.* she thought it was a spy letter about Sam
   - *c.* she thought it was too dangerous

5. Who tried to steal Mr. Meeker's cattle on the drive?
   - *a.* cowboys
   - *b.* Rebels
   - *c.* Lobsterbacks

6. British officers went to Mr. Heron's house to _____.
   - *a.* learn who the Rebel leaders were
   - *b.* arrest him
   - *c.* confiscate all his property

7. Tim felt he was Sam's equal when he _____.
   - *a.* had to be the man of the family
   - *b.* realized that Sam fought because he wanted to
   - *c.* fought out of a sense of duty

8. Tim decided he wouldn't be on anybody's side anymore after he _____.
   - *a.* and Mother lost the tavern
   - *b.* was wounded by a stray bullet
   - *c.* found out that Father was dead

9. Why was February 6 an important date to the family?
   - *a.* Sam's court-martial began.
   - *b.* They inherited money from relatives.
   - *c.* Tim turned 21.

10. Sam's girlfriend was _____.
    - *a.* Betsy Ross
    - *b.* Betsy Read
    - *c.* Betsy Ready

MY BROTHER SAM IS DEAD

I. *Directions:* Thousands of Americans who remained loyal to the crown fled to Canada because they were considered traitors. Trace the flight of these Loyalists from Castine, Maine to St. Andrews, St. John, and Fredericton in New Brunswick. Indicate each of these towns on the map below. Draw and label the Penobscot, St. Croix, and St. John Rivers. Draw a broken line to indicate the route of the Loyalists.

II. *Directions:* On a separate sheet of paper, write a report about the Loyalists and their flight to Canada. Include illustrations of the homes they built.

PROJECTS FOR *MY BROTHER SAM IS DEAD*

Directions: Choose one of the following projects or design your own. If you design your own project, fill out the form below and submit it to your teacher for approval.

1. Eliphalet Meeker said he fought in the battle of Louisbourg seventeen years before the beginning of the American Revolution. Write a report about this battle.

2. Sam and his father could not calmly debate the pros and cons of going to war with England because Mr. Meeker had such a hot temper. What if he controlled his temper long enough to have this debate? Choose two other class members who have read this book and present this debate to your class. (The three people taking part in this debate are Sam, Mr. Meeker, and Mr. Beach, the mediator.)

3. Newspapers such as the *Connecticut Journal* and *Rivington's Gazette* reported war news. Write an article about Sam's court-martial and execution for one of these newspapers.

4. Give a report and demonstration about children's games that were popular at the time of the American Revolution.

5. Draw illustrations of a Redcoat and a Continental soldier. Point out similarities and differences in their clothes, weapons, battle tactics, pay, and so on.

PROJECT PROPOSAL

Name _____ Beginning Date _____ Completion Date _____

Describe the project in detail: _____
_____

Why do you want to do this project? _____
_____

What will the final product be? _____
_____

How will you share your final product? _____
_____

Comments: _____
_____

THE WAR BETWEEN THE PITIFUL TEACHERS AND THE SPLENDID KIDS
Comprehension Test A

Directions: Read each question carefully. Circle the letter of the choice that best answers each question.

1. Who wrote this book?

   a. Robert Cormier   *b.* Stanley Kiesel   *c.* Robert Lipsyte

2. Mrs. Jerome gave Skinny a bucket and brush and told him to clean one lavatory wall, but he _____.

   a. dumped water on her shoes
   b. drank the soapy water and threw up on her
   c. licked the wall clean instead

3. Skinny and _____ decided it was time to declare war on the teachers.

   a. Curly   *b.* Fritzie   *c.* Margery

4. Curly explained that kings and popes who became allies to fight the infidels signed a _____.

   a. concordent   *b.* concordat   *c.* contract

5. The 37th reunion of the 10th New York Cavalry was held on October 18, 1898 to commemorate the _____.

   a. Civil War   *b.* War of 1812   *c.* American Revolution

6. The Status Quo Solidifier, part of Project Metamorphosis, could _____.

   a. turn a kid into a rodent in ten seconds
   b. age a kid in ten seconds
   c. turn a kid into a statue in ten seconds

7. The score at the end of the second round was _____.

   a. Kids 2, Teachers 0
   b. Kids 0, Teachers 2
   c. Kids 1, Teachers 1

8. Miss Jenny began researching _____ from strange old books down in her cellar.

   a. spells   *b.* bites   *c.* magic

9. What did Miss Bumpy do that was just like a kid?

   a. rang a false fire alarm
   b. threw up in the cafeteria
   c. set the wastebasket in the restroom on fire

10. Skinny and Four Eyes developed a plan to change the Literary Flush to _____.

    a. the Terminator Flush
    b. the Academician Flush
    c. the Grand Flush

THE WAR BETWEEN THE PITIFUL TEACHERS AND THE SPLENDID KIDS
Comprehension Test B

Directions: Read each question carefully. Circle the letter of the choice that best answers each question.

1. Skinny was found in a box in the hallway of an apartment building when _____.
   - *a.* he was one day old
   - *b.* he was one week old
   - *c.* he was one month old

2. After war was declared, the first thing the kids did was mess with the _____.
   - *a.* flags
   - *b.* bells
   - *c.* cafeteria food

3. In just three years, Colonel Kratz rose from _____ to superintendent of schools.
   - *a.* hall monitor
   - *b.* crossing guard
   - *c.* playground aide

4. Big Alice Eyesore's parents dumped her at a wildlife preserve where she was adopted by a _____.
   - *a.* hippo
   - *b.* ferret
   - *c.* hyena

5. Mr. Foreclosure was a mutant who looked like a _____.
   - *a.* black beetle
   - *b.* red ant
   - *c.* roach

6. Who said the war should be decided by a tournament?
   - *a.* Ida
   - *b.* Skinny
   - *c.* Big Alice

7. The standards of the Substitute Teachers' Association, Blessed Martyr Division said _____.
   - *a.* We Came, We Saw, We Ran
   - *b.* We Came, We Saw, We Did Not Return
   - *c.* We Came, We Saw, We Conquered

8. Bookworms get their food from _____.
   - *a.* school cafeterias
   - *b.* restaurant kitchens
   - *c.* garbage pails

9. The sixty-eight kids who had "accidents" in the faulty solidifiers were converted into _____.
   - *a.* spitballs
   - *b.* breakfast cereal
   - *c.* kitty litter

10. The Dunphrys stopped worrying about the other teachers when they learned that _____.
    - *a.* the automatic coffeemakers were flushed with them
    - *b.* the ditto machines and lots of paper were flushed with them
    - *c.* their lesson plan books and chalkholders were flushed with them

THE WAR BETWEEN THE PITIFUL TEACHERS AND THE SPLENDID KIDS
Comprehension Test C

Directions: Read each question carefully. Circle the letter of the choice that best answers each question.

1. The one person at Ripley Street School who really cared about Skinny was _____.
   a. Mrs. Langley, a teacher
   b. Ida, the janitor
   c. Miss Swinley, the head cook

2. Mrs. Primrose, the vice-principal, had trained at _____ State Teachers College.
   a. Hangemhigh   b. Hara-kiri   c. Quasimodo

3. The teachers at Pangloss Polytechnic were so busy at the copy machines that the school was nicknamed _____.
   a. Mimeo   b. Ditto   c. Purple Inc.

4. The Status Quo Solidifier was a practical device that could harness the enormous power of _____.
   a. chocolate chip cookies   b. peanut butter   c. potato chips

5. Mrs. Jerome _____.
   a. took early retirement
   b. was taken away in a straitjacket
   c. was devoured by Big Alice

6. Curly told Skinny that *rococo* meant _____.
   a. mean-tempered   b. overdone   c. savage

7. Teachers sat in the bleachers for hours watching troublemakers go into the Solidifier and _____.
   a. be turned into retirees
   b. disappear from the face of the earth forever
   c. come out a Young Person

8. Why did Miss Bumpy and Miss Jenny tell Ida that Skinny had been tricked?
   a. Ida bribed them with new chalk, erasers, and felt-tip pens.
   b. They needed one real kid around.
   c. They wanted to get even with the administrators.

9. The Bookworms tried to unsolidify the Y.P.s, but their biggest achievement was getting one to _____.
   a. wear jeans and a T-shirt
   b. eat junk food
   c. pick his nose in public

10. Big Ida told Skinny _____
    a. "You'll find your own way."
    b. "Learn from your past mistakes."
    c. "Oh, grow up!"

THE WAR BETWEEN THE PITIFUL TEACHERS AND THE SPLENDID KIDS

I. Directions: Words from the story are hidden in the shield. Find the words and circle them. You may go across and down.

ART 26

```
                              s
                          a t c e
                     o t s v o l u m i n o u s
                   e s k i t t e r e d l m k l
                 q u a l m s a h r j c f e l m n
                 a h k b n g e s t i c u l a t e d e
               m b d e v o u r b n f l n o s t a l g i c l i
               e l s m u t c h e d a o d i p g k e o m i e n
             s c d m u t a n t t q s u a m b c r e x s t k s h
           s l o a m h k g s o n x t s t u p e f i e d i f i c e
           r a n s a c k e d l e a i e x c r u c i a t i n g z s
           e v e n o m o u s l t n d n m e a n d e r e d y n r t
       p l e n u m o h k u t v e i t w a s y n c h r o n i z e u
           n r i n s t i g a t e c o o a y c l k s t a c c a t o
           x e r s h m l o t v u d u m b x u h n u a u o s e r
           s d e c i p h e r l z o s o v c l z x k p s n p t h
           r q p w n o m k j i y t l l p a m o d m e p v a v e
           i n g e n i o u s h x a y o w l i n i l s i o s w l
           d e s p i c a b l e f l a g r a n t l y t c l m y d
             r p h e n o m e n a g e i b c a q i p r i u o d
           b l u d g e o n e d f d c c r t z g t i o t d r
             g u t t u r a l r q y a i i e s e e e u e i
             t n n p y g m i e s l l t d m n r d s d c
             s m e h x e w t r o v k y g o c o z y r
               p q o i m p e r i o u s h m e d a s
               r r s i t u v f c e d c e b a c
               b i a n e r u d i t i o n j c b
               c z e x w l k f v r u t m t
               d n y e u p e q s n o o y
               c t p f t o r p o r u n l
               l o g h i o q t u s e
               y m r k j u r n l
               y x u s v w y
               z t l s r
               e y o
```

edifice				staccato
skittered				ransacked
stupefied				culminated
pterodactyl				auspicious
despicable	plenum		unruly	ingenious
flagrantly	meandered	diligence	guttural	excruciating
entomological	scurrilous	shinnied	decipher	synchronize
devour	imperious	insignia	instigate	venomous
spasmodic	anecdotal	convoluted	qualms	gesticulated
momentous	phenomena	slavered	pygmies	tapestried
bludgeoned	torpor	nostalgic	mutant	melee
voluminous	mien	sabotage	smutched	fastidiously
alacrity	vociferously	euphoric	erudition	eminently

II. Directions: Choose ten of the words above and use each one correctly in a sentence. Write your sentences on a separate sheet of paper.

PROJECTS FOR
THE WAR BETWEEN THE PITIFUL TEACHERS AND THE SPLENDID KIDS

Directions: Choose one of the following projects or design your own. If you design your own project, fill out the form below and submit it to your teacher for approval.

1. Rewrite this story as a picture book.

2. Rewrite this story as a comic book.

3. Make a mobile featuring characters from the book.

4. What if Phil, Oprah, Sally, or Geraldo had three representatives from the kids' side and three from the teachers' side make a guest appearance on his or her TV talk show? Simulate this guest appearance.

5. Reread the description of Big Alice's opponent in the tournament. Make a model of this person on whose shield were the words Le Chevalier Rococo.

6. Reread Beezer Martin's poem about a bird. Write three more stanzas to this poem or choose three different fuzzy, feathery, or scaly creatures to write poems about.

7. Reread the description of the good luck charm that Ida gave to Skinny. Make a model of this charm.

8. Choose three scenes from the story to illustrate. Include captions with your illustrations.

PROJECT PROPOSAL

Name _____ Beginning Date _____ Completion Date _____

Describe the project in detail: _____

_____

Why do you want to do this project? _____

_____

What will the final product be? _____

_____

How will you share your final product? _____

_____

Comments: _____

_____

Section 9

FAVORITE BOOKS
FOR
MAY

The following books are on "May Book List B" in *Ready-to-Use Reading Activities Through the Year*.

Activity Sheets	Book Title	Reading Level	Award
9-1 to 9-5	***All-of-a-Kind Family***	4.9	
9-6 to 9-10	***Call it Courage***	8	Newbery Medal
9-11 to 9-15	***Dirt Bike Racer***	5	
9-16 to 9-20	***Homesick: My Own Story***	4.8	Newbery Honor

All-of-a-Kind Family **by Sidney Taylor.**
Chicago: Follett, 1951. 189 pages.

This is a heartwarming story of a Jewish family living in a tenement in New York City in the early twentieth century. This warm, loving family consists of Mama, Papa, Ella, Henny, Sarah, Charlotte, and Gertie. We share their love and laughter as they celebrate various Jewish holidays and their surprise when a baby brother is born.

Call It Courage **by Armstrong Sperry.**
New York: Macmillan/Aladdin, 1940. 95 pages.

The sea claimed the life of Mafatu's mother when he was a young child. He has grown up being paralyzingly afraid of the sea. When it is time for boys his age to kill the great bonitos, Mafatu hesitates because he is afraid to go to sea. He overhears a conversation that stuns him into the realization that he either must face his fears and conquer them or he can no longer live on the island. He steals a canoe and heads to sea with his dog. He faces dangers that challenge him to the limit of his strength, but he triumphs. He returns home with the comfort of knowing that no one will ever again refer to him as Mafatu, the Boy Who Was Afraid. He has earned the right to be known as Mafatu, Stout Heart.

Dirt Bike Racer **by Matt Christopher.**
Boston: Little, Brown, 1979. 149 pages.

Twelve-year-old Ron Baker is delighted when he finds a minibike while he is scuba diving. After learning that he can legally keep it, he sets about getting it in running order. He advertises in the newspaper for a job so that he can afford to buy parts for his bike. He is hired by Mr. Perkins, a rich, elderly man who used to race bikes when he was young. Ron and Mr. Perkins become friends. Ron can't figure out why this friendship upsets Mark, who is the nephew of Mr. Perkins. Mark's obvious dislike of Ron escalates to threats and harassment. When Ron sees Mark paying another rider to make things rough for him on the track, Ron wonders if he'll be able to figure out how to keep from getting hurt in the race. Can Ron handle this on his own?

Homesick: My Own Story **by Jean Fritz.**
New York: Putnam, 1982. 163 pages.

Author Jean Fritz was born in China and grew up there during a turbulent period when opposing forces were vying for control of the country. She says that she felt as if she lived on the wrong side of the world and longed to go to America and be a real American. Yet, when war breaks out in 1927 and twelve-year-old Jean learns that she and her parents will be leaving, she realizes that there are many things she will miss about China. She also worries about whether she will fit in and be accepted in her new life in America. This concern about fitting in and being accepted by one's peers will strike a responsive chord in the heart and mind of each reader. Jean tells her story with such warmth and wit that this book can truly be described as a "good read."

ALL-OF-A-KIND FAMILY
Comprehension Test A

Directions: Read each question carefully. Circle the letter of the choice that best answers the question.

1. Who wrote this book?
   a. Patricia Reilly Giff
   b. Sydney Taylor
   c. Betsy Byars

2. Papa was a _____.
   a. junk dealer
   b. dock worker
   c. doctor

3. Papa's best friend was _____.
   a. Joe
   b. Picklenose
   c. Charlie

4. Which girl didn't have to share a bed with one of her sisters?
   a. Henny
   b. Sarah
   c. Gertie

5. When did they read by candlelight?
   a. on the Sabbath
   b. when they couldn't pay their light bill
   c. when their kerosene ran out

6. Which sister did not get scarlet fever?
   a. Ella
   b. Gertie
   c. Henny

7. What special treat did Charlie buy the girls for the Fourth of July?
   a. Roman candles
   b. pizza
   c. comic books

8. The family built a wooden hut in the backyard for the holiday of _____.
   a. Rosh Hashana
   b. Yom Kippur
   c. Succos

9. When Charlie found his sweetheart, they left to make up with _____.
   a. each other
   b. his family
   c. her family

10. Mama had her new baby _____.
    a. in the front room
    b. in the hospital
    c. in the carriage on the way to the hospital

ALL-OF-A-KIND FAMILY
Comprehension Test B

Directions: Read each question carefully. Circle the letter of the choice that best answers the question.

1. Sarah learned that she shouldn't _____.
    a. offer to pay for a lost library book
    b. check out a book from the public library
    c. lend her library book to anyone

2. The family was _____.
    a. Catholic   *b.* Jewish   *c.* Protestant

3. Mr. Basch didn't speak any English, only _____.
    a. Russian   *b.* Italian   *c.* Yiddish

4. Who disappeared for days at a time?
    a. Picklenose   *b.* Mr. Basch   *c.* Papa's friend Charlie

5. Women were allowed to go to synagogue _____.
    a. whenever they wanted
    b. only on important holidays
    c. only during Purim

6. Charlie was unhappy because _____.
    a. he lost his money in the stock market crash
    b. his doctor told him he was terminally ill
    c. he couldn't find the woman he loved

7. Who got lost at Playland?
    a. Henny   *b.* Gertie   *c.* Ella

8. Where did Charlie find his long-lost love?
    a. in the library
    b. in the family's backyard
    c. in the junk store

9. Which Jewish holiday falls between Rosh Hashana and Succos?
    a. Passover   *b.* Yom Kippur   *c.* Hanukkah

10. Which sister had the hardest time accepting the new baby?
    a. Charlotte   *b.* Sarah   *c.* Gertie

ALL-OF-A-KIND FAMILY
Comprehension Test C

Directions: Read each question carefully. Circle the letter of the choice that best answers the question.

1. How did Mama get the girls to dust the front room thoroughly?
   a. She threatened to punish sloppy work.
   b. She made it a game.
   c. She watched them as they worked.

2. Why did the rainy day turn out to be so much fun?
   a. They got to stay home from school.
   b. They found a 5-dollar bill on the sidewalk.
   c. They found books in Papa's junk store.

3. The family lived above a _____.
   a. grocery store   b. candy store   c. junk store

4. What did the girls buy Papa for his birthday?
   a. a tie   b. a moustache cup   c. a pocket knife

5. Charlie said that Ella sang like _____.
   a. a sick cow
   b. Picklenose
   c. an opera singer

6. When one sister got lost at Playland, where was she found?
   a. at the freak show
   b. in the police station
   c. on the carousel

7. The family found relief from the heat _____.
   a. at Coney Island
   b. at Atlantic City
   c. in the subway

8. What was the name of the woman Charlie loved?
   a. Charlotte O'Reilly   b. Rose Feenberg   c. Kathy Allen

9. Papa cried when Tanta brought the new baby to him because _____.
   a. he had the son he wanted
   b. the baby was deformed
   c. the baby was another girl

10. The family lived in a tenement in _____.
    a. Chicago   b. New York City   c. Newark

ALL-OF-A-KIND FAMILY

Directions: As you read the book, you may have noticed how often food was mentioned. The girls loved spending their pennies on candy, shopping at the street market, and watching Mama prepare festive holiday foods. Some of these foods are named in the puzzle below. We'll give you the letters *R, S, T, L, N,* and *E.* You have to fill in the missing letters.

1	S				E		▉	S		L			N	▉			
2	R	E		▉			E	R	R	Y	▉		E		R	T	S
3				L	E		▉	T				T		E	S	▉	
4			T		T		▉			E	L	S	▉				
5	L				R		E	R	▉			E	E	S	E		
6	S			R	▉	R		E		▉	R	E			▉		
7		R	E	T		E	L	S						▉			
8			N			E	▉		R			E	S	▉			
9	T		N		E	R		N	E	S	▉						
10			T			T	H	▉			L	L	S				
11	S		L	T	▉		E	R	R		N		S				
12		R		N				R	T	E	R	S	▉				
13						L		T	E	▉		E	N	N		E	S
14		R				E	R	S	▉								
15		E	L	L		▉		E		N	S	▉					
16	S			R	▉					L	E	S	▉				
17	S			E	R		R			T		▉					
18	S		E	E	T	▉			T		T		E	S	▉		
19			R						L	E	▉		E			S	
20		E		N		T	▉			R	S	▉					

© 1993 by Sue Jones Erlenbusch

PROJECTS FOR *ALL-OF-A-KIND FAMILY*

Directions: Choose one of the following projects or design your own. If you design your own project, fill out the form below and submit it to your teacher for approval.

1. Make a cookbook of foods appropriate to various Jewish holidays. Choose one recipe to make and bring it to class to share.

2. Look at the illustrations of the family's living room and kitchen. Make a model of one of the rooms.

3. The girls bought a moustache cup for Papa. Today, moustache cups are a popular collectible. Write a report about these cups. Include several illustrations. Tell how much these cups cost at flea markets and antique shows. If you know a collector, ask this person to do a classroom presentation.

4. Make a bibliography of books the girls would have enjoyed reading. Do not include books copyrighted after 1910.

5. Choose classmates who have also read the book to become members of a five-piece band. Reread the description of the instruments the girls used. Your band will use the same instruments. Present a concert of music that was popular at the turn of the twentieth century.

6. Choose a scene from the story and illustrate it in the style of Helen John, the book's illustrator. Illustrate the same scene in your own style.

PROJECT PROPOSAL

Name _____ Beginning Date _____ Completion Date _____

Describe the project in detail: _____

_____

Why do you want to do this project? _____

_____

What will the final product be? _____

_____

How will you share your final product? _____

_____

Comments: _____

_____

CALL IT COURAGE
Comprehension Test A

Directions: Read each question carefully. Circle the letter of the choice that best answers each question.

1. Who wrote this book?
   a. Robert Lawson   b. Matt Christopher   c. Armstrong Sperry

2. Mafatu's constant companions were _____.
   a. Uri and Kivi   b. Kana and Kivi   c. Uri and Viri

3. While at sea, Mafatu got water from _____.
   a. a coconut   b. green drinking nuts   c. a canteen

4. What did Mafatu find in a clearing?
   a. a deserted village
   b. an ancient idol
   c. wild boars

5. Mafatu made cloth from _____.
   a. the bark of the mulberry tree
   b. palm fronds
   c. ferns

6. Mafatu killed _____ in order to save his dog's life.
   a. an octopus   b. a hammerhead shark   c. a wild boar

7. Uri ran around barking when he smelled _____ roasting.
   a. breadfruit   b. fish   c. wild pig

8. When did Mafatu decide it was time to leave the high island?
   a. when the eaters-of-men came
   b. when his food ran out
   c. when loneliness overtook him

9. What began swimming parallel to Mafatu's canoe?
   a. a whale
   b. a tiger shark
   c. dolphins

10. Mafatu knew he was home when he saw _____.
    a. land
    b. Kivi
    c. lagoon-fire

CALL IT COURAGE
Comprehension Test B

Directions: Read each question carefully. Circle the letter of the choice that best answers each question.

1. Mafatu was known as the _____.
   a. Boy Who Was Afraid
   b. Boy Who Ran With the Wind
   c. Boy Who Soared With Eagles

2. Why did Mafatu decide to face his biggest fear, the sea?
   a. Kana dared him.
   b. His father made him.
   c. He couldn't live on Hikueru otherwise.

3. Where did Mafatu find a spearhead?
   a. lodged in the skeleton of a wild pig
   b. at the base of an idol
   c. on the beach

4. Mafatu was determined to return home with a _____.
   a. boar's-tooth necklace   b. wife   c. fortune

5. Who stole fish out of Mafatu's bamboo trap?
   a. an octopus   b. a flock of albatross   c. a hammerhead shark

6. Mafatu was born on an atoll, which is a _____.
   a. low island   b. high island   c. reef

7. When Mafatu dove to retrieve his knife, he had to kill _____.
   a. an eel   b. a shark   c. an octopus

8. The canoes filled with eaters-of-men pursued Mafatu for almost _____ hours.
   a. 8   b. 12   c. 24

9. On the homeward journey, Mafatu ran out of water and _____.
   a. dried fish
   b. poi
   c. pork

10. Who caught Mafatu when he collapsed?
    a. his father
    b. his friend
    c. the shaman

CALL IT COURAGE
Comprehension Test C

Directions: Read each question carefully. Circle the letter of the choice that best answers each question.

1. Mafatu was afraid of _____.
   a. his father   *b.* war   *c.* the sea

2. Some islands were known as dark islands because _____.
   a. they were uncharted
   b. the vegetation was so dark and lush
   c. they were inhabited by eaters-of-men

3. Mafatu's leg was cut by a _____.
   a. shark   *b.* coral reef   *c.* jagged rock

4. What did Mafatu put on his cut?
   a. lime juice   *b.* banana peel   *c.* ashes

5. Mafatu knew it was time to leave when he was awakened by _____.
   a. chanting
   b. drums
   c. the splashing of many oars in the sea

6. As Mafatu ran desperately toward his canoe, he was pursued by _____.
   a. a wild boar   *b.* a mad dog   *c.* four black men

7. Mafatu steered a homeward course by the _____.
   a. North Star   *b.* Fishhook of Maui   *c.* Big Dipper

8. Tavana Nui was the Great Chief of _____.
   a. Hikueru
   b. Polynesia
   c. Easter Island

9. The reflection of a lagoon upon the lower sky is called _____.
   a. lagoon-light
   b. lagoon-fire
   c. lagoon-glow

10. Mafatu stood up and shouted that he was not afraid of _____.
    a. Maui
    b. anything
    c. Moana

CALL IT COURAGE

I. Directions: All of the clues in the puzzle are from the book. Read the clues and fill in the puzzle.

ACROSS

1. He made cloth from a ___ tree.
3. Mafatu knew how to make ___.
5. A ___ shark stole from his fish traps.
6. He made a ___ of bamboo.
8. A large disastrous fire: ___
11. Polynesians worshipped ___.
14. The ghost-spirit that possessed every child at birth: ___
15. He made a boar's-tusk ___.
16. He made a ___ from whale bones.

DOWN

1. The Sea God: ___
2. Tastes a little like bread and potato: ___
3. Mafatu landed on a ___ island.
4. Eaters-of-men: ___
7. Mafatu used purau leaves to make a healing ___.
9. A piece of ___ was used as an anchor.
10. Piece of clothing: ___
11. Tamanu wood made a ___.
12. Octopus: ___
13. God of the Fisherman: ___

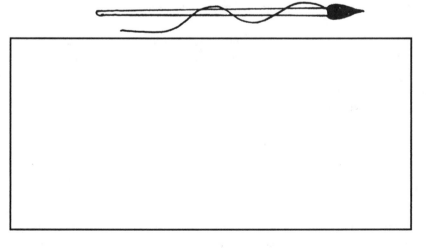

II. Directions: Draw a hammerhead shark, octopus, or one of the eaters-of-men in the box.

PROJECTS FOR *CALL IT COURAGE*

Directions: Choose one of the following projects or design your own. If you design your own project, fill out the form below and submit it to your teacher for approval.

1. Make a clay model of Uri.

2. Make a model of Mafatu's canoe.

3. Make a mural depicting the events in the story in chronological order.

4. Make a word search using words from the story.

5. Make a bibliography of at least ten other books about coming of age.

6. Write the next chapter of the book.

7. Make a mobile featuring Mafatu, Uri, Kivi, and his canoe.

8. Make a travel brochure about Polynesia.

9. Simulate the scene between Mafatu and his father upon his return home.

10. What if Mafatu had kept a diary about his adventure? Write the diary entries for him.

PROJECT PROPOSAL

Name _____ Beginning Date _____ Completion Date _____

Describe the project in detail: _____

_____

Why do you want to do this project? _____

_____

What will the final product be? _____

_____

How will you share your final product? _____

_____

Comments: _____

_____

DIRT BIKE RACER
Comprehension Test A

Directions: Read each question carefully. Circle the letter of the choice that best answers each question.

1. Who wrote this book?
   a. Richard Adams   *b.* Lloyd Alexander   *c.* Matt Christopher

2. Mike called Ron's bike a real _____.
   a. killer   *b.* klunker   *c.* loser

3. Who was Mark LaVerne?
   a. the most popular kid in Ronnie's class
   b. the nephew of Mr. Perkins
   c. the toughest bully in Ordell

4. Why did Mark give Glen Garner money after the race?
   a. for throwing the race
   b. for spilling Ron
   c. for the use of his bike

5. On the day of the cross-country race, Ron felt like _____.
   a. backing out   *b.* a winner   *c.* upchucking

6. Ron spilled during the cross-country race trying to avoid hitting _____.
   a. a rabbit that ran in front of him
   b. Glen, when he tried to cut Ron off
   c. a biker who sideswiped him

7. Whose fingerprints were found on Ron's bike?
   a. Lug Maneer   *b.* Skitch Bentley   *c.* Edward Bruning

8. Ron told his father that he didn't want to go to work because _____.
   a. Mark had embarrassed him
   b. Ollie didn't like his work
   c. the work was too hard

9. Mr. Perkins bought Ron a new _____.
   a. bike   *b.* tire   *c.* carburetor

10. Ron realized that Mr. Perkins _____.
    a. was a sucker for a sob story
    b. wasn't really blind
    c. filled a niche in his life

DIRT BIKE RACER
Comprehension Test B

Directions: Read each question carefully. Circle the letter of the choice that best answers each question.

1. Ron's best friend was _____.
   a. Lug Maneer   b. Skitch Bentley   c. Tony Franco

2. Mark acted hostile toward Ron and told him to stop _____.
   a. hanging around his uncle
   b. hanging around Turtleback Hill
   c. trying to take jobs away from him

3. Ron called his bike _____.
   a. the pony   b. Johnny Jo   c. the bronco

4. Ron's mother showed him an article announcing _____.
   a. a job opening at the local bike shop
   b. a reward for the return of his bike
   c. an 8-mile cross-country race

5. Ron had to drop out of the cross-country race because he _____.
   a. got a flat tire
   b. hurt himself in a spill
   c. lost his nerve

6. Ron's dad said that he might have to ride home on the hood because _____.
   a. he was so muddy
   b. his mom was so mad at him
   c. his bike had to fit in the back seat

7. When Ron was helping Ollie paint, Mark accused him of _____.
   a. stealing money from Mr. Perkins
   b. slashing the tires on his sports car
   c. weasling money from his uncle

8. In his second meet, Ron _____.
   a. hit a rock and broke his leg
   b. refused to let Glen stop him
   c. lost to Glen

9. When Mr. Perkins was sick, he felt better when he talked about _____.
   a. boxing   b. racing   c. making money

10. Ollie called _____ a codger.
    a. himself   b. Mr. Perkins   c. Mr. Baker

DIRT BIKE RACER
Comprehension Test C

Directions: Read each question carefully. Circle the letter of the choice that best answers each question.

1. Why was it okay for Ron to keep the bike that the Klines lost?
   a. They didn't want it any longer.
   b. They said he could have it.
   c. They had already collected insurance for it.

2. Ronnie discovered that Mr. Perkins used to _____.
   a. own a motorcycle shop
   b. race motorcycles and cars
   c. own a car dealership

3. Mark first threatened Ron at _____.
   a. his uncle's house   b. the race track   c. the pond

4. What woke Ron and his father up in the middle of the night?
   a. ambulance sirens
   b. a noise in the garage
   c. a motorcycle at full throttle

5. Ron suspected that _____ were involved in the break-in.
   a. Lug and Skitch   b. Mike and Tony   c. Mark and Glen

6. Ron needed money to replace his _____.
   a. carburetor   b. slashed tire   c. spark plugs

7. Ron's mother was afraid that his muddy clothes _____.
   a. would mess up the car seats forever
   b. were a lost cause
   c. would ruin her washing machine

8. Mrs. _____ took care of Mr. Perkins and his house.
   a. Kennedy   b. Johnson   c. Carter

9. Mark's main concern seemed to be _____.
   a. how to keep Ron from winning any races
   b. to make Ron look bad in everyone's eyes
   c. to keep Ron and Mr. Perkins from getting close

10. Ron was surprised to learn that Ollie spent his leisure time _____.
    a. reading biographies of famous painters
    b. photographing sports events for the local newspaper
    c. racing dirt bikes

DIRT BIKE RACER

Directions: Draw a six-panel cartoon showing how Ron gets Mark to stop harassing him. Don't forget to put the dialogue in bubbles.

PROJECTS FOR *DIRT BIKE RACER*

Directions: Choose one of the following projects or design your own. If you design your own project, fill out the form below and submit it to your teacher for approval.

1. Ollie liked to read biographies of famous painters. Choose a famous painter who you would like to know more about. Read about this person and write a report to share with others.

2. Matt Christopher is a well-known author of sports novels. Make a bibliography of his sports stories.

3. Write a chapter about Ron's next race.

4. Make a poster advertising this book. Make it eye-catching and attention-grabbing so others will want to read about Ron's adventures.

5. Draw a series of illustrations that tell this story in chronological order. Include a caption with each illustration.

6. Select a scene from the book to perform as a play.

7. Make a word search with words from the story.

8. Make a crossword puzzle based on the story.

PROJECT PROPOSAL

Name _____ Beginning Date _____ Completion Date _____

Describe the project in detail: _____

_____

Why do you want to do this project? _____

_____

What will the final product be? _____

_____

How will you share your final product? _____

_____

Comments: _____

_____

HOMESICK: MY OWN STORY
Comprehension Test A

Directions: Read each question carefully. Circle the letter of the choice that best answers each question.

1. Who wrote this book?
   a. Esther Forbes   *b.* Jean Fritz   *c.* Betsy Byars

2. Jean's father worked in the _____.
   a. Y.M.C.A.   *b.* American Embassy   *c.* British school

3. The best thing that happened to Jean on summer vacation was _____.
   a. she met a new best friend
   b. she got a kitten
   c. her baby sister was born

4. Jean's family and the Jordans were saved from a hostile crowd by the _____.
   a. navy   *b.* ricksha coolies   *c.* police

5. Communist soldiers tried to make the people of Wuchang surrender by _____.
   a. bombing them day and night
   b. using germ warfare
   c. starving them

6. Jean was shocked when her mother _____.
   a. did the Charleston
   b. bobbed her hair
   c. dressed like a flapper

7. Lin Nai-Nai's going-away gift to Jean was _____.
   a. a piece of handmade embroidery
   b. a bonsai tree
   c. a photograph

8. Jean's first taste of America was a _____.
   a. pizza   *b.* chocolate soda   *c.* hotdog

9. Jean felt like she was really home when _____.
   a. she saw the Golden Gate Bridge
   b. she saw her first cow grazing
   c. her grandmother said, "Welcome home."

10. On the first day of school, Jean fell in love with _____.
    a. Donald Burch   *b.* Andrew Carr   *c.* Charles Lindbergh

HOMESICK: MY OWN STORY
Comprehension Test B

Directions: Read each question carefully. Circle the letter of the choice that best answers each question.

1. Jean was born in _____, China.
   a. Peking   *b.* Shanghai   *c.* Hankow

2. How did Jean's mother learn that she had skipped school?
   a. The police phoned her.
   b. Jean's teacher came over.
   c. Jean's teacher sent a message.

3. Jean got up the mountain _____.
   a. in a sedan chair   *b.* on a mule   *c.* on foot

4. The worst thing that happened to Jean on summer vacation was that _____.
   a. her kitten got run over
   b. her new best friend moved away
   c. her baby sister died

5. Mother said she knew they'd leave for America on time because _____.
   a. they already had their tickets
   b. she could feel it in her bones
   c. the war was almost over

6. Why couldn't the men leave on the same boat with their families?
   a. They had to stay and fight.
   b. It was for women and children only.
   c. The soldiers dragged them off.

7. On the first day of school, Jean _____.
   a. punched Andrew Carr
   b. smart-mouthed the teacher
   c. corrected the teacher

8. Jean described her first day of school as _____.
   a. a bummer   *b.* a flop   *c.* the Cat's

9. Grandma imitated Miss Crofts by _____.
   a. scratching her head
   b. pursing her lips
   c. talking with a lisp

10. When anyone laughed near Josh, the rooster, he _____.
    a. pecked their ankles   *b.* flew at their face   *c.* croaked and flapped

HOMESICK: MY OWN STORY
Comprehension Test C

Directions: Read each question carefully. Circle the letter of the choice that best answers each question.

1. Ian Forbes ground his heel into Jean's toes to make her say _____

   a. "Uncle."   *b.* "God bless America."   *c.* "God save the King."

2. Jean told her mother that she really wanted _____ for Christmas.

   a. a new name   *b.* a new bike   *c.* a ticket home

3. The Communists wanted to _____.

   a. get out of China

   b. expel all foreigners from China

   c. kill all foreigners

4. Jean knew Yang Sze-Fu was a Communist when he _____.

   a. cut his spiky nails so he'd look like a worker

   b. demanded double his salary

   c. unionized the servants

5. Why did Lin Nai-Nai run like a stumbling duck?

   a. Her feet were bound.

   b. She was blind.

   c. She had a wooden leg.

6. Mother and Jean had to flee Hankow immediately because _____.

   a. the ricksha coolies were rampaging

   b. the Communists were going to start bombing

   c. soldiers were slaughtering foreigners nearby

7. Jean and her family set sail for America on the _____.

   a. President Van Buren   *b. President Taft*   *c. President Jackson*

8. The family drove over _____ miles to get from San Francisco, California, to the family farm in Washington, Pennsylvania.

   a. 2,000   *b.* 3,000   *c.* 4,000

9. Ruth and Marie made Jean upset by _____.

   a. asking stupid questions

   b. making fun of her clothes

   c. staring at her as if she were a freak

10. Miss Crofts forced Jean to _____.

    a. stand in the corner

    b. wear a dunce hat

    c. learn a new method of penmanship

HOMESICK: MY OWN STORY

Directions: Jean wanted to learn about America so she would fit in with her American classmates and friends. With her love of reading and learning, she would have had no problem finding the answers to the following questions about 1927. You may use an almanac to find the answers. Write your answers on the lines.

1. Who was president of the U.S.? _____

2. Who was Secretary of State? _____

3. Who was Director of the Federal Bureau of Investigation? _____

4. Which newspaper won a Pulitzer Prize for Meritorious Public Service? _____

5. Who won the Pulitzer Prize for American Poetry? _____

6. Who won the title of Miss America? _____

7. Who won an Academy Award for best actress? _____

8. Which picture won an Academy Award? _____

9. Who won an Academy Award for best actor? _____

10. Approximately how many marines landed in China on March 5 to protect property during the civil war? _____

11. Motion pictures up to this time were silent; which movie was the first part-talking motion picture? _____

12. Which famous singer was in this movie? _____

13. Who completed the first nonstop flight from New York to Paris on May 20–21? _____

14. Which famous musical opened in New York on December 27? _____

15. In 1927, the center of the U.S. was in the state of _____, 8 miles south-southwest of the city of _____.

16. Who was the Women's Singles U.S. Open Tennis Champion? _____

17. The results of the Davis Cup Challenge Round were _____–3, U.S.–2.

18. Which New York Yankee hit 60 home runs? _____

19. Who was the Heavyweight Champion? _____

20. Who won the Indianapolis 500? _____

21. What kind of car did this man drive? _____

22. Which golfer won the United States Open? _____

23. Who was the American League RBI leader? _____

PROJECTS FOR *HOMESICK: MY OWN STORY*

Directions: Choose one of the following projects or design your own. If you design your own project, fill out the form below and submit it to your teacher for approval.

1. Jean's mother had her hair bobbed, Jean had hers shingled, and Miss Crofts had her hair marcelled into stiff waves. Illustrate each of these 1920s hair styles and explain how hair was marcelled.

2. Perform a medley of songs that were popular in 1927.

3. Demonstrate dances that were popular in 1927.

4. Reread the chapter, "Background of Chinese History, 1913–1927." Put the events in this chapter on a time line.

5. Prepare a bibliography of books and magazines that were popular from 1917 to 1927.

6. Make a paper doll of Jean as she looked in 1927. Make a wardrobe of clothes to "dress" this paper doll.

7. Andrea wanted to see *The Phantom of the Opera*, but her mother said it was too scary and insisted they see *Rin-Tin-Tin* instead. Prepare a review of each of these movies.

8. Jean read the newspaper article about Charles Lindbergh. Write a feature article about this American hero.

PROJECT PROPOSAL

Name _____ Beginning Date _____ Completion Date _____

Describe the project in detail: _____
_____

Why do you want to do this project? _____
_____

What will the final product be? _____
_____

How will you share your final product? _____
_____

Comments: _____
_____

Section 10

FAVORITE BOOKS
FOR
JUNE

The following books are on "June Book List B" in *Ready-to-Use Reading Activities Through the Year*.

Activity Sheets	Book Title	Reading Level	Award
10-1 to 10-5	*Animal Farm*	9	
10-6 to 10-10	*The Boat Who Wouldn't Float*	9	
10-11 to 10-15	*The Summer of the Swans*	4.6	Newbery Medal
10-16 to 10-20	*Tiger Eyes*	4.4	

Animal Farm **by George Orwell.**
New York: Harcourt Brace Jovanovich, 1954. 128 pages.

A group of animals bands together to run off the human inhabitants of their farm. They take over and form a society based on the maxim that every animal is created equal. They adopt seven commandments to guide their daily lives. Unfortunately, the same evils that bedevil mankind befall these animals. They end up making as big a mess of their society as humans make of theirs.

The Boat Who Wouldn't Float by Farley Mowat.
New York: Bantam, 1970. 197 pages.

When Farley Mowat gives in to the urge to be a seafaring man and buys a boat, he gets more than he bargained for. He optimistically christens his boat *Happy Adventure*. He's blissfully unaware, however, that the two are about to develop a love-hate relationship the likes of which lift him to the heights of ecstasy and plunge him into the depths of despair. The boat seems to have a mind of its own. This leads to a clash of wills that is often hilarious, sometimes terrifying, and always entertaining. He begins to wonder why any sane person would want to be skipper of a boat that seems determined to commit suicide by sinking! He also wonders how he'll convince friends to accompany him on these attempted suicide missions. Can they set sail and keep the boat from achieving its goal?

The Summer of the Swans by Betsy Byars.
New York: Puffin, 1970. 142 pages.

Sara's fourteenth summer is the time of her discontent. She doesn't like herself, her older sister, her bossy aunt, her remote father, her retarded brother, or even her old dog Boysie. Her life is out of focus. Then, her brother Charlie gets lost. Her fear of losing Charlie forever helps Sara look at her life clearly. Sara learns that even though her life won't always glide along smoothly, she is capable of meeting any challenge head-on.

Tiger Eyes by Judy Blume.
New York: Dell, 1981. 222 pages.

When Davey's father is fatally shot during a robbery, she hides from life for weeks by taking to her bed. Davey, her mother, and little brother all need time to heal. They move to New Mexico to stay with relatives during the healing process. Davey is helped by Wolf, whose father is dying of cancer. Wolf helps her understand that when you lose a loved one, you should remember the love, joy, and laughter you shared, but you must get on with your own life. The year in New Mexico brings many changes to Davey. When the family returns home, she feels ready to begin building a new life.

ANIMAL FARM
Comprehension Test A

Directions: Read each question carefully. Circle the letter of the choice that best answers each question.

1. Who wrote this book?

   a. Carl Sagan   *b.* Aldous Huxley   *c.* George Orwell

2. The animals agreed that the cleverest among them were the _____.

   a. pigs   *b.* dogs   *c.* horses

3. Sugercandy Mountain was _____.

   a. the name of the farm owned by Mr. Jones

   b. the place animals supposedly went when they died

   c. a nearby amusement park

4. Napoleon accused _____ of destroying the windmill.

   a. Jones   *b.* Snowball   *c.* Mollie

5. Who acted as intermediary between Animal Farm and the outside world?

   a. Mr. Pilkington of Foxwood

   b. Mr. Frederick of Pinchfield

   c. Mr. Whymper from Willingdon

6. Why did Napoleon order the dogs to slaughter so many animals?

   a. They confessed to terrible crimes.

   b. They planned a rebellion against Napoleon.

   c. He wanted to show how powerful he had become.

7. Why did Napoleon order the others to stop singing "Beasts of England"?

   a. He had grown tired of it.

   b. He said it no longer had a purpose.

   c. He didn't want the animals to get worked up.

8. Why wasn't Napoleon accused of breaking the commandments?

   a. He changed the words to suit himself.

   b. Everyone was too afraid to say anything.

   c. No one noticed he was doing anything wrong.

9. Moses did no work, yet he was given an allowance of _____ a day.

   a. two apples

   b. two bowls of hot milk mash

   c. a gill of beer

10. Boxer dreamed of retiring on his _____ birthday.

    a. twelfth   *b.* fourteenth   *c.* sixteenth

ANIMAL FARM
Comprehension Test B

Directions: Read each question carefully. Circle the letter of the choice that best answers each question.

1. Old Major said the plain truth is that the life of an animal is _____.
   - *a.* happiness and leisure
   - *b.* misery and slavery
   - *c.* freedom and love

2. Old Major taught the other animals all of the verses to _____.
   - *a.* "Animals Arise"
   - *b.* "The Comrades' Rebellion"
   - *c.* "Beasts of England"

3. The farm was originally known as _____.
   - *a.* Jones Farm
   - *b.* Manor Farm
   - *c.* Animal Farm

4. When Jones and his friends came to reclaim the farm, Snowball led the defensive operations based on _____.
   - *a.* maneuvers of Attila the Hun
   - *b.* battle plans of Napoleon I
   - *c.* campaigns of Julius Caesar

5. The anniversary of the Battle of the Cowshed was observed on _____.
   - *a.* October twelfth
   - *b.* Midsummer's Eve
   - *c.* Boxing Day

6. What did Napoleon do to the plot of ground that was supposed to be for retirees?
   - *a.* sold it
   - *b.* plowed it up and planted barley
   - *c.* built a schoolroom on it

7. Napoleon was unanimously elected President because he _____.
   - *a.* stuffed the ballot boxes
   - *b.* bribed the voters
   - *c.* was unopposed

8. Sugarcandy Mountain supposedly had fields of clover and _____.
   - *a.* money growing on trees
   - *b.* buildings made of candy and gingerbread
   - *c.* linseed cake and lump sugar growing on hedges

9. Napoleon sold Boxer to the slaughterhouse so he could buy _____.
   - *a.* another case of whiskey
   - *b.* parts for the windmill
   - *c.* medals for himself

10. The animals overheard Mr. Pilkington say that they _____.
    - *a.* did more work and received less food than country animals
    - *b.* were much more equal than country animals
    - *c.* were better educated and better fed than country animals

ANIMAL FARM
Comprehension Test C

Directions: Read each question carefully. Circle the letter of the choice that best answers each question.

1. Old Major said that all men are _____ and all animals are _____.
   a. cruel; kind   b. sinners; saints   c. enemies; comrades

2. One thing that triggered the rebellion was _____.
   a. greed   b. hunger   c. selfishness

3. Who left Animal Farm for the comforts and luxuries to be found at Foxwood?
   a. Mollie   b. Muriel   c. Moses

4. Who took puppies away from their mother and raised them to do his bidding?
   a. Snowball   b. Napoleon   c. Squealer

5. Who kept declaring "I will work harder"?
   a. Napoleon   b. Squealer   c. Boxer

6. What did Frederick and his men destroy during their attack on Animal Farm?
   a. the still   b. the windmill   c. the house

7. Napoleon wanted to build a schoolroom for _____.
   a. anyone who wanted an education
   b. his children
   c. his guard dogs

8. Who awarded medals to Napoleon?
   a. the county farm bureau
   b. Napoleon
   c. Mr. Whymper

9. Boxer planned to spend his retirement years learning _____.
   a. the other twenty-two letters of the alphabet
   b. algebra
   c. Spanish

10. The van that took Boxer away was marked _____.
    a. " Retirement Home"
    b. "Willington Hospital"
    c. "Horse Slaughterer"

ANIMAL FARM

Directions: Several words from the story are hidden in the pig. Find the words and circle them. You may go across and down.

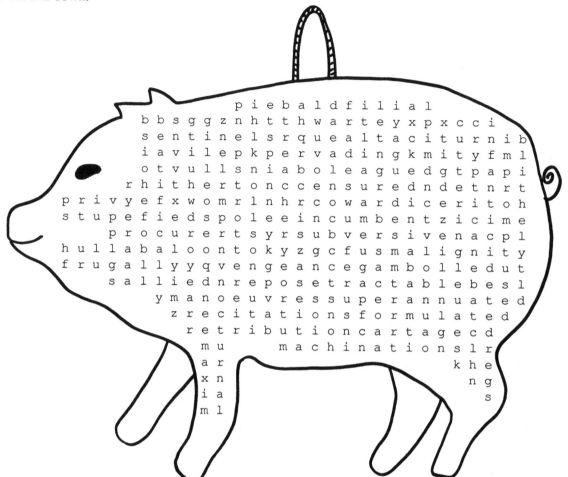

cowardice	leagued	censured	stupefied	piebald
treachery	sentinels	procure	filial	cartage
knoll	vile	manoeuvre*	cryptic	nocturnal
maxim	taciturn	retribution	malignity	tractable
thwart	infanticide	machinations	trotter	subversive
gill	frugally	privy	recitations	blithely
beatifically	spinney	vengeance	impromptu	superannuated
hullabaloo	gambolled	pervading	sallied	formulated
hitherto	repose	incumbent	uttering	dregs

_____

*British variation of *maneuver*.

Illustration based on Dresden Christmas ornament. Dresden ornaments were stamped cardboard with a gold or silver paper covering. Dresdens were made in Germany in the late nineteenth century and early twentieth century. If you find one of these ornaments today, prices often begin around $100.

PROJECTS FOR *ANIMAL FARM*

Directions: Choose one of the following projects or design your own. If you design your own project, fill out the form below and submit it to your teacher for approval.

1. Make clay models of Napoleon and Boxer.

2. At the end of the story, Napoleon and Mr. Pilkington were talking. The lower animals overheard this conversation. What if they became so upset that they made plans to change things? Write about their actions and the results of these actions.

3. What if you were a reporter sent to interview Napoleon and Clover? Simulate this interview.

4. Create a puppet show based on this story.

5. What if Napoleon wanted to make extra money by allowing people to tour the farm? Make a travel brochure that will make tourists want to spend their time and money at Animal Farm.

6. What if Napoleon wanted to turn Animal Farm into an amusement park? Create a brochure listing its attractions, rides, and restaurants.

7. Boxer wanted to learn the letters of the alphabet. Create a bulletin board display or a picture book that teaches the letters of the alphabet.

PROJECT PROPOSAL

Name _____ Beginning Date _____ Completion Date _____

Describe the project in detail: _____

_____

Why do you want to do this project? _____

_____

What will the final product be? _____

_____

How will you share your final product? _____

_____

Comments: _____

_____

THE BOAT WHO WOULDN'T FLOAT
Comprehension Test A

Directions: Read each question carefully. Circle the letter of the choice that best answers each question.

1. Who wrote this book?
   a. Robert Lipsyte   *b.* Farley Mowat   *c.* Robert Newton Peck

2. Wilbur wanted to be dropped off at _____.
   a. St. John's depot
   b. the shipyard in St. John's
   c. St. John's Mental Hospital

3. A quintal is a _____.
   a. type of seagoing vessel
   b. traditional measure used by cod fishermen
   c. type of cannon

4. Peter Easton was _____.
   a. a famous English pirate
   b. an infamous St. Shott's wrecker
   c. the ship's chief engineer

5. St. Pierre is twelve miles off the coast of _____.
   a. Canada   *b.* the U.S.   *c.* Greenland

6. Blanche was a _____.
   a. water dog   *b.* retriever   *c.* giant Newfoundland dog

7. Why weren't the villagers upset when Farley told them that he'd dumped their cargo?
   a. The cargo was only salt, sand, and rocks.
   b. The cargo would wash ashore because of the currents.
   c. They already had a scheme to steal it back from the Mounties.

8. Why did Martin, Théo, and Paulo rip part of *Itchy* off with crowbars?
   a. They had a fight with Farley.
   b. They needed the materials to repair another boat.
   c. They wanted the insurance money.

9. Who shipped out with Farley the second summer?
   a. Jack   *b.* Mike   *c.* Claire

10. The third summer, Farley managed to get *Itchy* only _____ miles west of Bay d'Espoir.
    a. 40   *b.* 80   *c.* 60

THE BOAT WHO WOULDN'T FLOAT
Comprehension Test B

Directions: Read each question carefully. Circle the letter of the choice that best answers each question.

1. The Hallohan brothers fed Farley salt beef and salt cod so he'd _____.
    a. drink too much and agree to buy their business
    b. drink too much and let them rob him blind
    c. drink lots of Screech and agree to buy their boat

2. The people of St. Shotts and St. Shores earned their living _____.
    a. as fishermen   b. as wreckers   c. from tourism

3. When Jack, Farley, and Enos took the *Happy Adventure* to sea, _____.
    a. the engine blew up
    b. the main mast broke
    c. she sprang a leak

4. Trepassay was known as _____.
    a. "the pirate's den"
    b. "the seafarer's coffin"
    c. "t'place where t'fog is made"

5. Why did the Manuel brothers think the Mounties were after them?
    a. They were smuggling rum.
    b. They were smuggling drugs.
    c. They were smuggling pure grain alcohol.

6. The saltwater lagoon Grand Barachois harbored thousands of _____.
    a. porpoises   b. blue whales   c. gray seals

7. The *Happy Adventure* stopped breaking down when she headed _____.
    a. east   b. west   c. north

8. When the *Happy Adventure* had to go from Raymond Pointe to Burgeo, Farley sent an S.O.S. to _____.
    a. Mike   b. Jack   c. Théo

9. When Jack heard that Farley intended to sail to Montreal, he _____.
    a. took out extra insurance
    b. wired good luck wishes
    c. sent life-saving equipment

10. When they couldn't buy a radar reflector, they substituted a _____.
    a. 10-gallon pail
    b. tin washboard
    c. zinc washtub

THE BOAT WHO WOULDN'T FLOAT
Comprehension Test C

Directions: Read each question carefully. Circle the letter of the choice that best answers each question.

1. *Passion Flower* was the name of a _____.
   a. tugboat   b. jeep   c. jack boat

2. Who told Farley about Ferryland's long history?
   a. Enos Coffin   b. Obie Murphy   c. Howard Morry

3. The children searched for the spectacles that Enos lost, and they found them _____.
   a. in a tree branch 10 feet off the ground
   b. hanging from a caribou's antler
   c. in the goat's mouth

4. Why did Jack leave the ship and send Mike Malloy as his replacement?
   a. He lost his nerve.
   b. He had to go back to work.
   c. He had to have a back operation.

5. The *Happy Adventure*'s name was changed to *Itchatchozale Alai* when she _____.
   a. became the flagship of the Basque mercantile marine
   b. hit a reef off St.Schott's and was "rescued" by the wreckers
   c. was sold to the French government

6. Farley and Mike panicked and _____.
   a. rammed the *Blue Iris* with a dozen policemen on board
   b. dumped their cargo in international waters
   c. ran aground off Pass Island

7. After spending the winter in Burgeo, Farley _____.
   a. married Claire
   b. sold his boat and moved to St. John's
   c. changed *Itchy* back to *Happy Adventure*

8. The townspeople of Burgeo turned on Farley after _____.
   a. they learned he was a reporter
   b. they killed a whale and were condemned by the press
   c. a reporter misquoted him about his opinion of Burgeo

9. Why did Dorman Collier's daughter give Farley an early wake-up call?
   a. to tell him that the *Happy Adventure* was sinking
   b. to tell him that a hurricane was coming
   c. to tell him that the Mounties were looking for him

10. Farley and Claire decided to take the *Happy Adventure* to _____.
    a. Cuba   b. Bermuda   c. Expo 67

THE BOAT WHO WOULDN'T FLOAT

Directions: Farley Mowat bought the *Happy Adventure* in Newfoundland. Answer the questions about Newfoundland by writing your answers on the correct lines. You may use an encyclopedia and an atlas for extra help.

1. Newfoundland became Canada's _____th province on_____.

2. The area of the island of Newfoundland is _____ square miles.

3. Memorial University of Newfoundland was founded in _____ and is located in the capital city,

   _____.

4. The Strait of _____ separates the island of Newfoundland from the Labrador

   portion of Newfoundland.

5. The largest single religious group in the Province of Newfoundland is _____.

6. The original inhabitants of the area were the _____ Indians, who were

   exterminated by settlers.

7. L'Anse-aux-Meadows is the site of a _____ village dating from

   approximately A.D. _____.

8. Port au Choix is the site of an _____ burial ground that is about _____ years old.

9. Lord Baltimore established the settlement of _____ in the 1620s.

10. The _____ Strait separating Newfoundland from Nova Scotia is _____ miles wide.

11. John Cabot first visited this region in _____.

12. Cabot Tower was built in _____ and stands in the _____ National

    Historic Park, which lies at the entrance to _____ Harbor.

13. Newfoundland's first daily newspaper, the _____, began

    publication in _____.

14. Newfoundland's four major rivers are the _____, _____,

    _____, and _____.

15. Newfoundland's floral emblem is the _____.

PROJECTS FOR *THE BOAT WHO WOULDN'T FLOAT*

Directions: Choose one of the following projects or design your own. If you design your own project, fill out the form below and submit it to your teacher for approval.

1. Draw a map of Newfoundland, Nova Scotia, and the east coast of Canada. Trace the route followed by Farley Mowat and his boat who wouldn't float.

2. Reread Farley's description of the plateau on top of Colombier. Make a diorama of this minute paradise.

3. Make a model of the *Happy Adventure*.

4. Make a crossword puzzle based on the story.

5. Make a word search using words from the story.

6. Dress as one of the characters and give a brief summary of the book.

7. Choose an adventure from the story to retell from the boat's point of view.

8. Rewrite this story in comic book form.

9. Wilbur was a natural raconteur who never stopped telling yarns. Make up a yarn about the wreckers who lived on St. Shotts and St. Shores. Tell this yarn to your class.

PROJECT PROPOSAL

Name _____ Beginning Date _____ Completion Date _____

Describe the project in detail: _____

_____

Why do you want to do this project? _____

_____

What will the final product be? _____

_____

How will you share your final product? _____

_____

Comments: _____

_____

THE SUMMER OF THE SWANS
Comprehension Test A

Directions: Read each question carefully. Circle the letter of the choice that best answers each question.

1. Who wrote this book?
   - *a.* Betsy Byars
   - *b.* Beverly Cleary
   - *c.* Katherine Peterson

2. Sara's fourteenth summer was when she realized that she was _____.
   - *a.* filled with discontent
   - *b.* slightly retarded
   - *c.* going to become a writer

3. Charlie was retarded as a result of _____.
   - *a.* high fevers when he was three
   - *b.* a birth defect
   - *c.* a mistake the doctor made when delivering him

4. Why did Charlie leave the house during the night?
   - *a.* He liked walking around when it was dark and quiet.
   - *b.* He wanted to see the swans again.
   - *c.* He was mad because no one sewed on his button.

5. When Wanda got a bad perm at the beauty school, Sara called her _____.
   - *a.* Wolfman
   - *b.* Sasquatch
   - *c.* Gentle Ben

6. Aunt Willie said that the worst thing about Sara was her _____.
   - *a.* know-it-all attitude
   - *b.* need for revenge
   - *c.* stubborn streak

7. Sara's legs and knees got badly skinned when she _____.
   - *a.* fell down the ravine
   - *b.* climbed to the top of the dirt bank
   - *c.* slid down the creek bank

8. Why didn't Wanda help look for Charlie?
   - *a.* She had a date.
   - *b.* She had classes.
   - *c.* She had to go to work.

9. When Sara talked to her father long distance, she suddenly realized _____.
   - *a.* that he no longer cared about his kids
   - *b.* that he had stopped trying to meet life's challenges
   - *c.* that he wanted to live his life without them around

10. This book won the _____.
    - *a.* Edgar Award
    - *b.* Caldecott Medal
    - *c.* Newbery Medal

THE SUMMER OF THE SWANS
Comprehension Test B

Directions: Read each question carefully. Circle the letter of the choice that best answers each question.

1. Charlie, Sara's and Wanda's brother, was _____.

    a. autistic   *b.* deaf   *c.* retarded

2. Sara said that the peak of her whole life was in third grade when she _____.

    a. got to be milk monitor

    b. got to be Donald Duck in the school play

    c. was the lead reindeer in the Christmas pageant

3. The one thing Sara disliked most about Aunt Willie was that _____.

    a. she was too old fashioned

    b. she never listened

    c. she always had to have her way

4. Aunt Willie promised Sara's mother that she would _____.

    a. help her get her job back

    b. make sure her husband paid child support

    c. look after her three children

5. Sara's father started acting remote after _____.

    a. Charlie's illness   *b.* he lost his job   *c.* his wife divorced him

6. Why did Sara hose down Gretchen Wyant?

    a. She called Sara "Big Foot."

    b. She called Sara "Dumbo."

    c. She called Charlie "retard."

7. Sara's best friend was _____.

    a. Mary   *b.* Gretchen   *c.* Wanda

8. Who helped Sara most when she was looking for Charlie?

    a. Mary   *b.* Joe   *c.* Boysie

9. Before going home, Aunt Willie and Charlie stopped at the Carsons to _____.

    a. eat watermelon

    b. use their phone

    c. be interviewed by Mr. Carson, the newspaper reporter

10. Bennie Hoffman was having a party _____.

    a. so he could play his guitar for everyone

    b. for his birthday

    c. the last day before school started

THE SUMMER OF THE SWANS
Comprehension Test C

Directions: Read each question carefully . Circle the letter of the choice that best answers each question.

1. Sara didn't feel pretty and she hated her big _____.
   a. hands   *b.* feet   *c.* ears

2. When Sara tried to dye her orange sneakers baby blue, they turned out _____.
   a. puce   *b.* pomegranate   *c.* Pomeranian

3. Sara wanted revenge on Joe Melby because she thought that he _____.
   a. made fun of her to all the other kids
   b. had dognapped Boysie
   c. stole Charlie's watch

4. After Aunt Willie made a missing person's report to the police, she called _____.
   a. Charlie's mother   *b.* Charlie's father   *c.* Uncle Bert

5. Charlie felt safe and well when _____.
   a. his father hugged him
   b. he hid under the covers
   c. his routine was kept up

6. How did Sara break her nose?
   a. She fell off her bike.   *b.* A baseball hit her.   *c.* She was in a fight.

7. Charlie wouldn't leave the ravine until _____.
   a. Joe fixed his broken watch
   b. Joe lent him his watch
   c. Sara found his lost watch

8. Sara thought the flying swans looked like _____.
   a. balloons with the air hissing out
   b. deflated soccer balls
   c. frying pans with their necks stretched out

9. Sara got a big surprise when Joe _____.
   a. kissed her on the cheek
   b. asked her to go to a party with him
   c. said he liked her

10. Wanda didn't know Charlie was lost until _____.
   a. she heard it on the radio
   b. Frank phoned her
   c. her boss told her

THE SUMMER OF THE SWANS

I. *Directions:* Sara had a very poor self-concept. Surveys have shown that teens across the country fall into this same category. Almost everyone would like to change something about himself or herself. In the space below, tell what you would change about yourself if you could. Explain how you hope to benefit from this change.

_____

_____

_____

_____

_____

_____

_____

_____

_____

_____

_____

_____

_____

_____

_____

_____

II. *Directions:* Put these events in the correct order. Write the numeral *1* in front of the event that happened first. Continue numbering the remaining items.

_____ Sara stuck a sign on Joe's back that said "fink."

_____ Joe asked Sara out.

_____ Aunt Willie went for a ride on a motor scooter.

_____ Charlie went to look for the swans by himself.

_____ Aunt Willie called the police.

_____ Joe loaned Charlie his watch.

PROJECTS FOR *SUMMER OF THE SWANS*

Directions: Choose one of the following projects or design your own. If you design your own project, fill out the form below and submit it to your teacher for approval.

1. Write Sara's diary entry telling about her first date with Joe Melby when he took her to Bennie Hoffman's party.

2. Betsy Byars is a very popular author. Make a bibliography of her books.

3. Make a poster advertising this book.

4. Rewrite this story as a picture book.

5. Rewrite this story as a comic book.

6. Write a letter to Betsy Byars telling her how you felt as you read the book. Mail the letter to her in care of the publishing company.

7. Draw a map showing the town, houses, lake, woods, ravine, dirt bank, and so on. Mark the route Charlie took when he left the house and became lost.

8. Write a report about childhood diseases, traumas, and birth defects that can cause retardation.

9. Draw a large swan. Make a word search about the story inside the swan.

PROJECT PROPOSAL

Name _____ Beginning Date _____ Completion Date _____

Describe the project in detail: _____

_____

Why do you want to do this project? _____

_____

What will the final product be? _____

_____

How will you share your final product? _____

_____

Comments: _____

_____

TIGER EYES
Comprehension Test A

Directions: Read each question carefully. Circle the letter of the choice that best answers each question.

1. Who wrote this book?
    a. Fran Arrick   *b.* Susan Beth Pfeffer   *c.* Judy Blume

2. After her husband was shot, Gwen couldn't _____.
    a. cry   *b.* eat or sleep   *c.* reopen the store

3. Bitsy and Walter were Davey's _____.
    a. best friends   *b.* aunt and uncle   *c.* neighbors

4. Davey didn't feel glad to be alive again until she _____.
    a. met Wolf
    b. got away from the scene of the tragedy
    c. volunteered to work in the Bradbury Science Museum

5. Davey wanted to form a new group at school called the _____.
    a. Left-overs   *b.* No-shows   *c.* Brain-trust

6. Minka liked to sleep in Davey's _____.
    a. hiking boots   *b.* dresser drawers   *c.* knapsack

7. After Davey was rude to Ned, Mom suggested that she _____.
    a. move out of the house
    b. see the school guidance counselor
    c. see a shrink

8. Mom took Davey to a nice restaurant so she could _____.
    a. break the news of her engagement to Ned
    b. talk about going home
    c. celebrate Davey's success in the school play

9. Davey told Jane that it was unhealthy to become _____.
    a. too dependent on someone else
    b. afraid of life
    c. too attached to anyone or anything

10. Davey told her aunt that life _____.
    a. wasn't for the timid
    b. wasn't fair
    c. was a good adventure

TIGER EYES
Comprehension Test B

Directions: Read each question carefully. Circle the letter of the choice that best answers each question.

1. Davey's father was killed _____.
   a. in a car wreck
   b. during a robbery
   c. by a massive heart attack

2. Davey's mother took the family to stay with relatives in _____.
   a. Los Alamos   b. Las Vegas   c. Phoenix

3. Davey was shocked to learn that her uncle _____.
   a. was terminally ill
   b. was a Ku Klux Klan member
   c. designed weapons

4. When Davey spent the night with her friend Jane, they double dated with _____.
   a. Wolf and Howard   b. Hugh and Robby   c. Ted and Ruben

5. The family celebrated Christmas and _____ at the same time.
   a. Hanukkah
   b. Jason's birthday
   c. the anniversary of the death of Mr. Wexler

6. Davey was upset when her mother agreed to have lunch with Ned, _____.
   a. who was Hispanic
   b. who was Davey's chemistry teacher
   c. the Nerd

7. When Walter saw Davey's grades, he said she'd end up like her father and _____.
   a. be a loser   b. have a wasted life   c. be on welfare

8. Davey's picture appeared in the weekly newspaper *The Monitor* because _____.
   a. she was lost in the mountains
   b. she was listed as a missing person
   c. she was such a success in the school play

9. When he learned they were moving back home, Jason worried that _____.
   a. his old friends wouldn't like him any longer
   b. no one would help him bake cookies
   c. he might be put back a grade in school

10. Mother explained that they had come to Los Alamos mostly because _____.
    a. they were destitute
    b. she wanted to start a new life
    c. it was better for her

TIGER EYES
Comprehension Test C

Directions: Read each question carefully. Circle the letter of the choice that best answers each question.

1. Davey's best friend was _____.
   a. Lenaya   b. Bitsy   c. Gwen

2. During the first few days of high school, Davey _____ every day.
   a. threw up   b. fainted   c. ran away

3. Gwen broke her toes when she _____.
   a. ran over them with Bitsy's bike
   b. fell down a canyon
   c. kicked the wall

4. Davey volunteered at the _____.
   a. daycare center   b. homeless shelter   c. hospital

5. Davey exploded with anger when she was not allowed to _____.
   a. hang out with Jane anymore
   b. take Driver's Ed
   c. date Wolf

6. Mr. Ortiz left Davey _____.
   a. a thousand dollars
   b. a dancing bear toy
   c. a stuffed tiger

7. Davey wanted to try out for a part in _____.
   a. *South Pacific*   b. *Grease*   c. *Oklahoma*

8. Davey's friend Jane had a problem with _____.
   a. drinking   b. her parents   c. drugs

9. The first person Davey talked to about her father's death was _____.
   a. Miriam   b. Jane   c. Ruben

10. Davey's mother said she had been afraid to be alone with Davey because _____.
    a. they always ended up fighting
    b. she reminded her so much of Adam
    c. of the questions she might ask

TIGER EYES

Directions: Davey enjoyed studying astronomy. She probably could answer the questions below. Can you? You may use an encyclopedia or almanac for extra help. Write your answers on the correct lines.

1. Which five planets were discovered before the invention of the telescope?

   (1) _____ (2) _____ (3) _____

   (4) _____ (5) _____

2. What is the term for a body in orbit around the sun? _____

3. What is the term for a body in orbit around another body? _____

4. The word *satellite* can sometimes be used interchangeably with the term _____.

5. Name the book written by Copernicus in 1543. _____

6. What instrument, developed in the nineteenth century, gives information about the chemical composition and motions of heavenly bodies? _____

7. What planet did Sir William Herschel discover in 1781? _____

8. Which planet has the largest number of natural moons? _____

9. German physicist _____ invented the spectroscope in 1814.

10. Who was the American physicist who, in 1938, advanced the theory that solar energy is produced by the nuclear fusion of hydrogen atoms into helium? _____

11. Neptune lies an average distance of _____ billion miles from the sun.

12. The _____ appears in southern skies at the same time the Aurora Borealis appears in northern skies.

13. What is the radiating surface of the sun called? _____

14. What is the fifth largest planet and the third from the sun?

    _____

15. The moon completes a circuit around the earth in _____ days, _____ hours, and _____ minutes on the average.

© 1993 by Sue Jones Erlenbusch

_____

Illustration based on a wind-up dancing bear by Schuco. He wears a bellhop outfit and is made of mohair over metal.

PROJECTS FOR *TIGER EYES*

Directions: Choose one of the following projects or design your own. If you design your own project, fill out the form below and submit it to your teacher for approval.

1. Make a diorama of your favorite scene in the book.

2. Make a time line of events in Davey's life.

3. Prepare a travel brochure for Atlantic City, Los Alamos, or Santa Fe.

4. Prepare a bibliography of at least ten other books about the loss of a loved one.

5. Make a board game featuring books by Judy Blume.

6. Write a bio-poem about Davey.

7. Write about Davey's summer and how Lenaya and Hugh react to her return.

8. Davey enjoyed shopping in Doodlets, a shop filled with objects sporting cat motifs. She bought a pot holder with a cat face on it, a set of catnip toys, some cat wrapping paper, and a cat mobile. Make each of these items.

9. Reread the description of the unusual candle Davey bought. Make this candle.

PROJECT PROPOSAL

Name _____ Beginning Date _____ Completion Date _____

Describe the project in detail: _____

_____

Why do you want to do this project? _____

_____

What will the final product be? _____

_____

How will you share your final product? _____

_____

Comments: _____

_____

Section 11

FAVORITE BOOKS FOR

JULY

The following books are on "July Book List B" in *Ready-to-Use Reading Activities Through the Year*.

Activity Sheets	Book Title	Reading Level
11-1 to 11-5	**Summer of My German Soldier**	5
11-6 to 11-10	**Summer of the Monkeys**	4.9
11-11 to 11-15	**Pursuit**	6.5
11-16 to 11-20	**Wuthering Heights**	8

Summer of My German Soldier by Betty Greene.
New York: Bantam, 1973. 199 pages.

Patty Bergen's parents make her feel ugly and unloved. Their cruelty sometimes goes beyond verbal abuse, and Patty receives severe beatings at the hands of her father. Patty tries to figure out what is so bad about herself that her parents aren't able to love her. The only person who loves her just as she is is their housekeeper Ruth. Patty meets a German prisoner of war when he tries to escape from the nearby prison camp. She helps him by giving him a hiding place, bringing him food, and giving him clothes to replace his POW garb. When it is time for him to leave, he gives Patty a ring that is his most prized and valuable possession. He tells her to wear it and remember that she is a person of value. When Patty's aid to the enemy is discovered, she is sent to reform school. The townspeople turn on Patty and her parents. They wonder how she, a Jewish girl, could have helped a Nazi. Her parents are horrified by her behavior and act as though she is no longer alive. The only person who visits Patty at the reform school is Ruth. Ruth tells Patty that she truly is a person of value and that it's her parents, not her, who are not people of quality. The realization that Ruth is speaking the truth gives Patty the strength to endure.

Summer of the Monkeys by Wilson Rawls.
New York: Dell, 1976. 283 pages.

Jay Berry is growing up in the Ozarks in the late nineteenth century. He lives on a farm with his parents and sister Daisy, who has a crippled leg. When he discovers that he can make $156 by catching some monkeys who have escaped from a circus, he decides it's about the only way he'll ever be able to earn enough money to buy the pony and .22 gun he's always wanted. After he catches the monkeys and collects the reward, Jay Berry surprises himself by handing over the entire amount to his parents so they can pay for the operation Daisy needs. When Daisy comes home with her leg fixed, Jay Berry knows he'll never regret his decision.

Pursuit by Michael French.
New York: Dell, 1982. 181 pages.

Gordy's parents agree to let him go on a camping trip in the Sierra Nevada Mountains with Roger and Luke on the condition that Gordy's younger brother Martin gets to go, too. This arrangement doesn't bother Gordy or Luke, but Roger is extremely impatient with Martin. Martin is the only one who sees Roger as the phony he really is. Martin continually taunts Roger. Roger snaps and, in one reckless act, causes Martin's death. Roger immediately starts trying to convince the others that Martin's fatal fall was an accident. Luke is easily coerced, but Gordy insists that Roger is a murderer and will have to pay for what he did. The three split up. Roger convinces Luke to head for town on his own. With Luke gone, Roger has a free hand to track down Gordy and eliminate the one witness who seems determined to get him into trouble with the law and ruin his plans for the future. Gordy, though cold, thirsty, hungry, and badly injured, doggedly makes his way toward La Porte to report to the sheriff. Roger relentlessly pursues him. Gordy's survival instincts take over because he has no doubt that Roger would kill him to prevent him from telling the truth. When Gordy sees two fishermen, hope flares in his heart, but Roger gets to the men first. When Gordy finally gets to talk to them, they are reluctant to believe him or offer help. Roger has always been able to talk his way out of anything and he seems to have done it again. In one final effort, Gordy starts running toward La Porte. Roger comes after him. Gordy climbs a butte and desperately kicks at some boulders, sending an avalanche down on Roger. Roger is knocked unconscious. Gordy climbs down and pockets Roger's knife. He is about to tie Roger's wrists when rescuers arrive. Roger comes to and tells the sheriff *his* version of what happened. The sheriff appears about ready to charge Gordy for making an attempt on Roger's life. Why won't anyone believe Gordy? Is Luke going to tell the truth or side with Roger?

Wuthering Heights **by Emily Brontë.**
Mahwah, NJ: Watermill Press, 1983. 345 pages.

This classic tale of tortured lovers is set on the bleak, windswept moors of northern England in the late 1700s. Emily Brontë has created two of the most memorable characters in all of literature. As Heathcliff and Catherine's engrossing love story unfolds, readers will understand why this novel is on every student of literature's "must read" list.

SUMMER OF MY GERMAN SOLDIER
Comprehension Test A

Directions: Read each question carefully. Circle the letter of the choice that best answers each question.

1. Who wrote this book?

    a. Bette Greene   *b.* Zibby Oneal   *c.* Barbara Cohen

2. Where did Patty first meet Anton?

    a. in church   *b.* in her father's store   *c.* at the train station

3. Patty's father gave her a terrible beating for _____.

    a. being friendly with a Nazi   *b.* daring to stand up to him   *c.* breaking a car window

4. The infirmary doctor told Charlene that Anton _____.

    a. seemed like a decent man

    b. was a fanatical Nazi

    c. was arrogant and dangerous

5. Patty's father beat her again when he saw _____.

    a. Anton's hiding place above the garage

    b. Freddy sitting on the porch with her

    c. how much the FBI men frightened her

6. The FBI agent _____.

    a. accused Patty of treason

    b. brought back the shirt that she had given to Anton

    c. arrested Patty

7. The FBI agents took Patty to _____.

    a. the prison camp

    b. her grandmother's house in Memphis

    c. the state penitentiary

8. Charlene Madlee told Patty and her grandparents that _____.

    a. Patty might go to reform school

    b. all charges against Patty had been dropped

    c. Patty was going to have to stand trial for treason

9. When Ruth came to visit Patty, she brought her _____.

    a. pork chops, hush puppies, and chocolate chip cookies

    b. a sweater, slacks, and chocolate cake

    c. fried chicken, gingersnaps, and Anton's ring

10. Ruth told Patty that her parents _____.

    a. sold the store and moved to Memphis

    b. were not people of quality

    c. had disinherited her

SUMMER OF MY GERMAN SOLDIER
Comprehension Test B

Directions: Read each question carefully. Circle the letter of the choice that best answers each question.

1. What did the townspeople do to Mr. Lee?

   a. elected him mayor   *b.* ran him out of town   *c.* boycotted his store

2. Patty's ambition was to _____.
   a. know the meaning of every word in the English language
   b. marry the richest man in Memphis
   c. get away from her cold-hearted parents

3. When Patty talked back to her mother, she was forced to _____.
   a. apologize in a store full of customers
   b. do extra chores for a month
   c. have a perm that fried her hair

4. Ruth couldn't go to teacher's college because _____.
   a. her father gambled all their money away
   b. Mr. Jackson stole the family's savings
   c. the family lost everything in the stock market crash

5. Anton told Patty that she _____.
   a. was beautiful
   b. should get away from her cruel parents
   c. was a person of value

6. Patty found out from _____ that Anton had been killed.

   a. an FBI agent   *b.* her father   *c.* the sheriff

7. Patty told her father that she helped Anton _____.
   a. because he was kind to her
   b. because she hated being Jewish
   c. out of hatred for her family

8. Mr. Bergen said that a lot of Patty's meanness was _____ fault.

   a. her mother's   *b.* Ruth's   *c.* her grandmother's

9. Patty saw that the windows of the reform school were _____.
   a. boarded over
   b. barred
   c. covered with wire screen like cages at the zoo

10. Charlene Madlee gave Patty a _____.
    a. bouquet of roses
    b. trip to the best beauty shop in Memphis
    c. newspaper subscription

SUMMER OF MY GERMAN SOLDIER
Comprehension Test C

Directions: Read each question carefully. Circle the letter of the choice that best answers each question.

1. Mrs. Burton Benn accused Ruth of being _____.
    a. a Communist   *b.* bigoted   *c.* uppity

2. Patty's hideout was _____.
    a. in a cave   *b.* above the garage   *c.* a treehouse

3. Anton's father was _____.
    a. an S.S. officer   *b.* a double agent   *c.* a history professor

4. Ruth discovered that Anton was in the garage when _____.
    a. Mr. Bergen heard him
    b. Patty told her
    c. he ran out to help Patty

5. When he left to catch the ten-fifteen, Anton gave Patty a _____.
    a. pin   *b.* ring   *c.* gold watch

6. Patty said she got her new ring _____.
    a. from an old man
    b. near the railroad tracks
    c. from the lady reporter from Memphis

7. Patty said that being in the same room with her mother was like _____.
    a. looking into the face of a monster
    b. a visit to the dentist
    c. being a feast for a thousand starving insects

8. Mr. Pierce was _____.
    a. an FBI agent
    b. a newspaper reporter
    c. the sheriff

9. Mr. Grimes drove Patty to _____.
    a. the hospital
    b. her grandmother's house
    c. reform school

10. Patty's mother said she couldn't come visit her because she _____.
    a. was busy working in the store
    b. had a bad back and the trip was too long
    c. never wanted to lay eyes on Patty again

SUMMER OF MY GERMAN SOLDIER

Directions: Patty was an avid newspaper reader. The answers to the following questions about World War II could have been found in newspapers between 1941 and 1945. You can find the answers in an encyclopedia. Write your answers on the lines.

1. During the infamous attack by the Japanese on Pearl Harbor, _____ battleships were sunk and _____ more were damaged.

2. Germany and Italy declared war on the U.S. on _____.

3. What three major powers made up the Axis Coalition? _____

    _____

4. Name the two types of heavy bombers built by the British especially for night bombing.

    _____

5. Give the meaning of the term *Holocaust.* _____

    _____

6. In 1943, the leaders of the three major allied powers met in Tehran, Iran. Name the leaders and their

    countries. _____

    _____

7. When and what was D-Day? _____

8. Name the general who was the supreme commander of Allied forces in Europe.

    _____

9. On what date did a bomb explode in Hitler's headquarters during an attempt to assassinate him?

    _____

10. On what date did Americans liberate Paris? _____

11. Name the leader of the Free French. _____

12. Name the Associated Press photographer who won a Pulitzer Prize for his photo of Marines raising the

    flag on Iwo Jima in 1945. _____

13. Name the date on which President Franklin D. Roosevelt died. _____

14. On what date did Hitler commit suicide in his Berlin Bunker? _____

15. Name the general who signed an unconditional surrender of all German armed forces on May 7, 1945.

    _____

16. When and what was V-E Day? _____

17. The Japanese formally signed their unconditional surrender on September 2, 1945 aboard the U.S.

    battleship _____.

PROJECTS FOR *SUMMER OF MY GERMAN SOLDIER*

Directions: Choose one of the following projects or design your own. If you design your own project, fill out the form below and submit it to your teacher for approval.

1. Draw illustrations of Patty before her permanent wave, while the machine is on, and after her hair has been frizzled.

2. Patty made lists of Thin Words (ago, ode), Fat Words (harmonic, palatable), Beautiful Words (rendezvous, dementia praecox), and Ugly Words (grief, degrade). On a separate sheet of paper, draw four columns and label them as above. Write at least twenty-five words in each column. (Do not use the same words that Patty used.)

3. People watch soap operas on TV today. In the 1940s, they listened to them on radio. Make a list of at least five soaps that Patty could have listened to. Choose an episode from one of these old radio shows and perform it with other classmates.

4. Write diary entries for Patty telling about her life between the ages of 13 and 18 years.

5. Create a newspaper based on the time period and events of this story. Be sure to include cartoons, society news, entertainment information, letters to the editor, editorials, and so on.

6. Write a report on the Holocaust.

PROJECT PROPOSAL

Name _____ Beginning Date _____ Completion Date _____

Describe the project in detail: _____

_____

Why do you want to do this project? _____

_____

What will the final product be? _____

_____

How will you share your final product? _____

_____

Comments: _____

_____

SUMMER OF THE MONKEYS
Comprehension Test A

Directions: Read each question carefully. Circle the letter of the choice that best answers each question.

1. Who wrote this book?
   a. Wilson Rawls   b. Farley Mowat   c. Donald J. Sobol

2. Jay Berry's favorite hero was _____.
   a. Kit Carson   b. Daniel Boone   c. Davy Crockett

3. After the traps were stolen, Jay Berry tried to catch the monkeys with _____.
   a. bananas strewn over a pit
   b. a stuffed monkey and a cage
   c. a net

4. Why did Grandpa almost go broke when the butterfly professor stayed with him?
   a. Customers thought he was crazy and wouldn't come near the store.
   b. The bank called in his loan.
   c. He brought bad luck.

5. While Rowdy and Jay Berry were hiding in the hole, along came a _____ followed by a _____.
   a. copperhead; wasp   b. black snake; hornet   c. rattler; bee

6. After he got drunk, Jay Berry woke up and discovered that the monkeys _____.
   a. had shaved his head
   b. had tied him to a tree
   c. had stolen his britches

7. Sour mash is made of things animals like, such as _____.
   a. sugar, corn, malt, and yeast
   b. salt, hops, rye, and yeast
   c. sugar, hops, salt, and yeast

8. Who got to make the first wish in the fairy ring?
   a. Daisy   b. Jay Berry   c. Mama

9. What is the first thing that Jay Berry did with his money?
   a. ran to the store to buy his pony
   b. handed Daisy $6
   c. gave Mama and Papa $100 for Daisy's operation

10. Mama brought Daisy's old crutch from the hospital _____.
    a. because Daisy still needed it
    b. so they could have a ceremony and bury it
    c. as a reminder to be thankful

SUMMER OF THE MONKEYS
Comprehension Test B

Directions: Read each question carefully. Circle the letter of the choice that best answers each question.

1. How did Mama and Papa get 60 acres of land?
   a. Her father traded a Cherokee Indian for it.
   b. It was a wedding present.
   c. They bought it with their savings.

2. There was a reward worth _____ for twenty-eight little monkeys and Jimbo.
   a. $96   b. $156   c. $66

3. After Grandpa wrapped the steel trap so it wouldn't hurt a monkey, he _____.
   a. made Jay Berry stick his finger in it
   b. placed Rowdy's paw in it
   c. stuck his finger in it to test it

4. After Jay Berry got bitten all over by monkeys, Mama said she was afraid _____.
   a. he'd get hydrophobia
   b. he'd met his match
   c. to ever let him go back to the bottom

5. The third thing Jay Berry tried was _____.
   a. putting down a trail of apples leading to the smokehouse
   b. making friends with Jimbo
   c. wooden traps

6. What happened to the coconuts?
   a. Grandpa and Jay Berry used them in a trap.
   b. The monkeys stole them.
   c. They fell off the back of the wagon and rolled away.

7. What did Daisy find when she went to clean her playhouse after the storm?
   a. that it had been completely destroyed
   b. that Jimbo had moved in
   c. a fairy ring

8. Who made the last wish in the fairy ring?
   a. Rowdy   b. Papa   c. Jay Berry

9. The monkeys were caught because _____.
   a. Grandpa outsmarted them
   b. they wanted to be caught
   c. Daisy made friends with them

10. Who came to pick up the monkeys?
    a. Ben and Tom Johnson
    b. P.T. Barnum and Tom Thumb
    c. the Ringling brothers

SUMMER OF THE MONKEYS
Comprehension Test C

Directions: Read each question carefully. Circle the letter of the choice that best answers each question.

1. Rowdy was Jay Berry's_____.

   a. redbone coon hound   *b.* basset hound   *c.* old bluetick hound

2. How did the monkeys come to be in Cherokee Bottoms?

   a. They escaped from a circus train.

   b. Wild monkeys had been there for decades.

   c. They were pets left behind by fishermen.

3. The first time Jay Berry set traps for the monkeys, _____.

   a. he accidentally caught Rowdy

   b. the chimp sprang all of them

   c. he caught one monkey, but it escaped from the sack

4. Jay Berry caught two monkeys in the net, but _____.

   a. the chimp rescued them

   b. they figured out how to open it and ran off

   c. he caught it on a branch and it tore open

5. Why did Jay Berry and Rowdy get drunk on sour mash?

   a. Monkey see; monkey do.

   b. They got drunk every time they found a still.

   c. Jimbo demanded it.

6. Grandpa said that no matter what the problem, you could always find the answer _____.

   a. at the library   *b.* in church   *c.* in school

7. Grandpa got the idea to use coconuts for bait from _____.

   a. the animal trainer in the circus

   b. a book in the library

   c. a professor at the college in Tahlequah

8. Grandpa said that from now on he was going to spend time _____.

   a. sitting and rocking

   b. dealing in horses and mules

   c. looking for a fairy ring

9. Rowdy showed he was jealous of the new pony by _____.

   a. trying to stay between it and Jay Berry

   b. hiding under the porch and howling

   c. growling and nipping at it

10. Jay Berry named his new pony _____.

   a. Dolly   *b.* Cutie Pie   *c.* Little One

SUMMER OF THE MONKEYS

I. *Directions:* When Daisy saw a drunken Jay Berry coming home, she yelled to Mama that he was "as drunk as a boiled owl" and "as naked as a jaybird." Complete each simile below. Write the correct letter on the line.

Column A

_____ 1. as sick as
_____ 2. as strong as
_____ 3. as blind as
_____ 4. as thin as
_____ 5. as sly as
_____ 6. as slow as
_____ 7. as slippery as
_____ 8. as mad as
_____ 9. as cool as
_____10. as drunk as
_____11. as clear as
_____12. as deaf as
_____13. as weak as
_____14. as stiff as
_____15. as happy as
_____16. as stubborn as
_____17. as neat as
_____18. as clean as
_____19. as pretty as
_____20. as fresh as

Column B

a. a bat
b. a skunk
c. a fox
d. a daisy
e. a board
f. a mule
g. a dog
h. a cucumber
i. a kitten
j. an ox
k. a lark
l. a whistle
m. a bell
n. a post
o. a hornet
p. a picture
q. a pin
r. an eel
s. molasses
t. a rail

II. *Directions:* On a separate sheet of paper, write at least ten more similes.

III. *Directions:* Choose ten of the above similes to use in complete sentences. Write your sentences on a separate sheet of paper.

PROJECTS FOR *SUMMER OF THE MONKEYS*

Directions: Choose one of the following projects or design your own. If you design your own project, fill out the form below and submit it to your teacher for approval.

1. Make a corn shuck or a corncob doll and dress it appropriately for the late nineteenth century. For directions on making a corncob doll, see page 97 in the August 1991 issue of *Colonial Homes* magazine.

2. Read *Where the Red Fern Grows*. Tell how these two stories by Wilson Rawls are alike and how they're different.

3. Reread the description of the monkey-catching net. Make a model just like the one Grandpa gave to Jay Berry.

4. When Grandpa and Jay Berry came to the river, Grandpa let Jay Berry drive the team because he was reminded of a painting called "The Big Moment." Draw this picture.

5. You are a reporter who has come to the farm to ask Jay Berry about catching the monkeys and his plans for spending the reward money. First, simulate this interview. Next, write a feature article about Jay Berry's adventure.

6. Select at least twenty-five of your favorite dog jokes and combine them into a joke book to share with your class. Illustrate each joke. Include a footnote for each joke giving its source.

PROJECT PROPOSAL

Name _____ Beginning Date _____ Completion Date _____

Describe the project in detail: _____

_____

Why do you want to do this project? _____

_____

What will the final product be? _____

_____

How will you share your final product? _____

_____

Comments: _____

_____

PURSUIT
Comprehension Test A

Directions: Read each question carefully. Circle the letter of the choice that best answers each question.

1. Who wrote this book?
   a. Gary Paulsen   b. Milton Meltzer   c. Michael French

2. Roger made all-American and planned on being a _____ at USC in the fall.
   a. quarterback   b. tight end   c. running back

3. Gordy felt that he was in control of himself except for his _____.
   a. imagination   b. rage   c. fear

4. Roger cooked _____ over the fire to bait Gordy into coming out of the cave.
   a. two squirrels   b. two trout   c. sausage and eggs

5. In a desperate attempt to attract attention, Gordy set fire to _____.
   a. an old abandoned shack
   b. Roger's tent
   c. a pile of pine needles

6. Roger told the fishermen that he was _____ from Salinas.
   a. Hank Brown   b. Mike Johnson   c. Steve Wilson

7. The two fishermen told Gordy that they weren't going north toward La Porte, but _____ toward Quincy.
   a. south   b. east   c. west

8. When Luke demanded to sign a statement, _____.
   a. the sheriff stalled for time
   b. Roger shot him
   c. Roger tackled him

9. Roger could be tried for _____.
   a. first-degree murder
   b. manslaughter or second-degree murder
   c. assault and battery

10. Roger's sentence might be _____.
    a. a couple of years
    b. twenty years
    c. life

PURSUIT
Comprehension Test B

Directions: Read each question carefully. Circle the letter of the choice that best answers each question.

1. Whose father was on unemployment most of the time?

   a. Roger   *b.* Luke   *c.* Martin

2. Luke stole money from _____ to buy equipment for the trip.

   a. the petty cash fund in the school office

   b. his father's hardware store

   c. the collection basket at church

3. Gordy survived on berries, bird eggs, clover, and _____.

   a. rodent   *b.* roots   *c.* wild onions

4. When Gordy thought he was going to die in the river, he was surprised at _____.

   a. how calm he was

   b. how happy he was

   c. how terrified he was

5. Gordy's _____ made him leave the cave and approach Roger's camp.

   a. fear   *b.* hunger   *c.* rage

6. In Roger's first attempt to scale the rocks and reach the cave, Gordy was saved when _____.

   a. he hit Roger in the eye with a rock

   b. a helicopter flew over

   c. two fishermen appeared and Roger climbed down

7. The fishermen told Gordy that he was only _____ miles away from La Porte.

   a. 4   *b.* 5   *c.* 6

8. Gordy started running toward La Porte but saw Roger close behind, so he _____.

   a. jumped in the Yuba and floated underwater

   b. hid in the undergrowth

   c. climbed a butte to push boulders down on Roger

9. Roger said he'd file charges against Gordy _____.

   a. and he'd kill Luke if he didn't back his story

   b. unless he agreed that Martin's death was an accident

   c. and Luke for being accessories to Martin's death

10. Luke was sickened when he realized that _____.

    a. Roger was setting him up

    b. the sheriff didn't believe him

    c. he'd do anything to have an important friend

PURSUIT
Comprehension Test C

Directions: Read each question carefully. Circle the letter of the choice that best answers each question.

1. Who said Roger was a phony and others were blind if they couldn't see it?
   a. Gordy *b.* Luke *c.* Martin

2. Gordy knew he had to _____ Roger.
   a. outwit *b.* outrun *c.* kill

3. Gordy was bleeding profusely from a wound on his _____.
   a. ankle *b.* chin *c.* wrist

4. Gordy realized that when he saw Roger move along the bank of the river, he had _____.
   a. gathered pebbles to use in self-defense
   b. gathered driftwood for a fire
   c. picked everything edible

5. Roger tried to poison Gordy, but _____ stole the food and saved his life.
   a. a mountain lion *b.* an eagle *c.* a hawk

6. Just as Gordy was about to tie Roger's wrists, he saw _____ coming toward them.
   a. two fishermen *b.* two campers *c.* Luke and his father

7. Roger told the sheriff that Gordy _____.
   a. had tried to kill him
   b. was the person responsible for Martin's death
   c. had suffered a concussion and was talking nonsense

8. Gordy told the sheriff to get Roger's backpack and check _____.
   a. for poisoned food
   b. the rope
   c. for the statement Roger wanted him to sign

9. Gordy's father told him that he was too _____ to understand the real world.
   a. naive
   b. stupid
   c. blind

10. When Gordy was lost, he stumbled upon a _____.
    a. fisherman *b.* hermit *c.* man panning for gold

PURSUIT

Directions: Words from the story are hidden in the puzzle. Find the hidden words and circle them. You may go across and down.

apparition
colloquially
arbitrarily
protuberance
bellicose
incomprehension
ploy
discrepancy
feigned
wearisome
mesmerized
buffered
innocuous
sallies
predominant
precipice
queasiness
futile
unpremeditated
skepticism
immobilized
hallucinating
duress
fusillade
acoustics
haughty
futilely
cajoled
rationalization
undeterred
camaraderie
foraged
pummeled

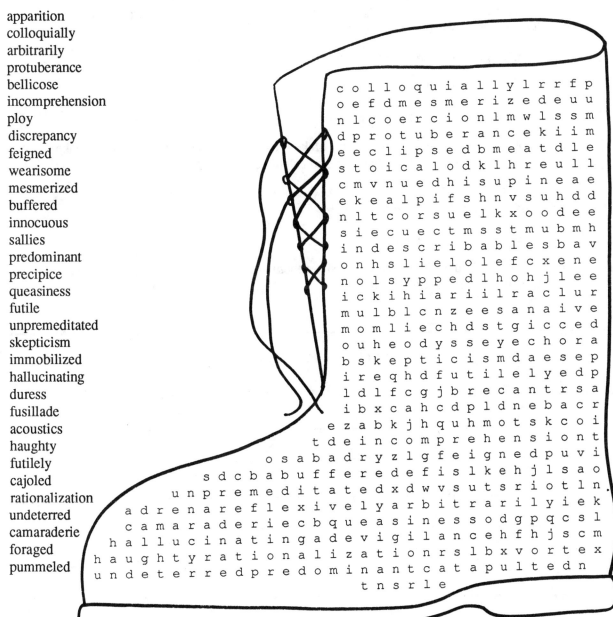

```
c o l l o q u i a l l y l r r f p
o e f d m e s m e r i z e d e u u
n l c o e r c i o n l m w l s s m
d p r o t u b e r a n c e k i i m
e e c l i p s e d b m e a t d l e
s t o i c a l o d k l h r e u l l
c m v n u e d h i s u p i n e a e
e k e a l p i f s h n v s u h d d
n l t c o r s u e l k x o o d e e
s i e c u e c t m s s t m u b m h
i n d e s c r i b a b l e s b a v
o n h s l i e l o l e f c x e n e
n o l s y p p e d l h o h j l e e
i c k i h i a r i i l r a c l u r
m u l b l c n z e e s a n a i v e
m o m l i e c h d s t g i c c e d
o u h e o d y s s e y e c h o r a
b s k e p t i c i s m d a e s e p
i r e q h d f u t i l e l y e d p
l d l f c g j b r e c a n t r s a
i b x c a h c d p l d n e b a c r
e z a b k j h q u h m o t s k c o i
t d e i n c o m p r e h e n s i o n t
o s a b a d r y z l g f e i g n e d p u v i
s d c b a b u f f e r e d e f i s l k e h j l s a o
u n p r e m e d i t a t e d x d w v s u t s r i o t l n
a d r e n a r e f l e x i v e l y a r b i t r a r i l y i e k
c a m a r a d e r i e c b q u e a s i n e s s o d g p q c s l
h a l l u c i n a t i n g a d e v i g i l a n c e h f h j s c m
h a u g h t y r a t i o n a l i z a t i o n r s l b x v o r t e x
u n d e t e r r e d p r e d o m i n a n t c a t a p u l t e d n
t n s r l e
```

coercion	inaccessible	disembodied	meticulously	irrelevant
catapulted	stoical	recant	mechanicalness	convalesce
condescension	supine	coveted	veered	maneuvered
cache	odyssey	naive	vigilance	tenuous
indescribable	residue	eclipsed	reflexively	vortex

PROJECTS FOR *PURSUIT*

Directions: Choose one of the following projects or design your own. If you design your own project, fill out the form below and submit it to your teacher for approval.

1. What if Luke had fallen and struck his head, causing amnesia? Rewrite the last chapter, telling what would likely have happened under these circumstances.

2. Rewrite this book as a picture book.

3. Make a diorama of a scene from the story.

4. What if a TV or newspaper reporter interviewed Gordy in La Porte? Simulate this interview.

5. You are going on a one-week camping trip. Make a list of equipment that you plan to take in your backpack. Estimate the weight of each item and calculate a grand total. (Catalogs will show various camping items plus their weights.)

6. Rewrite this book as an adventure comic book.

7. Write the next chapter of the book.

8. When school starts in the fall, Gordy's English teacher has everyone write a report about their summer vacation. Write Gordy's report for him.

PROJECT PROPOSAL

Name _____ Beginning Date _____ Completion Date _____

Describe the project in detail: _____

_____

Why do you want to do this project? _____

_____

What will the final product be? _____

_____

How will you share your final product? _____

_____

Comments: _____

_____

WUTHERING HEIGHTS
Comprehension Test A

Directions: Read each question carefully. Circle the letter of the choice that best answers each question.

1. Who wrote this book?

    a. Mary Shelley   *b.* Emily Brontë   *c.* Catherine Cookson

2. Mr. Earnshaw, the old master, had two children who were named _____.

    a. Hindley and Cathy

    b. Hareton and Zillah

    c. Hadley and Nelly

3. Hareton's mother _____.

    a. ran away with the village doctor

    b. committed suicide

    c. died shortly after his birth

4. Catherine's primary motive for marrying was _____.

    a. love   *b.* money   *c.* revenge

5. The doctor told Nelly that Isabella was planning to _____.

    a. write Catherine out of her will

    b. go live with a relative because of Catherine's tantrums

    c. elope with Heathcliff

6. Nelly said it would be better if Catherine died than to _____.

    a. continually heap anguish upon all who loved her

    b. be a lingering burden and misery-maker to all about her

    c. linger on expecting everyone to do her bidding

7. Why did Heathcliff want Linton and Cathy to marry?

    a. to make Edgar miserable

    b. to get the weakling Linton out of his sight

    c. so Heathcliff could gain control of Thrushcross Grange

8. Heathcliff was afraid that _____.

    a. Linton would die before Cathy's father

    b. Cathy's father would die before Linton

    c. Cathy would refuse Linton's marriage proposal

9. In his will, Linton signed over _____ to his father.

    a. all of his and all of his wife's property

    b. all of his and all of his wife's movable property

    c. his property

10. When Cathy was teaching Hareton to read, she _____ him if he made a mistake.

    a. belittled   *b.* cursed   *c.* slapped

WUTHERING HEIGHTS
Comprehension Test B

Directions: Read each question carefully. Circle the letter of the choice that best answers each question.

1. Why did Mr. Lockwood stay overnight when Heathcliff obviously disliked his company?
   a. because of the fog
   b. because of the snow
   c. because of the pouring rain

2. Catherine married _____.
   a. Edgar Linton   b. Ethan Lockwood   c. Edward Landon

3. While Catherine was willfully making herself ill, she was angered to learn that _____.
   a. her husband was quietly reading in the library
   b. no one cared
   c. her husband had invited friends over

4. What did Nelly discover hanging from a bridle hook?
   a. a love letter from Catherine to Heathcliff
   b. Isabella's springer Fanny
   c. Mr. Linton's Persian cat Fluffy

5. Who was Mr. Kenneth?
   a. the lawyer   b. the tutor   c. the doctor

6. Isabella wrote to Nelly to tell her that her marriage to Heathcliff _____.
   a. was a marriage made in heaven
   b. was a disappointment
   c. made her feel wretched

7. When Mr. Lockwood visited Wuthering Heights in 1802, the first difference he noticed _____.
   a. was an unlocked gate
   b. was a light on in every room
   c. was music and laughter coming from the open windows

8. Who got hurt when his gun burst while he was hunting?
   a. Lockwood   b. Heathcliff   c. Hareton

9. When Joseph discovered that his shrubs had been dug up, he was so angry that _____.
   a. he had a stroke
   b. he had an apoplectic fit
   c. his jaws worked like a cow chewing its cud

10. After they married, Cathy and Hareton decided to _____.
    a. move to London
    b. move to the south of France
    c. move to Thrushcross Grange

WUTHERING HEIGHTS
Comprehension Test C

Directions: Read each question carefully. Circle the letter of the choice that best answers each question.

1. When Mr. Earnshaw first saw Heathcliff, he was homeless and starving _____.
   - *a.* in the streets of London
   - *b.* in the streets of Edinburgh
   - *c.* in the streets of Liverpool

2. When Catherine's husband said she had to choose between Heathcliff or him, she _____.
   - *a.* poisoned herself
   - *b.* went on a hunger strike
   - *c.* laughed in his face

3. Who was first to discover that Isabella had eloped with Heathcliff?
   - *a.* Nelly
   - *b.* Edgar
   - *c.* Catherine

4. The doctor said Mrs. Linton suffered from _____.
   - *a.* brain fever
   - *b.* insanity
   - *c.* palsy

5. Catherine died _____.
   - *a.* while walking across the moor
   - *b.* two hours after her baby was born
   - *c.* when she tried to ride to Wuthering Heights

6. Catherine was buried _____.
   - *a.* on the moor
   - *b.* in the kirkyard
   - *c.* inside the chapel

7. How did Mrs. Heathcliff get a cut near her ear?
   - *a.* Her husband threw a knife at her.
   - *b.* She fell while running across the moor.
   - *c.* She cut herself on a broken window.

8. Linton was the son of _____.
   - *a.* Edgar
   - *b.* Heathcliff
   - *c.* Hindley

9. Who did Heathcliff refer to as a whey-faced whining wretch?
   - *a.* Linton
   - *b.* Hareton
   - *c.* Edgar

10. When Heathcliff kept Cathy and Ellen locked up for days, he told people _____.
    - *a.* he hadn't seen them for months
    - *b.* they had probably gone to London to see the sights
    - *c.* they'd fallen in a bog

WUTHERING HEIGHTS

I. *Directions:* The English language changes over the years. If you read *Frankenstein* and *Wuthering Heights*, you noticed that nineteenth-century authors used phrases that sound archaic today. Read each phrase below. Write what you think each phrase means.

1. subdue the maxillary convulsions _____

2. resuming my garments _____

3. quit the chamber _____

4. ever and anon _____

5. perused the epistle _____

6. importuned me _____

7. she essayed another method _____

8. I was cogitating _____

9. I durst not _____

10. to bid adieu _____

II. *Directions:* Many words from the novel are given below. Use each of these words in a word search. First, draw a large heart on a separate sheet of paper. Next, incorporate each word into the puzzle.

perseverance	assiduity	cudgel	discomfiture	magnanimity
misanthropist	sagacity	lachrymose	blackguard	equanimity
manifested	taciturn	appellation	ignoble	assiduously
sinewy	diabolical	orisons	purification	vagaries
penetralium	gruel	impalpable	expostulated	vociferating
actuate	beneficent	indigenae	prognosticate	perdition
stalwart	reprobate	whinstone	provincialisms	clamorously
physiognomy	malignity	usurper	zealous	phalanx
parrying	ensconcing	wheedle	dissipation	vials
egress	palaver	interloper	vivisection	averred
vexations	copestone	prattled	laconic	fastidiousness
phlegm	miscreants	tyrannical	swoon	presentiment
signet	virulency	annihilate	catgut	petulance
laconic	hieroglyphics	execrations	soliloquy	alleviation
churlish	initiatory	heathenism	saturnine	abjured
vehemently	sobriety	mire	winsome	changeling
corrugated	asseverated	beclouded	malappropriated	peevishness

PROJECTS FOR *WUTHERING HEIGHTS*

Directions: Choose one of the following projects or design your own. If you design your own project, fill out the form below and submit it to your teacher for approval.

1. Mr. Lockwood had terrible nightmares when he spent the night in the oak closet. Make a model of this closet.

2. Write a report about women's rights between 1780–1800. Explain why Catherine could not inherit her father's property after her marriage.

3. Write a bio-poem about one of the characters in the story. Illustrate this poem with a sketch of the person.

4. Cathy and Linton found tops, hoops, battledores, and shuttlecocks to play with. Make a chart showing at least twelve toys children played with in the late eighteenth century. Draw each toy and label it.

5. *Wuthering Heights* is considered a classic. Writers of today use this story as a text in how to write a romance novel. Write a report explaining what elevates this story into the realm of a classic and why modern authors study it to hone their craft.

6. Emily Brontë was a member of a famous literary family. Write a report about Emily, Charlotte, Anne, and Branwell Brontë.

PROJECT PROPOSAL

Name _____ Beginning Date _____ Completion Date _____

Describe the project in detail: _____

_____

Why do you want to do this project? _____

_____

What will the final product be? _____

_____

How will you share your final product? _____

_____

Comments: _____

_____

Section 12

FAVORITE BOOKS
FOR
AUGUST

The following books are on "August Book List B" in *Ready-to-Use Reading Activities Through the Year*.

Activity Sheets	Book Titles	Reading Level	Award
12-1 to 12-5	*The Hero and the Crown*	7	Newbery Medal
12-6 to 12-10	*Hitty: Her First Hundred Years*	5	Newbery Medal
12-11 to 12-15	*National Velvet*	7	
12-16 to 12-20	*The Red Pony*	4	

The Hero and the Crown by Robin McKinley.
New York: Greenwillow, 1984. 227 pages.

Aerin slays dragons, learns magic, becomes not quite mortal, rescues her country, overcomes evil, falls in love, marries a king, and is crowned queen. Thus, she fulfills her destiny as a mortal. Quiet whisperings in the far reaches of her mind hint of a destiny yet to be attained by the part of her that is not quite mortal.

Hitty: Her First Hundred Years by Rachel Field.
New York: Macmillan, 1929. 207 pages.

In the early nineteenth century, an old peddler carves Hitty out of mountain-ash, which is supposed to bring good luck. Hitty survives many owners, both young and old, and experiences many exciting adventures. She travels on a square-rigged whaling ship, by horse and buggy, steamship, train, and automobile. At the age of 100, she finds herself in an antique shop where she is looked upon as a rare bit of early Americana. Hitty is waiting for her next owner and her next adventure. Maybe she'll get to ride in one of those newfangled airplanes that she sees from the front window of the shop.

National Velvet by Enid Bagnold.
New York: Scholastic, 1953. 251 pages.

Velvet Brown's life revolves around horses. She is overjoyed when she inherits five horses and wins one in a raffle. She develops a special relationship with one of the horses and begins dreaming of riding him in the Grand National. There is one problem, however; girls are not allowed to enter this race. In her heart, Velvet knows that she and Pie could win it. She follows her heart and sets about getting around the problem. When the world discovers that a girl has won the Grand National, Velvet is caught up in a media circus. After the frenzy dies down, she quietly plans her next adventure.

The Red Pony by John Steinbeck.
New York: Bantam, 1933. 120 pages.

Jody's dream of having a pony of his very own finally comes true. He tries to take good care of his pony, but one day he makes a fatal error in judgment. He decides to leave Gabilan outside in the corral while he goes to school. When it starts raining, Jody desperately wants to race home to put his pony in the barn, but decides not to risk getting in trouble with the teacher. When he finally gets home, he finds a very sick pony. Although he and the hired man fight tirelessly to save the pony, it dies. Jody is devastated. He hardly dares to dream of one day getting another pony. Can his dream of having a pony of his own come true a second time?

THE HERO AND THE CROWN
Comprehension Test A

Directions: Read each question carefully. Circle the letter of the choice that best answers each question.

1. Who wrote this book?
   a. J.R.R. Tolkien   *b.* Robin McKinley   *c.* Lloyd Alexander

2. If you touched the leaves of the surka plant, you would die unless _____.
   a. you had royal blood
   b. you had the witchwoman quickly cast a spell
   c. you had the antidote at hand

3. Aerin wanted to take a short trip so she could _____.
   a. secretly meet Tor
   b. shop in the city
   c. test kenet on herself and Tolat

4. Aerin got careless with the fifth dragon and it marked her _____.
   a. by swiping her with its tail
   b. by biting her arm
   c. by burning her where her tunic was torn

5. A dragon's babies were called _____.
   a. kits   *b.* kids   *c.* pups

6. In order to restore Aerin's life, Luthe had to _____.
   a. use healers from several villages
   b. immerse her in dragon's blood
   c. turn her into an immortal

7. What did Aerin hurl at Agsded?
   a. water from the silver lake and dragonfire
   b. the surka wreath and the dragon stone
   c. kenet and the skull of one of the Great Ones

8. Luthe said the red stone was _____.
   a. the last drop of blood from Maur's heart
   b. the bloodstone of the great mage Goriolo
   c. the one stolen centuries before from the Hero's Crown

9. Luthe traveled by _____.
   a. air currents   *b.* walking   *c.* horse

10. As king, Tor was known for his even handedness and was called the _____.
    a. Judge   *b.* Wise One   *c.* Just

THE HERO AND THE CROWN
Comprehension Test B

Directions: Read each question carefully. Circle the letter of the choice that best answers each question.

1. Aerin's father was _____.
   a. Albert *b.* Arlbeth *c.* Alfred

2. Aerin's maid was _____.
   a. Teka *b.* Talat *c.* Torina

3. When Aerin first tried to spear the dragon, _____.
   a. she struck a mortal blow
   b. she missed entirely
   c. she hit it in the neck

4. When Aerin encountered her first dragon, she almost died because _____.
   a. she didn't put enough kenet on
   b. she was so afraid she couldn't move
   c. she forgot about its mate

5. How did Aerin's father reprimand her for going out alone to slay dragons?
   a. He put her in a dungeon for a fortnight.
   b. He hit her on both cheeks with the flat of a sword.
   c. He took Talat away from her.

6. Aerin killed Maur by _____.
   a. spearing him in the neck
   b. knifing him through the eye and into the brain
   c. using the kenet to turn the dragonfire back on him

7. Why did Aerin get out of her sickbed and sneak away in the night?
   a. to fight another Black Dragon
   b. to find the man who said he could help her
   c. to run away from the people who hated her and wished her harm

8. The foothills of Airdthmar were lush with _____ grass.
   a. purple *b.* red *c.* orange

9. Kelar was _____.
   a. a potion *b.* a spell *c.* the Gift

10. Agsded was the brother of _____.
    a. Maur *b.* Aerin's mother *c.* Luthe

THE HERO AND THE CROWN
Comprehension Test C

Directions: Read each question carefully. Circle the letter of the choice that best answers each question.

1. An ointment called kenet was _____.
   a. a burn medicine
   b. a deadly poison for those of royal blood
   c. protection against dragonfire

2. The war stallion Talat had been _____.
   a. slashed in a battle
   b. burned by a Great One
   c. blinded by eating some leaves from the surka

3. Why did Teka tie ankle ribbons on Aerin?
   a. to hide the lumpy darns on her stockings
   b. to outdo Galana and the ladies of the court
   c. to catch Tor's eye

4. A messenger told the king the shocking news that _____.
   a. the black plague had been sent from the North
   b. enemy soldiers were only a mile outside the City
   c. Maur, the Black Dragon, had returned

5. Aerin lost her voice when _____.
   a. she caught the black plague   b. she swallowed dragonfire   c. the witchwoman enspelled her

6. A *folstra* is a _____ and a *yerig* is a _____.
   a. horse; donkey   b. cat; dog   c. dragon; deer

7. As Aerin climbed the stairs in the dark tower, she _____.
   a. walked slowly so Luthe could catch up
   b. stumbled and fell backwards
   c. knew that evil was with her

8. Agsded told Aerin that she couldn't defeat him because _____.
   a. he wore the Hero's Crown
   b. she was foolish enough to come alone
   c. she was a mere female

9. What did the Yerigs drop at Aerin's feet after her encounter with Agsded?
   a. game for breakfast
   b. a charred surka wreath and the Hero's Crown
   c. Agsded's red sword and red dragon stone

10. When Aerin rode away, Luthe lay on the ground and _____.
    a. sobbed
    b. disintegrated into the earth
    c. listened to Talat's hoofbeats carrying her away

THE HERO AND THE CROWN

Directions: Words from the story are hidden in the puzzle. Find the words and circle them. You may go across and down.

Kenet

```
s d i w              o s t r a c i z e f i d g e t i e s t
l e t h a r g y a r i m e a s c r i b e d s c u r r i l o u s
a f b i k a l m p i t e i n s i d i o u s p b j i o n a b z u
n t f f c z n s r s e l f a g g r a n d i z e m e n t l h l r
g e g f j e t h e r e l n b m j a c e k y r m i d w r i t h e
u r i l u d o u c z q i e v a l o r o u s t u n o e a h a a
o d s e n h p n a a r f g a g k b i a l o e s i c q n q t s
r e t a d r q t r y y l d z e l c d d r i q e o i u s e r p
o g r e i s h i i c o u r t i e r s h t w s d n l n i u o e
u u i s l x o n o b s o s t r a c i z t z n l s e b g r c r
s t n v u w y g u c u u k y s m d t l e h u y k l c e s i i
l u g z t z d m s i n s i n u a t e d m e w e d y d n b t t
y v e y e q e l o j u g g e r n a u t e v o m i h e c r y y
a e n b d p n k h a b t r a c o s k m r x q u a i l e d s k
a n t i q u a t e d w e t h e r e a l i n a l t e r a b l e
r t l c r s o j w e p m i v a p g m s t e r m a g a n t k n
t r n x t u n i b a s i l i s k h i w y c a c o p h o n y s
i n g l o r i o u s x o h b e l e a g u e r e d g f l e r
f s k v s p u r b l i n d u r i n s c r u t a b l y n s
a e h w u e f f i c a c y t s q i m o r g a n a t i c h
c h l d e r e l i c t i o n f q h a n t i p a t h y b
t a s e t t
```

ascribed	valorous	writhe	usurper	hew
atrocity	hoyden	miasma	antiquated	inglorious
razed	languorously	basilisk	minions	shunting
beleaguered	defter	ostracize	aloes	purblind
docilely	artifact	acrid	bemusedly	ethereal
whiffle	cacophony	antipathy	dereliction	insinuated
rime	ogreish	mewed	inscrutably	juggernaut
asperity	scurrilous	courtiers	stringent	undiluted
fidgetiest	surcease	temerity	precarious	intransigence
efficacy	insidious	lethargy	morganatic	quailed
termagant	mellifluous	mage	inalterable	self-aggrandizement

PROJECTS FOR *THE HERO AND THE CROWN*

Directions: Choose one of the following projects or design your own. If you design your own project, fill out the form below and submit it to your teacher for approval.

1. Rewrite the story as a picture book.

2. Prepare a time line of Aerin's life.

3. Draw a mural depicting scenes from the story in chronological order.

4. Make a mobile featuring a Great One, smaller dragons, war horses, a folstra, and a yerig.

5. Make a clay model of Maur.

6. Draw a map showing where the events in this story took place.

7. Prepare a scroll featuring the menu for Aerin and Tor's wedding celebration. Write the menu items in both Damarian and English.

8. Make sketches of costumes Aerin and Tor would have worn for everyday use, court ceremonials, and battle.

9. Paint a wedding portrait of Aerin and Tor.

PROJECT PROPOSAL

Name _____ Beginning Date _____ Completion Date _____

Describe the project in detail: _____

_____

Why do you want to do this project? _____

_____

What will the final product be? _____

_____

How will you share your final product? _____

_____

Comments: _____

_____

HITTY: HER FIRST HUNDRED YEARS
Comprehension Test A

Directions: Read each question carefully. Circle the letter of the choice that best answers each question.

1. Who wrote this book?
   a. Rachel Field   *b.* Bernice Selden   *c.* P.L. Travers

2. A peddler carved Hitty for a little girl named _____.
   a. Phoebe Preble   *b.* Lucy Larcom   *c.* Sarah Bagley

3. Where did Phoebe lose Hitty the second time?
   a. in church
   b. in a raspberry patch
   c. in a boat

4. Who had a clipper ship tattooed across his chest?
   a. Jeremy Folger   *b.* Andy Preble   *c.* Bill Buckle

5. Hitty never suffered more in her life than when _____.
   a. Thankful hid her in the sofa
   b. natives painted her face
   c. the cobra coiled itself around her body

6. Clarissa and Hitty went to a concert to hear the famous singer _____.
   a. Jenny Lind   *b.* Adelina Patti   *c.* Enrico Caruso

7. After being rescued from the hayloft, Hitty became _____.
   a. an artist's model
   b. a doll of fashion
   c. a high-priced antique in a shop

8. Sally stole Hitty and then tried to give her back by _____.
   a. mailing her back to the Cotton Exposition
   b. giving her to the preacher to return
   c. setting her adrift in a basket on the Mississippi

9. The ticket agent's wife _____.
   a. gave Hitty to her daughter
   b. turned Hitty into a pincushion
   c. sold Hitty to an antique dealer

10. Hitty joined the famous doll collection of _____.
    a. Miss Pamela Wellington
    b. Miss Maggie Arnold
    c. Miss Louella Larraby

HITTY: HER FIRST HUNDRED YEARS
Comprehension Test B

Directions: Read each question carefully. Circle the letter of the choice that best answers each question.

1. Hitty said that mountain-ash brings good luck and has power _____.
   a. to ward off sickness and death
   b. to provide health and happiness
   c. over witchcraft and evil

2. Phoebe's father said the square balconies built around roofs and chimneys were called _____.
   a. Lookout walks   b. Captain's walks   c. Widow's walks

3. When sailors say they're going to "join the fishes," they mean they're going _____.
   a. to die   b. whaling   c. swimming

4. Hitty became lost in India when _____.
   a. someone grabbed her from Phoebe's hand
   b. Phoebe fell asleep and dropped her in the street
   c. she was left behind on a jewelry store counter

5. Hitty was rescued from the sofa by _____.
   a. Clarissa   b. Thankful   c. Paul

6. Hitty met poet _____.
   a. Henry Wadsworth Longfellow
   b. Elizabeth Barrett Browning
   c. John Greenleaf Whittier

7. Miss _____ turned Hitty into a doll of fashion like those in "Godey's Lady's Book."
   a. Isabella Van Rensselaer   b. Milly Pinch   c. Camilla Calhoun

8. Hitty traveled to New Orleans on a _____.
   a. boat with a big paddle wheel
   b. train run by steam
   c. clipper ship

9. Hitty returned to the state of Maine in _____.
   a. a horse and buggy
   b. an automobile
   c. an airplane

10. Hitty was surprised to hear herself referred to as a _____.
    a. fine piece of American folk art
    b. reproduction
    c. very rare bit of early Americana

HITTY: HER FIRST HUNDRED YEARS
Comprehension Test C

Directions: Read each question carefully. Circle the letter of the choice that best answers each question.

1. Hitty began writing her memoirs while in _____.
   a. an antique shop   *b.* a sailing vessel   *c.* a valise

2. Why did Captain Preble want his wife to go on the voyage with him?
   a. She was ill and he had to take care of her.
   b. He was lonely.
   c. He wanted her to be the ship's cook.

3. After being lost in church, carried away by a crow, and shipwrecked, Hitty _____.
   a. became a heathen idol
   b. was swallowed by a whale
   c. was eaten by a cannibal

4. Thankful sailed from India to live with her grandparents in _____.
   a. New York City   *b.* Philadelphia   *c.* Boston

5. The Pryces were _____ who felt that all slaves should be freed.
   a. Quakers   *b.* Amish   *c.* Shakers

6. Toward the end of the Civil War, Hitty was _____.
   a. sent to a little southern girl
   b. put in camphor
   c. scorched when the house was set on fire

7. Isabella dropped Hitty at the feet of the famous author _____.
   a. Charles Dickens
   b. Sir Arthur Conan Doyle
   c. A.A. Milne

8. After Sally Loomis took her from the display case, Hitty was taken aboard a _____.
   a. clipper ship
   b. square-rigged whaling vessel
   c. river steamboat

9. At the auction, an old gentleman had to pay _____ to outbid the fat lady for Hitty.
   a. $50   *b.* $51   *c.* $52

10. At the age of 100, Hitty was looking forward to _____.
    a. further adventures
    b. a comfortable life in a museum case
    c. being put in camphor and stored away

HITTY: HER FIRST HUNDRED YEARS

Directions: Poet John Greenleaf Whittier wrote a poem about Hitty. Write a poem of your own about this remarkable doll. Your poem can be a cinquain, diamante, haiku, or any other form you choose.

PROJECTS FOR *HITTY: HER FIRST HUNDRED YEARS*

Directions: Choose one of the following projects or design your own. If you design your own project, fill out the form below and submit it to your teacher for approval.

1. Make a model of Hitty and dress her as Phoebe, Thankful, Clarissa, Isabella, Miss Pinch, or Miss Annette and Miss Hortense did.

2. Make a time line for Hitty from the time she was "born" in the early nineteenth century until she ended up in the antique shop in the early twentieth century. Show her various owners, the way they dressed, and the way they dressed Hitty.

3. Write a report about daguerreotypes. Give the report orally to your class. Include several examples of old daguerreotypes. Tell where daguerreotypes are made today and how much they cost.

4. Write Hitty's next adventure in which she gets to ride in an airplane.

5. Choose an adventure from the story and present it as a puppet show.

6. Dress as Hitty (in various costumes) and tell the story from her point of view.

7. One of the many things on display at the Shelburne Museum is a large doll collection. Write to this museum and ask for information. (Shelburne Museum, Inc., Rt. 7, Shelburne, Vermont 05482.) After reading the information, plan a schedule for a one-day visit to this outstanding museum.

PROJECT PROPOSAL

Name _____ Beginning Date _____ Completion Date _____

Describe the project in detail: _____

_____

Why do you want to do this project? _____

_____

What will the final product be? _____

_____

How will you share your final product? _____

_____

Comments: _____

_____

NATIONAL VELVET
Comprehension Test A

Directions: Read each question carefully. Circle the letter of the choice that best answers each question.

1. Who wrote this book?
   a. Enid Bagnold   *b.* Marjorie Kinnan Rawlings   *c.* John Steinbeck

2. Mr. Brown _____.
   a. ran a stable   *b.* was a butcher   *c.* owned the grocery

3. Right after Mr. Cellini signed his horses over to Velvet, he _____.
   a. shot himself to death
   b. had a heart attack and died
   c. had a stroke and died

4. The girls got the money to enter various events _____.
   a. by selling Ada
   b. from Mi
   c. from Donald's piggy bank

5. Who made Velvet's outfit to wear in the Grand National?
   a. Mi   *b.* Mi's sister   *c.* Mi's sweetheart

6. After Mi cut Velvet's hair, he covered the telltale white nape with _____.
   a. iodine   *b.* shoe polish   *c.* dirt

7. Who was the first to discover that a girl had just won the Grand National?
   a. the ambulance attendant
   b. the nurse
   c. the doctor

8. Reuters was a _____.
   a. jockey   *b.* hospital   *c.* wire service

9. The most important thing to Velvet was _____.
   a. becoming famous
   b. the prize money
   c. getting Pie into the record books

10. Which member of the National Hunt Committee admitted to being a Velvet fan?
    a. Mits Schreiber
    b. Lord Tunmarsh
    c. Sir Harry Hall

NATIONAL VELVET
Comprehension Test B

Directions: Read each question carefully. Circle the letter of the choice that best answers each question.

1. Velvet had _____ sisters.
    a. two   *b.* three   *c.* four

2. Velvet's favorite horses were _____.
    a. bays   *b.* blacks   *c.* chestnuts

3. A gymkhana is a _____.
    a. hot spell
    b. meeting with sporting events
    c. type of pony

4. Mi pawned his _____ when he really needed money.
    a. teeth   *b.* gold watch   *c.* leather coat

5. Which sister did Terry like?
    a. Edwina   *b.* Velvet   *c.* Meredith

6. Why couldn't Mi see much of the Grand National race?
    a. The crowds were too thick.
    b. The fog was too thick.
    c. He was too drunk.

7. While in the hospital, Velvet refused to tell her name to _____.
    a. anyone at all
    b. anyone but the doctor
    c. anyone but the nurse

8. Mrs. Brown never let the spaniels in the house, but she let them in _____.
    a. during the hurricane
    b. when crowds surrounded the house
    c. when they started biting reporters

9. When the sisters were being compared, Velvet was referred to as the _____.
    a. plain one   *b.* pretty one   *c.* talented one

10. The sisters started _____.
    a. a fan club
    b. collecting Velvet novelties
    c. a scrapbook about Velvet and Pie

NATIONAL VELVET
Comprehension Test C

Directions: Read each question carefully. Circle the letter of the choice that best answers each question.

1. Which sister loved birds?
   a. Meredith   *b.* Malvolia   *c.* Edwina

2. Why was Mr. Ede going to raffle off the piebald?
   a. because he was lame
   b. because he wouldn't stay tied up or shut in
   c. because he was mean and temperamental

3. What did Donald carry around in a bottle for several weeks?
   a. a dead newt   *b.* a drop of sherry   *c.* his spit

4. Velvet won her first event ever riding _____.
   a. Pie   *b.* Sir Pericles   *c.* Mrs. James

5. Where did Velvet get the money to enter the Grand National?
   a. from her mother   b. from Mi   c. from her father

6. When Velvet slipped off Piebald at the finish of the race _____.
   a. she didn't break anything
   b. she struck her head and got a concussion
   c. she broke her ankle

7. Velvet had to go to London to attend an enquiry held by the _____.
   a. Grand National Committee
   b. National Racing Commission
   c. National Hunt Committee

8. During the enquiry, a crowd gathered in the street and demanded that _____.
   a. Velvet's win be made official
   b. Velvet be arrested for fraud
   c. the Grand National be run again

9. Velvet and Mi escaped the crowds by _____.
   a. crawling out the coal chute
   b. going over rooftops
   c. climbing down the drainpipes in back

10. As soon as the enquiry was dropped, Velvet _____.
    a. started planning the next race she'd enter disguised as a boy
    b. became old news
    c. became depressed because she was no longer the center of attention

NATIONAL VELVET

Directions: Velvet thought about horses all day and dreamed about them at night. She could have answered the following questions about horses. Can you? You may use an encyclopedia or the *Guinness Book of World Records*. Write your answers on the lines.

1. The horse is a mammal of the genus _____, of the family _____.

2. A systematic attempt to breed Arabian stallions with mares of English native stock took place at the end of the _____ century.

3. An Arabian horse stands between _____ and _____ inches at the shoulder.

4. Name five breeds of small horses commonly called ponies that are native to Great Britain.

   (1) _____ (2) _____ (3) _____

   (4) _____ (5) _____

5. The smallest of the ponies native to Great Britain is the _____ which stands _____ inches high at the shoulder.

6. Racetracks in England are _____ courses that are _____ in shape.

7. Name the three races in Britain's triple crown: (1) _____

   (2) _____ (3) _____

8. Women were not granted jockey licenses until the _____.

9. British jockey Dick Francis was born in _____ and later became well

   known for writing mysteries with _____ settings.

10. Name the parent body of British racing: _____

11. The _____, the first public racecourse built since Roman times, was built in London in 1174.

12. Old Billy foaled in 1760 in the United Kingdom and lived for _____ years. The skull of this famous

    horse is in the _____ Museum and his stuffed head is in the _____ Museum.

    Name the company that Old Billy worked for: _____. What was Old Billy's job?

    _____ In what year did he retire? _____

13. The tallest horse on record was born in the United Kingdom in 1846 and measured _____ hands in 1850. He reportedly weighed _____ pounds.

14. American colt Man o' War was defeated only once in _____ starts. He was retired in 1921 after amassing total winnings of _____.

15. Name the monarch known as the "father of the British turf": _____.

PROJECTS FOR *NATIONAL VELVET*

Directions: Choose one of the following projects or design your own. If you design your own project, fill out the form below and submit it to your teacher for approval.

1. Make a clay model of Pie.

2. Write about Velvet's and Pie's next race.

3. You are a reporter determined to get an interview with Velvet. Simulate this interview.

4. Create a board game about horses.

5. If you think it was unfair that Velvet was denied the prize money just because she was a female, rewrite the ending of the story.

6. Make a bibliography of at least ten other books about horses. Be sure to include several that are considered classics.

7. Make a mural showing Velvet and Pie competing in the Grand National. Show the events from the starting gate to the finish.

8. Reuters was the wire service that sent news of Velvet's win around the world. Explain how wire services work.

9. Create a word search using words from the story.

PROJECT PROPOSAL

Name _____ Beginning Date _____ Completion Date _____

Describe the project in detail: _____

_____

Why do you want to do this project? _____

_____

What will the final product be? _____

_____

How will you share your final product? _____

_____

Comments: _____

_____

THE RED PONY
Comprehension Test A

Directions: Read each question carefully. Circle the letter of the choice that best answers each question.

1. Who wrote this book?
   a. Walter Farley   *b.* John Steinbeck   *c.* Marguerite Henry

2. What morning ritual changed after Jody got the pony?
   a. He put off chores until dark.
   b. He skipped breakfast to spend time with his pony.
   c. He got up before his mother rang the triangle.

3. Jody got his pony late in the summer, but wasn't allowed to ride him _____.
   a. until Halloween   *b.* until Thanksgiving   *c.* until Christmas

4. In an effort to save the pony, Billy _____.
   a. cut a hole in his throat
   b. gave him a massive dose of penicillin
   c. called the best vet in town

5. After Jody's first pony died, his father said _____.
   a. he didn't take good care of them
   b. he just didn't have a feel for horses
   c. he could raise one of Nellie's colts

6. Nellie's colt was _____.
   a. red   *b.* black   *c.* dappled

7. Junius Maltby moved from San Francisco to _____ for health reasons.
   a. Salinas   *b.* The Pastures of Heaven   *c.* Tucson

8. When Junius suggested that Robbie and his friends play Spy, they _____.
   a. organized a club to spy on Japanese
   b. organized a club to spy on Germans
   c. organized a club to spy on Italians

9. When Miss Morgan went to Robbie's house, she saw _____ tied to a stake.
   a. Junius   *b.* Jacob Stutz   *c.* Guenevere

10. Junius worked as _____ when he lived in San Francisco.
    a. a shoe salesman
    b. a professor
    c. an accountant

THE RED PONY
Comprehension Test B

Directions: Read each question carefully. Circle the letter of the choice that best answers each question.

1. What did Jody want to name his new pony at first?

   a. Fleetfoot   *b.* Running Deer   *c.* Gabilan Mountains

2. Carl Tiflin hated weakness and sickness and had a violent contempt _____.

   a. for dependency   *b.* for helplessness   *c.* for selfishness

3. Jody knew his pony was going to die when _____.

   a. he saw how dry and dead his hair looked

   b. Billy packed up the medicine and left

   c. his mother started sobbing

4. Gitano returned to the ranch to _____.

   a. work as a cowhand

   b. buy back the house where he was born

   c. stay until he died

5. Billy had to kill Nellie _____.

   a. in order to save her colt

   b. because she broke her front leg

   c. because she tried to stomp her colt to death

6. What did his parents call Jody?

   a. Knucklehead   *b.* Mr. Know-it-all   *c.* Big Britches

7. When he was getting ready to kill mice, Jody made a _____.

   a. grave   *b.* trap   *c.* flail

8. Jody's dogs were named _____.

   a. Sunspot and Gopher

   b. Riley and Buck

   c. Doubletree Mutt and Smasher

9. The word that best describes Junius Maltby is _____.

   a. lazy   *b.* ambitious   *c.* sly

10. Junius decided to move back to San Francisco _____.

    a. so Robbie wouldn't grow up in poverty

    b. so he could find a new mother for Robbie

    c. so Robbie could go to a better school

THE RED PONY
Comprehension Test C

Directions: Read each question carefully. Circle the letter of the choice that best answers each question.

1. Billy Buck was _____.
   - *a.* the sheriff
   - *b.* Jody's teacher
   - *c.* a cowhand

2. When the pony was left in the corral on a stormy day, he _____.
   - *a.* got sick
   - *b.* escaped and ran off
   - *c.* kicked a hole in the side of the barn

3. Jody baited a trap knowing that Doubletree Mutt would get caught in it because he _____.
   - a. was mad at him
   - b. was bored
   - c. had a cruel streak

4. Easter was the first horse _____ ever owned.
   - *a.* Billy
   - *b.* Carl
   - *c.* Gitano

5. When Jody's mother opened his lunch pail filled with toads, grasshoppers, a snake, and a newt, she _____.
   - *a.* screamed and threw it out of the window
   - *b.* fell over in a dead faint
   - *c.* gasped with rage

6. It took Nellie approximately _____ months to have a colt.
   - *a.* nine
   - *b.* ten
   - *c.* eleven

7. Who bored people by talking about Indians and crossing the plains?
   - *a.* Mr. Tiflin's father
   - *b.* Mrs. Tiflin's father
   - *c.* Billy Buck

8. Jody's grandfather had hurt feelings when _____.
   - *a.* he heard Carl say it was time to stop telling stories over and over
   - *b.* he heard Jody say he'd heard all the stories before
   - *c.* Billy got up and left in the middle of a story

9. Robbie didn't know he was poor until _____.
   - *a.* the kids taunted him
   - *b.* the county tried to put him in a foster home
   - *c.* members of the school board tried to give him clothes

10. Junius married the widow, Mrs. Quaker, for _____.
    - *a.* love
    - *b.* a home and a golden future
    - *c.* her brilliant mind

THE RED PONY

I. *Directions:* It's no wonder that this story is considered a classic. John Steinbeck's masterful use of language weaves a powerful and unforgettable tale. This is one of those stories that makes a reader want to look up the meanings of unknown words so as not to lose a thread in the rich tapestry of the tale. Some words from the story are hidden in the puzzle. Find the words and circle them. You may go across and down.

```
              r c e s b i p                         l s b d
      r a m b u n c t i o u s n e s s d e c a p i t a t i o n l i
      b p e o n a g e a t d l r a n c o r s c a c o p h o n o u s d
      d p z y h a t a r e a o s g i s h r i v e l e d m i k n n e i
  r t r e l l i s m x s n s t h l v i r t u o u s x i r j l w d m s
  a f c n a x j b l i t c h e o e s p i o n a g e g e n i i e b c
  n j u d i c i o u s l y a f e r l a m e n t e d s o l e g n r o o
  k g e a m i a b l e u l r u p i i n e x t r i c a b l y n i s w n
  l i a g u e k c k h v m d l i o n x r a k f a h r x i r z t e e s
  y b b e r u d i t e w n l n s u g y s p l g b l b w s f s i h l o
  b o n f w l d c r x o y e h s t z t a m h p a i s a n o a l m l
  e m e e v m e o z y p i s l o v e n l y i c k t q l o m t p e a
  r i f r q c o n v a l e s c e n c e l n j d d r x b k b i a n t
  i n a v u n f j c o v e t o u s l y e o s q u a l o r r v l t e
  n a r p r o f u n d i t y r t m r u d p p k b t r l s e e a b l
  g b i n t f u n e r e a l f e r o c i o u s r e i t e c m t n y
      l o t s u c c u m b e d e s n t i m b r e s d v e u d q e t
      e u o r s g t r a v e s t i e d v y q l e r h i d e o u s o
        s t r e p i d a t i o n s z d u m p i l y d i c t i o n s
        r e c o l l e c t i o n l w m o n s t r o u s s p r
        t s u n c o m p r e h e n d i n g l y f e r v e n t
```

glorious	slovenly	travestied	covetously	erudite
diction	espionage	hideous	timbre	appendage
shriveled	cacophonous	disembowelment	ferocious	judiciously
dastardly	purling	gibbering	rambunctiousness	virtuous
fervent	genii	initiative	axis	paisano
amiable	lamented	profundity	peonage	conjunction
monstrous	succumbed	funereal	potency	slothfulness
sombre	recollection	trepidations	trellis	convalescence
blunders	decapitation	disconsolately	inextricably	arbitrated
rankly	palates	dumpily	ague	sniveling
	bolted	sheepish	rancor	uncomprehendingly
	abominable	nefarious	squalor	

II. *Directions:* John Steinbeck's characters are multidimensional. We see both their strengths and their weaknesses. Choose your favorite character from the story and write a character sketch about this person. Tell how this character made you feel as you followed the events in the story.

PROJECTS FOR *THE RED PONY*

Directions: Choose one of the following projects or design your own. If you design your own project, fill out the form below and submit it to your teacher for approval.

1. Jody carried his lunch to school in a golden lard bucket. Write a report about school lunch buckets from the early nineteenth century through today. Include illustrations of each type discussed. Tell which types are eagerly sought by collectors and their approximate price range.

2. Jody's mother was making cottage cheese. Write a report about how this was done by farm wives in the late nineteenth century and early twentieth century. How was the finished product stored to prevent spoilage? What special kitchen utensils were required? Include illustrations with your report.

3. Write a bio-poem about Jody, Mr. or Mrs. Tiflin, Billy Buck, Junius, or Robbie Maltby.

4. Write a chapter telling about what happened to Junius and Robbie after they moved to San Francisco.

5. Create a mural depicting the events in this story in chronological order.

6. Make a crossword puzzle based on the story.

7. Make a diorama of a scene from the story.

PROJECT PROPOSAL

Name _____ Beginning Date _____ Completion Date _____

Describe the project in detail: _____

_____

Why do you want to do this project? _____

_____

What will the final product be? _____

_____

How will you share your final product? _____

_____

Comments: _____

_____

ANSWER KEYS

Section 1

1-1 *THE INDIAN IN THE CUPBOARD* Comprehension Test A

1. c	6. a
2. b	7. b
3. a	8. a
4. c	9. b
5. c	10. c

1-2 *THE INDIAN IN THE CUPBOARD* Comprehension Test B

1. b	6. a
2. b	7. a
3. c	8. b
4. b	9. a
5. a	10. c

1-3 *THE INDIAN IN THE CUPBOARD* Comprehension Test C

1. a	6. b
2. b	7. b
3. a	8. c
4. b	9. b
5. c	10. a

1-4 *THE INDIAN IN THE CUPBOARD* Activity Sheet

Part I:
5, 2, 4, 1, 3, 6, 7

Part II:

Feelings	Objects	Size	Actions
baffled	longhouse	gigantic	tottered
appreciate	bullet	minute	rummaged
stupefaction	battle-ax	infinitesimal	boasting
astonishment	lorry	great	dashed

stunned	crosspieces	microscopic	carried
triumphant	Minnie	huge	stamped
horror	hypodermic		kneeling
anxious	cupboard		gnawing
cheerfully	tepee		scalping
petrified	tomahawk		writhed
	breechcloth		pocketed
			scuttering

1-5 *THE INDIAN IN THE CUPBOARD* Projects

Answers will vary.

1-6 *IT'S LIKE THIS, CAT* Comprehension Test A

1. c	6. c
2. b	7. c
3. c	8. a
4. a	9. c
5. b	10. b

1-7 *IT'S LIKE THIS, CAT* Comprehension Test B

1. a	6. b
2. b	7. a
3. a	8. b
4. c	9. a
5. c	10. c

1-8 *IT'S LIKE THIS, CAT* Comprehension Test C

1. c	6. b
2. c	7. a
3. c	8. b
4. a	9. c
5. a	10. b

1-9 *IT'S LIKE THIS, CAT* Activity Sheet

Answers will vary.

1-10 *IT'S LIKE THIS, CAT* Projects

Answers will vary.

1-11   *THIMBLE SUMMER* Comprehension Test A

1. b	6. b
2. a	7. a
3. a	8. c
4. b	9. c
5. c	10. c

1-12   *THIMBLE SUMMER* Comprehension Test B

1. b	6. b
2. b	7. a
3. a	8. a
4. c	9. c
5. c	10. a

1-13   *THIMBLE SUMMER* Comprehension Test C

1. b	6. c
2. c	7. b
3. a	8. c
4. b	9. b
5. b	10. b

1-14   *THIMBLE SUMMER* Activity Sheet

Part I:

1. j	6. g
2. d	7. c
3. h	8. e
4. b	9. f
5. a	10. i

Part II:
   Answers will vary.

Part III:
   Answers will vary.

1-15   *THIMBLE SUMMER* Projects

Answers will vary.

1-16   *WHERE THE RED FERN GROWS* Comprehension Test A

1. c	6. c
2. c	7. b
3. a	8. b
4. a	9. b
5. b	10. a

1-17   *WHERE THE RED FERN GROWS* Comprehension Test B

1. b	6. a
2. a	7. c
3. b	8. a
4. c	9. a
5. b	10. c

1-18   *WHERE THE RED FERN GROWS* Comprehension Test C

1. b	6. c
2. c	7. a
3. c	8. c
4. a	9. b
5. b	10. a

1-19   *WHERE THE RED FERN GROWS* Activity Sheet

Across

1. Cherokee
3. angel
6. cat
10. Illinois
11. jawbreaker
12. themselves
14. churn
15. smokehouse
18. Ann
19. magazine
20. sixty

Down

2. Ozarks
4. lantern
5. disease
7. language
8. Dan
9. redbone
13. lion
14. come
16. home
17. fifty

1-20   *WHERE THE RED FERN GROWS* Projects

Answers will vary.

Section 2

2-1 *BUNNICULA: A RABBIT TALE OF MYSTERY* Comprehension Test A

1. a   6. a
2. c   7. c
3. c   8. b
4. b   9. a
5. b   10. c

2-2 *BUNNICULA: A RABBIT TALE OF MYSTERY* Comprehension Test B

1. c   6. b
2. b   7. b
3. c   8. a
4. c   9. c
5. b   10. a

2-3 *BUNNICULA: A RABBIT TALE OF MYSTERY* Comprehension Test C

1. a   6. c
2. b   7. a
3. a   8. c
4. b   9. b
5. c   10. c

2-4 *BUNNICULA: A RABBIT TALE OF MYSTERY* Activity Sheet

Part I:
  Answers will vary.
Part II:
  Answers will vary.

2-5 *BUNNICULA: A RABBIT TALE OF MYSTERY* Projects

  Answers will vary.

2-6 *JUST ONE FRIEND* Comprehension Test A

1. a   6. b
2. c   7. b
3. a   8. c
4. a   9. b
5. b   10. c

2-7 *JUST ONE FRIEND* Comprehension Test B

1. a   6. a
2. c   7. c
3. c   8. a
4. b   9. c
5. a   10. b

2-8 *JUST ONE FRIEND* Comprehension Test C

1. a   6. c
2. a   7. a
3. b   8. b
4. b   9. a
5. c   10. a

2-9 *JUST ONE FRIEND* Activity Sheet

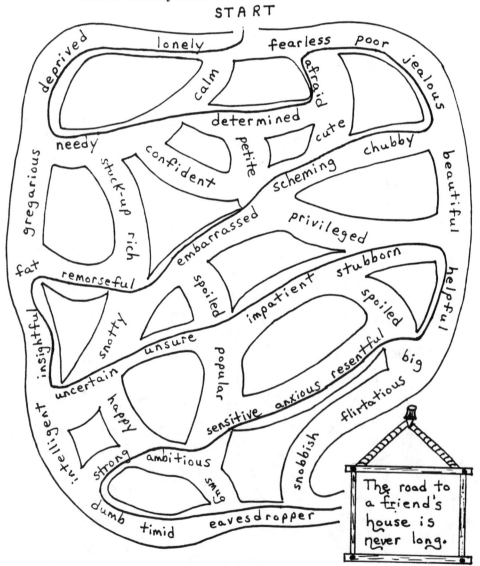

2-10 *JUST ONE FRIEND* Projects

Answers will vary.

2-11 *LEIF THE UNLUCKY* Comprehension Test A

1. a	6. a
2. b	7. b
3. a	8. b
4. c	9. c
5. a	10. c

2-12 *LEIF THE UNLUCKY* Comprehension Test B

1. b	6. c
2. a	7. c
3. a	8. c
4. b	9. a
5. c	10. b

2-13 *LEIF THE UNLUCKY* Comprehension Test C

1. c	6. b
2. c	7. a
3. a	8. b
4. b	9. a
5. a	10. b

2-14 *LEIF THE UNLUCKY* Activity Sheet

Answers will vary.

2-15 *LEIF THE UNLUCKY* Projects

Answers will vary.

2-16 *M.C. HIGGINS, THE GREAT* Comprehension Test A

1. b	6. c
2. c	7. a
3. c	8. a
4. a	9. b
5. a	10. a

2-17 *M.C. HIGGINS, THE GREAT* Comprehension Test B

1. c	6. b
2. a	7. c

3. b	8. b
4. b	9. a
5. a	10. a

2-18 *M.C. HIGGINS, THE GREAT* Comprehension Test C

1. a	6. c
2. a	7. c
3. b	8. c
4. c	9. b
5. a	10. b

2-19 *M.C. HIGGINS, THE GREAT* Activity Sheet

Part I:

1. F	6. O
2. O	7. O
3. F	8. F
4. O	9. F
5. F	10. O

Part II:

Answers will vary.

2-20 *M.C. HIGGINS, THE GREAT* Projects

Answers will vary.

Section 3

3-1 *THE GREAT GILLY HOPKINS* Comprehension Test A

1. b	6. b
2. c	7. a
3. a	8. a
4. b	9. a
5. c	10. b

3-2 *THE GREAT GILLY HOPKINS* Comprehension Test B

1. b	6. c
2. a	7. c
3. b	8. c
4. c	9. a
5. b	10. a

3-3 *THE GREAT GILLY HOPKINS* Comprehension Test C

1. c	6. b
2. c	7. b
3. c	8. b
4. a	9. a
5. a	10. a

3-4 *THE GREAT GILLY HOPKINS* Activity Sheet

Part I:
    1, 3, 4, 2, 10, 8, 6, 9, 7, 5

Part II:
    Answers will vary.

3-5 *THE GREAT GILLY HOPKINS* Projects

    Answers will vary.

3-6 *HOW TO EAT FRIED WORMS* Comprehension Test A

1. b	6. a
2. b	7. b
3. c	8. a
4. c	9. a
5. b	10. c

3-7 *HOW TO EAT FRIED WORMS* Comprehension Test B

1. a   6. b
2. b   7. a
3. c   8. c
4. b   9. b
5. a   10. a

3-8 *HOW TO EAT FRIED WORMS* Comprehension Test C

1. b   6. c
2. a   7. c
3. a   8. b
4. c   9. c
5. b   10. a

3-9 *HOW TO EAT FRIED WORMS* Activity Sheet

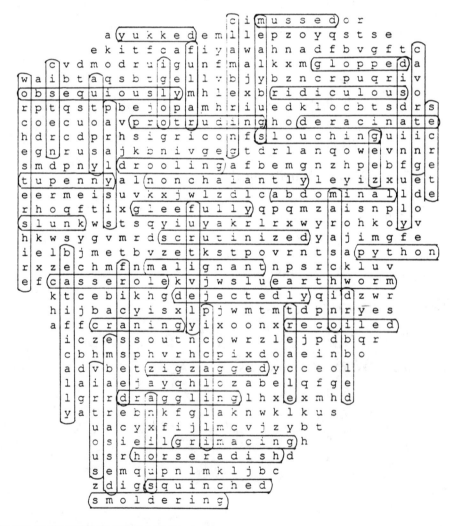

3-10 *HOW TO EAT FRIED WORMS* Projects

Answers will vary.

3-11   *SARAH, PLAIN AND TALL* Comprehension Test A

1. a	6. b
2. b	7. a
3. a	8. a
4. b	9. b
5. a	10. c

3-12   *SARAH, PLAIN AND TALL* Comprehension Test B

1. c	6. a
2. a	7. c
3. c	8. b
4. b	9. c
5. b	10. b

3-13   *SARAH, PLAIN AND TALL* Comprehension Test C

1. b	6. c
2. c	7. b
3. c	8. c
4. a	9. b
5. c	10. a

3-14   *SARAH, PLAIN AND TALL* Activity Sheet

Part I:
   1. c   2. a   3. b   4. c   5. a

Part II:
   Answers will vary.

Part III:
   1. Answers will vary, but may include such as comments as: Jacob has been married and had children, but Sarah has always been single. Jacob loves the land, and Sarah loves the sea. Jacob is poor at expressing his feelings, but Sarah isn't.
   2. Answers will vary, but may include such comments as: Both are lonely. Both like to sing. Both are hard working and dependable. Both are thoughtful and kind. Both are handy with tools. Both are good with children.
   3. Answers will vary.

3-15   *SARAH, PLAIN AND TALL* Projects

   Answers will vary.

3-16 *TALES OF A FOURTH GRADE NOTHING* Comprehension Test A

1. b	6. a
2. b	7. a
3. c	8. c
4. c	9. a
5. c	10. b

3-17 *TALES OF A FOURTH GRADE NOTHING* Comprehension Test B

1. c	6. c
2. c	7. b
3. a	8. b
4. b	9. a
5. a	10. c

3-18 *TALES OF A FOURTH GRADE NOTHING* Comprehension Test C

1. b	6. c
2. a	7. a
3. c	8. c
4. a	9. a
5. b	10. a

3-19 *TALES OF A FOURTH GRADE NOTHING* Activity Sheet

Part I:

1. past	6. present
2. present	7. past
3. present	8. present
4. past	9. past
5. past	10. past

Part II:

　Answers will vary.

Part III:

1. My mother puts her arm around me.
2. The teachers are at a special meeting.
3. I lived at 25 West 68th Street.
4. He knew everybody in the building.
5. He spent a lot of time watching commercials on TV.

3-20 *TALES OF A FOURTH GRADE NOTHING* Projects

　Answers will vary.

Section 4

4-1 *ANNE FRANK: DIARY OF A YOUNG GIRL* Comprehension Test A

1. c	6. c
2. b	7. a
3. c	8. a
4. a	9. c
5. b	10. b

4-2 *ANNE FRANK: DIARY OF A YOUNG GIRL* Comprehension Test B

1. b	6. a
2. a	7. c
3. c	8. c
4. c	9. b
5. a	10. c

4-3 *ANNE FRANK: DIARY OF A YOUNG GIRL* Comprehension Test C

1. c	6. c
2. b	7. b
3. b	8. b
4. a	9. a
5. c	10. a

4-4 *ANNE FRANK: DIARY OF A YOUNG GIRL* Activity Sheet

1. James Cagney	11. Fragaria Vesca
2. Greer Garson	12. southwest
3. 5.6 million	13. Gandhi
4. Gemini	14. Anfa
5. It was not awarded.	15. with honor
6. Henry VIII	16. Elizabeth
7. August 28, 1749	17. toga
8. vichyssoise	18. Apollo
9. Romulus and Remus	19. Saturn
10. Hephaestus	20. John

4-5 *ANNE FRANK: DIARY OF A YOUNG GIRL* Projects

Answers will vary.

4-6 *THE BEST CHRISTMAS PAGEANT EVER* Comprehension Test A

1. c	6. a
2. a	7. b
3. b	8. a
4. c	9. b
5. c	10. c

4-7 *THE BEST CHRISTMAS PAGEANT EVER* Comprehension Test B

1. c	6. c
2. a	7. b
3. b	8. c
4. a	9. b
5. c	10. c

4-8 *THE BEST CHRISTMAS PAGEANT EVER* Comprehension Test C

1. b	6. c
2. c	7. a
3. a	8. a
4. b	9. c
5. b	10. c

4-9 *THE BEST CHRISTMAS PAGEANT EVER* Activity Sheet

Part I:

1. The Herdmans smoked cigars and cussed their teachers.
2. The cat shot straight up in the air and tore up the room.
3. Alberta passed out while whistling "What Child Is This?"
4. Every time you go in the girls' room, the air is blue.
5. Christmas came over Imogene all at once, like a case of chills.

Part II:
Answers will vary.

4-10 *THE BEST CHRISTMAS PAGEANT EVER* Projects

Answers will vary.

4-11 *JOHNNY TREMAIN* Comprehension Test A

1. a	6. c
2. c	7. a
3. c	8. b
4. b	9. b
5. c	10. a

4-12 *JOHNNY TREMAIN* Comprehension Test B

1. a	6. a
2. c	7. c
3. a	8. c
4. a	9. a
5. b	10. b

4-13 *JOHNNY TREMAIN* Comprehension Test C

1. b	6. c
2. b	7. c
3. b	8. a
4. c	9. a
5. c	10. b

4-14 *JOHNNY TREMAIN* Activity Sheet

1. snuff	7. palsy
2. hippogriffs	8. placard
3. sillabubs	9. chaise
4. surtout	10. paroxysm
5. atrophying	11. sedition
6. tipsy parson	12. abets

4-15 *JOHNNY TREMAIN* Projects

Answers will vary.

4-16 *RACSO AND THE RATS OF NIMH* Comprehension Test A

1. b	6. c
2. a	7. b
3. c	8. b
4. c	9. a
5. a	10. c

4-17 *RACSO AND THE RATS OF NIMH* Comprehension Test B

1. c	6. b
2. b	7. c
3. a	8. c
4. a	9. a
5. b	10. b

4-18   *RACSO AND THE RATS OF NIMH* Comprehension Test C

1.	a	6.	a
2.	c	7.	a
3.	b	8.	b
4.	b	9.	a
5.	a	10.	c

4-19   *RACSO AND THE RATS OF NIMH* Activity Sheet

Part I:

1. scientists
2. cinder-block house
3. peppermint
4. streambed
5. quill pen
6. laboratory worker
7. corn-husks
8. playground
9. teachers
10. chocolate
11. doctor
12. dictionary

Part II:
Answers will vary.

4-20   *RACSO AND THE RATS OF NIMH* Projects

Answers will vary.

Section 5

5-1 *ACROSS FIVE APRILS* Comprehension Test A

1. b	6. b
2. a	7. b
3. a	8. b
4. c	9. c
5. c	10. a

5-2 *ACROSS FIVE APRILS* Comprehension Test B

1. a	6. c
2. b	7. a
3. c	8. b
4. b	9. b
5. a	10. c

5-3 *ACROSS FIVE APRILS* Comprehension Test C

1. a	6. c
2. b	7. a
3. a	8. c
4. c	9. b
5. c	10. a

5-4 *ACROSS FIVE APRILS* Activity Sheet

Part I:

1. p	11. c
2. g	12. i
3. f	13. r
4. m	14. e
5. s	15. k
6. d	16. l
7. o	17. b
8. a	18. j
9. t	19. h
10. q	20. n

Part II:
Answers will vary.

Part III:
Answers will vary.

5-5 *ACROSS FIVE APRILS* Projects

Answers will vary.

5-6 *FROM THE MIXED-UP FILES OF MRS. BASIL E. FRANKWEILER* Comprehension Test A

1. b	6. a
2. b	7. a
3. a	8. b
4. b	9. a
5. b	10. c

5-7 *FROM THE MIXED-UP FILES OF MRS. BASIL E. FRANKWEILER* Comprehension Test B

1. c	6. b
2. a	7. c
3. b	8. a
4. a	9. b
5. a	10. c

5-8 *FROM THE MIXED-UP FILES OF MRS. BASIL E. FRANKWEILER* Comprehension Test C

1. a	6. c
2. a	7. b
3. c	8. c
4. c	9. b
5. a	10. b

5-9 *FROM THE MIXED-UP FILES OF MRS. BASIL E. FRANKWEILER* Activity Sheet

Part I:

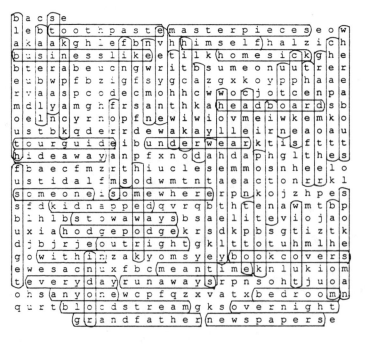

Part II:
Answers will vary.

Part III:
Answers will vary.

5-10 *FROM THE MIXED-UP FILES OF MRS. BASIL E. FRANKWEILER* Projects

Answers will vary.

5-11 *IN THE YEAR OF THE BOAR AND JACKIE ROBINSON* Comprehension Test A

1. a		6. a
2. c		7. b
3. b		8. b
4. b		9. b
5. c		10. a

5-12 *IN THE YEAR OF THE BOAR AND JACKIE ROBINSON* Comprehension Test B

1. b		6. b
2. c		7. c
3. a		8. c
4. c		9. b
5. a		10. b

5-13 *IN THE YEAR OF THE BOAR AND JACKIE ROBINSON* Comprehension Test C

1. a		6. c
2. c		7. a
3. b		8. b
4. c		9. b
5. a		10. a

5-14 *IN THE YEAR OF THE BOAR AND JACKIE ROBINSON* Activity Sheet

1. Abner Doubleday
2. June 2, 1883
3. 1905
4. Joe DiMaggio
5. football, basketball, and track
6. 1947
7. .311 in 1,382 games
8. 1962
9. 1949
10. 10

11. William A. (Candy) Cummings
12. 1875
13. 1876
14. 1885
15. Cooperstown, New York
16. Mickey Mantle
17. Ralph Kiner and John Mize
18. Harry Walker
19. New York Yankees
20. 60 feet 6 inches

5-15 *IN THE YEAR OF THE BOAR AND JACKIE ROBINSON* Projects

Answers will vary.

5-16 *THE SLAVE DANCER* Comprehension Test A

1. c	6. c
2. a	7. a
3. a	8. b
4. b	9. b
5. c	10. c

5-17 *THE SLAVE DANCER* Comprehension Test B

1. a	6. b
2. b	7. c
3. c	8. a
4. b	9. c
5. a	10. b

5-18 *THE SLAVE DANCER* Comprehension Test C

1. c	6. c
2. a	7. a
3. b	8. b
4. c	9. b
5. b	10. c

5-19 *THE SLAVE DANCER* **Activity Sheet**

Part I:

1. holystone
2. becalmed
3. impale
4. mizzenmast
5. spyglass
6. blockade
7. mortify
8. taffrail
9. carronade
10. jettison
11. cabociero
12. turbulence
13. lament
14. davits
15. keening
16. revivified
17. zenith
18. apothecary
19. chandler
20. envisage
21. dirge
22. impertinent

Part II:
Answers will vary.

5-20 *THE SLAVE DANCER* **Projects**

Answers will vary.

Section 6

6-1   *ROLL OF THUNDER, HEAR MY CRY* Comprehension Test A

1. b   6. c
2. c   7. a
3. b   8. b
4. a   9. c
5. b   10. c

6-2   *ROLL OF THUNDER, HEAR MY CRY* Comprehension Test B

1. a   6. b
2. c   7. c
3. b   8. a
4. c   9. b
5. b   10. b

6-3   *ROLL OF THUNDER, HEAR MY CRY* Comprehension Test C

1. c   6. a
2. b   7. c
3. b   8. a
4. c   9. a
5. c   10. c

6-4   *ROLL OF THUNDER, HEAR MY CRY* Activity Sheet

Part I:

1. raucous   9. motley
2. pensively   10. ebbed
3. undaunted   11. penchant
4. amiable   12. monotonously
5. disdainfully   13. quivered
6. dismal   14. temerity
7. traverse   15. furrowed
8. reverberated

Part II:
Answers will vary.

6-5 *ROLL OF THUNDER, HEAR MY CRY* Projects

Answers will vary.

6-6 *SOUNDER* Comprehension Test A

1. a   6. c
2. b   7. a
3. c   8. a
4. a   9. b
5. c   10. c

6-7 *SOUNDER* Comprehension Test B

1. b   6. b
2. a   7. c
3. b   8. b
4. b   9. c
5. c   10. a

6-8 *SOUNDER* Comprehension Test C

1. c   6. a
2. b   7. a
3. a   8. b
4. c   9. a
5. a   10. c

6-9 *SOUNDER* Activity Sheet

1. Mme. Jenkins   8. Benjamin Banneker
2. W. Johnson   9. Crispus Attucks
3. Thurgood Marshall   10. Phillis Wheatley
4. Marian Anderson   11. Rosa Lee Parks
5. Scott Joplin   12. Jackie Robinson
6. Jesse Owens   13. George Washington Carver
7. Harriet Tubman   14. Martin Luther King, Jr.

6-10 *SOUNDER* Projects

Answers will vary.

6-11 *TO BE A SLAVE* Comprehension Test A

1. b   6. c
2. a   7. a
3. c   8. c
4. b   9. a
5. b   10. b

6-12 *TO BE A SLAVE* Comprehension Test B

1. a	6. c
2. b	7. b
3. c	8. a
4. a	9. c
5. b	10. a

6-13 *TO BE A SLAVE* Comprehension Test C

1. c	6. b
2. a	7. b
3. b	8. c
4. a	9. a
5. a	10. a

6-14 *TO BE A SLAVE* Activity Sheet

Part I:

Across	**Down**
1. ammunition	1. America
2. plantations	3. territory
5. Indian	4. Pizarro
8. Balboa	6. master
9. dehumanizing	7. Union
10. suicide	9. Desire
11. block	
12. indentured	
13. Jamestown	

Part II:
Indentured servants signed a contract agreeing to work for a specific number of years. At the end of this term, they were free.

6-15 *TO BE A SLAVE* Projects

Answers will vary.

6-16 *WITH YOU AND WITHOUT YOU* Comprehension Test A

1. a	6. b
2. c	7. b
3. c	8. c
4. a	9. b
5. b	10. a

6-17 *WITH YOU AND WITHOUT YOU* Comprehension Test B

1. c		6. c
2. a		7. a
3. a		8. c
4. b		9. b
5. c		10. a

6-18 *WITH YOU AND WITHOUT YOU* Comprehension Test C

1. b		6. b
2. c		7. a
3. b		8. c
4. a		9. b
5. b		10. a

6-19 *WITH YOU AND WITHOUT YOU* Activity Sheet

1. latchkey	10. sarcasm
2. gullible	11. eulogy
3. cardiomyopathy	12. valedictorian
4. prognosis	13. morbid
5. quavering	14. conspiratorially
6. sympathetic	15. miser
7. aneurysm	16. inflict
8. awed	17. martyred
9. eavesdrop	

6-20 *WITH YOU AND WITHOUT YOU* Projects

Answers will vary.

Section 7

7-1   *THE CAT ATE MY GYMSUIT* Comprehension Test A

1. a	6. c
2. b	7. a
3. b	8. c
4. c	9. a
5. a	10. b

7-2   *THE CAT ATE MY GYMSUIT* Comprehension Test B

1. b	6. b
2. c	7. b
3. b	8. c
4. b	9. a
5. a	10. c

7-3   *THE CAT ATE MY GYMSUIT* Comprehension Test C

1. a	6. b
2. c	7. b
3. a	8. c
4. b	9. b
5. c	10. a

7-4   *THE CAT ATE MY GYMSUIT* Activity Sheet

Part I:
Answers will vary.

Part II:
Answers will vary.

7-5   *THE CAT ATE MY GYMSUIT* Projects

Answers will vary.

7-6   *JAMES AND THE GIANT PEACH* Comprehension Test A

1. a	6. a
2. c	7. b
3. b	8. a
4. b	9. b
5. c	10. c

7-7 *JAMES AND THE GIANT PEACH* Comprehension Test B

1. b	6. c
2. a	7. a
3. c	8. c
4. b	9. b
5. a	10. c

7-8 *JAMES AND THE GIANT PEACH* Comprehension Test C

1. b	6. c
2. c	7. c
3. a	8. a
4. b	9. c
5. c	10. a

7-9 *JAMES AND THE GIANT PEACH* Activity Sheet

Answers will vary.

7-10 *JAMES AND THE GIANT PEACH* Projects

Answers will vary.

7-11 *JULIE OF THE WOLVES* Comprehension Test A

1. c	6. b
2. b	7. c
3. a	8. a
4. a	9. b
5. b	10. c

7-12 *JULIE OF THE WOLVES* Comprehension Test B

1. c	6. b
2. a	7. c
3. c	8. a
4. a	9. b
5. b	10. c

7-13 *JULIE OF THE WOLVES* Comprehension Test C

1. b	6. a
2. c	7. b
3. a	8. c
4. a	9. b
5. b	10. c

7-14 *JULIE OF THE WOLVES* Activity Sheet

Part I:

1. F	6. F
2. O	7. O
3. F	8. O
4. F	9. F
5. O	10. O

Part II:
Answers will vary.

Part III:
Answers will vary.

7-15 *JULIE OF THE WOLVES* Projects

Answers will vary.

7-16 *ONE FAT SUMMER* Comprehension Test A

1. a	6. c
2. a	7. b
3. c	8. a
4. b	9. a
5. a	10. c

7-17 *ONE FAT SUMMER* Comprehension Test B

1. b	6. b
2. a	7. c
3. b	8. b
4. c	9. a
5. a	10. c

7-18 *ONE FAT SUMMER* Comprehension Test C

1. a	6. a
2. c	7. c
3. a	8. b
4. b	9. a
5. c	10. b

7-19 *ONE FAT SUMMER* **Activity Sheet**

1. ES; 99; 254
2. Villa Maria College
3. J.P. McGranery
4. Sam Rayburn
5. Harry S. Truman
6. General Walter Bedell Smith
7. Archer J.P. Martin and Richard L.M. Synge
8. *St. Louis Post-Dispatch*
9. Marianne Moore; Collected Poems
10. Paul R. Williams
11. Coleen Kay Hutchins; Salt Lake City, Utah
12. Gary Cooper
13. John Ford
14. the nation's steel mills
15. Paul Arizin

7-20 *ONE FAT SUMMER* **Projects**

Answers will vary.

Section 8

8-1 *CHARLIE AND THE CHOCOLATE FACTORY* Comprehension Test A

1. a	6. b
2. c	7. a
3. c	8. b
4. b	9. c
5. c	10. b

8-2 *CHARLIE AND THE CHOCOLATE FACTORY* Comprehension Test B

1. b	6. a
2. a	7. c
3. c	8. b
4. a	9. b
5. c	10. c

8-3 *CHARLIE AND THE CHOCOLATE FACTORY* Comprehension Test C

1. c	6. a
2. c	7. b
3. b	8. c
4. a	9. b
5. a	10. a

8-4 *CHARLIE AND THE CHOCOLATE FACTORY* Activity Sheet

Part I:
Answers will vary.

Part II:
Answers will vary.

Part III:
Answers will vary.

8-5 *CHARLIE AND THE CHOCOLATE FACTORY* Projects

Answers will vary.

8-6 *FRANKENSTEIN* Comprehension Test A

1. c	6. a
2. b	7. c
3. a	8. b
4. a	9. a
5. b	10. c

8-7 *FRANKENSTEIN* Comprehension Test B

1. a	6. c
2. b	7. b
3. c	8. a
4. c	9. c
5. b	10. a

8-8 *FRANKENSTEIN* Comprehension Test C

1. c	6. c
2. b	7. b
3. a	8. c
4. c	9. a
5. a	10. b

8-9 *FRANKENSTEIN* Activity Sheet

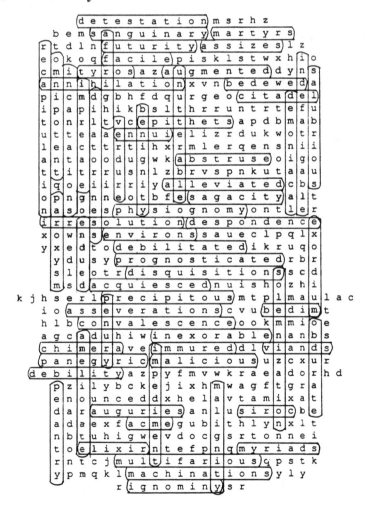

8-10 *FRANKENSTEIN* Projects

Answers will vary.

8-11 *MY BROTHER SAM IS DEAD* Comprehension Test A

1. c	6. b
2. b	7. c
3. c	8. b
4. a	9. b
5. b	10. b

8-12 *MY BROTHER SAM IS DEAD* Comprehension Test B

1. b	6. c
2. c	7. c
3. a	8. b
4. b	9. b
5. c	10. a

8-13 *MY BROTHER SAM IS DEAD* Comprehension Test C

1. c	6. a
2. a	7. b
3. b	8. c
4. b	9. a
5. a	10. b

8-14 *MY BROTHER SAM IS DEAD* Activity Sheet

Part I:

Part II:
Answers will vary.

8-15 *MY BROTHER SAM IS DEAD* **Projects**

Answers will vary.

8-16 *THE WAR BETWEEN THE PITIFUL TEACHERS
AND THE SPLENDID KIDS*
Comprehension Test A

1. b	6. b
2. c	7. c
3. a	8. b
4. b	9. a
5. a	10. c

8-17 *THE WAR BETWEEN THE PITIFUL TEACHERS
AND THE SPLENDID KIDS*
Comprehension Test B

1. b	6. c
2. a	7. b
3. c	8. a
4. c	9. b
5. b	10. b

8-18 *THE WAR BETWEEN THE PITIFUL TEACHERS
AND THE SPLENDID KIDS*
Comprehension Test C

1. b	6. b
2. c	7. c
3. a	8. b
4. b	9. c
5. c	10. a

8-19   *THE WAR BETWEEN THE PITIFUL TEACHERS*
           AND THE SPLENDID KIDS
           Activity Sheet

Part I:

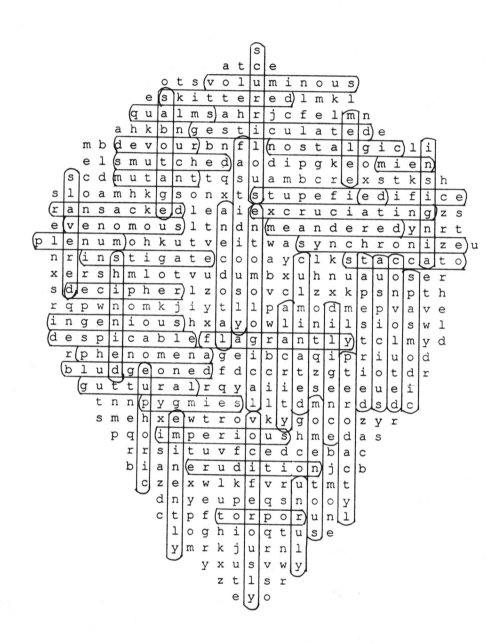

Part II:
Answers will vary.

8-20   *THE WAR BETWEEN THE PITIFUL TEACHERS AND THE SPLENDID KIDS* **Projects**

Answers will vary.

Section 9

9-1 *ALL-OF-A-KIND FAMILY* **Comprehension Test A**

1. b	6. c
2. a	7. a
3. c	8. c
4. a	9. b
5. a	10. a

9-2 *ALL-OF-A-KIND FAMILY* **Comprehension Test B**

1. c	6. c
2. b	7. a
3. c	8. b
4. c	9. b
5. b	10. c

9-3 *ALL-OF-A-KIND FAMILY* **Comprehension Test C**

1. b	6. b
2. c	7. a
3. a	8. c
4. b	9. a
5. c	10. b

9-4 *ALL-OF-A-KIND FAMILY* **Activity Sheet**

1. smoked salmon	11. salt herrings
2. red cherry hearts	12. frankfurters
3. pickled tomatoes	13. chocolate pennies
4. potato kugels	14. crackers
5. limburger cheese	15. jelly beans
6. sour rye bread	16. sour pickles
7. pretzels	17. sauerkraut
8. candied grapes	18. sweet potatoes
9. tangerines	19. hard-boiled eggs
10. matzoth balls	20. peanut bars

9-5 *ALL-OF-A-KIND FAMILY* **Projects**

Answers will vary.

9-6   *CALL IT COURAGE* Comprehension Test A

1. c   6. b
2. a   7. c
3. b   8. a
4. b   9. b
5. a   10. c

9-7   *CALL IT COURAGE* Comprehension Test B

1. a   6. a
2. c   7. c
3. b   8. c
4. a   9. b
5. c   10. a

9-8   *CALL IT COURAGE* Comprehension Test C

1. c   6. c
2. c   7. b
3. b   8. a
4. a   9. b
5. b   10. c

9-9   *CALL IT COURAGE* Activity Sheet

Across   **Down**

  1. mulberry   1. Moana
  3. fire   2. breadfruit
  5. hammerhead   3. forbidden
  6. raft   4. savages
  8. conflagration   7. bandage
11. courage   9. coral
14. tupapau   10. pareu
15. necklace   11. canoe
16. knife   12. feke
                        13. Maui

9-10   *CALL IT COURAGE* Projects

Answers will vary.

9-11 *DIRT BIKE RACER* Comprehension Test A

1. c	6. a
2. a	7. c
3. b	8. a
4. b	9. a
5. c	10. c

9-12 *DIRT BIKE RACER* Comprehension Test B

1. c	6. a
2. a	7. c
3. b	8. b
4. c	9. b
5. a	10. a

9-13 *DIRT BIKE RACER* Comprehension Test C

1. c	6. b
2. b	7. c
3. b	8. a
4. b	9. c
5. a	10. a

9-14 *DIRT BIKE RACER* Activity Sheet

Answers will vary.

9-15 *DIRT BIKE RACER* Projects

Answers will vary.

9-16 *HOMESICK: MY OWN STORY* Comprehension Test A

1. b	6. b
2. a	7. a
3. c	8. b
4. b	9. c
5. c	10. a

9-17 *HOMESICK: MY OWN STORY* Comprehension Test B

1. c	6. b
2. b	7. c
3. a	8. b
4. c	9. a
5. b	10. c

9-18 *HOMESICK: MY OWN STORY* Comprehension Test C

1. c	6. c
2. a	7. b
3. b	8. b
4. a	9. a
5. a	10. c

9-19 *HOMESICK: MY OWN STORY* Activity Sheet

1. Calvin Coolidge
2. Frank B. Kellogg
3. J. Edgar Hoover
4. Canton (Ohio) *Daily News*
5. Leonora Speyer, "Fiddler's Farewell"
6. Lois Delaner of Joliet, Illinois
7. Janet Gaynor
8. *Wings*
9. Emil Jannings
10. 1,000
11. *The Jazz Singer*
12. Al Jolson
13. Charles Lindbergh
14. *Show Boat*
15. Indiana; Spencer
16. Helen Wills
17. France
18. Babe Ruth
19. Gene Tunney
20. George Souders
21. Dusenberg
22. Tommy Armour
23. Lou Gehrig

9-20 *HOMESICK: MY OWN STORY* Projects

Answers will vary.

Section 10

10-1 *ANIMAL FARM* Comprehension Test A

1. c	6. a
2. a	7. b
3. b	8. a
4. b	9. c
5. c	10. a

10-2 *ANIMAL FARM* Comprehension Test B

1. b	6. b
2. c	7. c
3. b	8. c
4. c	9. a
5. a	10. a

10-3 *ANIMAL FARM* Comprehension Test C

1. c	6. b
2. b	7. b
3. a	8. b
4. b	9. a
5. c	10. c

10-4 *ANIMAL FARM* Activity Sheet

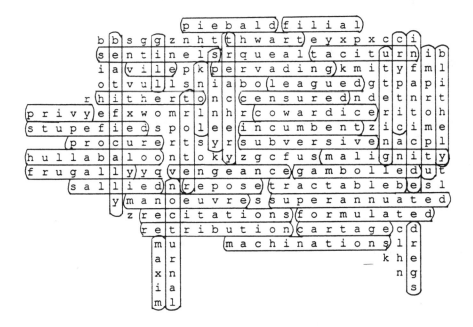

10-5 *ANIMAL FARM* Projects

Answers will vary.

10-6 *THE BOAT WHO WOULDN'T FLOAT* Comprehension Test A

1. b	6. a
2. c	7. a
3. b	8. c
4. a	9. c
5. a	10. b

10-7 *THE BOAT WHO WOULDN'T FLOAT* Comprehension Test B

1. c	6. c
2. b	7. a
3. c	8. b
4. c	9. c
5. c	10. a

10-8 *THE BOAT WHO WOULDN'T FLOAT* Comprehension Test C

1. b	6. b
2. c	7. c
3. a	8. b
4. b	9. a
5. a	10. c

10-9 *THE BOAT WHO WOULDN'T FLOAT* Activity Sheet

1. 10; March 31, 1949
2. 43,359
3. 1925; St. John's
4. Belle Isle
5. Roman Catholic
6. Beothuk
7. Viking; 1000
8. Indian; 4000
9. Ferryland
10. Cabot; 90
11. 1497
12. 1897; Signal Hill; St. John's
13. *Evening Telegram*; 1879
14. Churchill, Exploits, Naskaupi, Gander
15. Pitcher plant

10-10 *THE BOAT WHO WOULDN'T FLOAT* Projects

Answers will vary.

10-11 *THE SUMMER OF THE SWANS* Comprehension Test A

1. a	6. b
2. a	7. b
3. a	8. c
4. b	9. b
5. c	10. c

10-12 *THE SUMMER OF THE SWANS* Comprehension Test B

1. c	6. c
2. a	7. a
3. b	8. b
4. c	9. a
5. a	10. a

10-13 *THE SUMMER OF THE SWANS* Comprehension Test C

1. b	6. b
2. a	7. b
3. c	8. c
4. b	9. b
5. c	10. a

10-14 *THE SUMMER OF THE SWANS* Activity Sheet

Part I:
Answers will vary.

Part II:
2, 6, 1, 3, 4, 5

10-15 *THE SUMMER OF THE SWANS* Projects

Answers will vary.

10-16 *TIGER EYES* Comprehension Test A

1. c	6. b
2. c	7. c
3. b	8. b
4. a	9. a
5. a	10. c

10-17 *TIGER EYES* Comprehension Test B

1. b	6. c
2. a	7. b
3. c	8. c
4. c	9. b
5. a	10. c

10-18 *TIGER EYES* Comprehension Test C

1. a	6. b
2. b	7. c
3. c	8. a
4. c	9. a
5. b	10. c

10-19 *TIGER EYES* Activity Sheet

1. Mercury, Venus, Mars, Jupiter, Saturn
2. planet
3. satellite
4. moons
5. *On the Revolution of the Heavenly Bodies*
6. spectroscope
7. Uranus
8. Saturn
9. Joseph von Fraunhofer
10. Hans Bethe
11. 2.8
12. Aurora Australis
13. photosphere
14. Earth
15. 27; 7; 43.2

10-20 *TIGER EYES* Projects

Answers will vary.

Section 11

11-1 *SUMMER OF MY GERMAN SOLDIER* Comprehension Test A

1. a	6. b
2. b	7. b
3. c	8. a
4. a	9. c
5. b	10. b

11-2 *SUMMER OF MY GERMAN SOLDIER* Comprehension Test B

1. b	6. a
2. a	7. a
3. c	8. b
4. b	9. c
5. c	10. c

11-3 *SUMMER OF MY GERMAN SOLDIER* Comprehension Test C

1. c	6. a
2. b	7. c
3. c	8. a
4. c	9. c
5. b	10. b

11-4 *SUMMER OF MY GERMAN SOLDIER* Activity Sheet

1. 4; 4
2. December 11, 1941
3. Germany, Italy, Japan
4. Lancasters and Halifaxes
5. the destruction of Jews in Europe by Nazi Germany
6. Premier Joseph Stalin, USSR; President Franklin D. Roosevelt, U.S.; Prime Minister Winston Churchill, Great Britain
7. June 6, 1944; beginning of Allied invasion of German-occupied western Europe
8. General Dwight D. Eisenhower
9. July 20, 1944
10. August 25, 1944
11. General Charles de Gaulle
12. Joe Rosenthal
13. April 12, 1945
14. April 30, 1945
15. General Alfred Jodl
16. May 8, 1945; Victory in Europe
17. *Missouri*

11-5   *SUMMER OF MY GERMAN SOLDIER* Projects

Answers will vary.

11-6   *SUMMER OF THE MONKEYS* Comprehension Test A

1. a	6. c
2. b	7. a
3. c	8. a
4. a	9. a
5. b	10. c

11-7   *SUMMER OF THE MONKEYS* Comprehension Test B

1. a	6. b
2. b	7. c
3. c	8. a
4. a	9. b
5. b	10. a

11-8   *SUMMER OF THE MONKEYS* Comprehension Test C

1. c	6. a
2. a	7. b
3. b	8. c
4. a	9. a
5. c	10. a

11-9   *SUMMER OF THE MONKEYS* Activity Sheet

Part I:

1. g	11. m
2. j	12. n
3. a	13. i
4. t	14. e
5. c	15. k
6. s	16. f
7. r	17. q
8. o	18. l
9. h	19. p
10. b	20. d

Part II:
Answers will vary.

Part III:
Answers will vary.

11-10 *SUMMER OF THE MONKEYS* Projects

Answers will vary.

11-11 *PURSUIT* Comprehension Test A

1. c	6. c
2. c	7. a
3. a	8. c
4. b	9. b
5. c	10. a

11-12 *PURSUIT* Comprehension Test B

1. a	6. c
2. b	7. c
3. c	8. c
4. a	9. b
5. b	10. c

11-13 *PURSUIT* Comprehension Test B

1. c	6. c
2. a	7. a
3. b	8. b
4. c	9. a
5. c	10. c

11-14 *PURSUIT* Activity Sheet

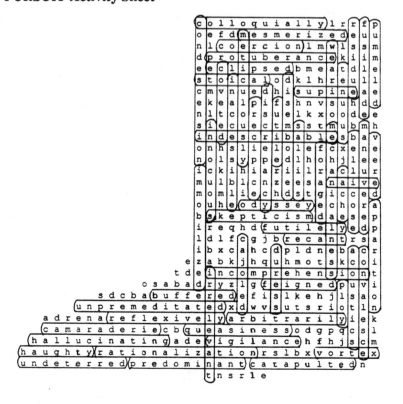

11-15 *PURSUIT* Projects

   Answers will vary.

11-16 *WUTHERING HEIGHTS* Comprehension Test A

   1. b   6. b
   2. a   7. c
   3. c   8. a
   4. b   9. b
   5. c   10. c

11-17 *WUTHERING HEIGHTS* Comprehension Test B

   1. b   6. c
   2. a   7. a
   3. a   8. c
   4. b   9. c
   5. c   10. c

11-18 *WUTHERING HEIGHTS* Comprehension Test C

   1. a   6. b
   2. b   7. a
   3. a   8. b
   4. a   9. a
   5. b   10. c

11-19 *WUTHERING HEIGHTS* Activity Sheet

   Part I: Answers will vary slightly but will be similar to the following:
   1. stop teeth from chattering
   2. putting my clothes back on
   3. leave/left the room
   4. now and then
   5. read the letter
   6. begged me
   7. she tried another way
   8. I was thinking about
   9. I didn't dare
   10. to say goodbye

   Part II:
   Answers will vary.

11-20 *WUTHERING HEIGHTS* Projects

   Answers will vary.

Section 12

12-1 *THE HERO AND THE CROWN* Comprehension Test A

1. b	6. c
2. a	7. b
3. c	8. a
4. b	9. b
5. a	10. c

12-2 *THE HERO AND THE CROWN* Comprehension Test B

1. b	6. b
2. a	7. b
3. c	8. a
4. c	9. c
5. b	10. b

12-3 *THE HERO AND THE CROWN* Comprehension Test C

1. c	6. b
2. a	7. c
3. a	8. a
4. c	9. b
5. b	10. c

12-4 *THE HERO AND THE CROWN* Activity Sheet

12-5 *THE HERO AND THE CROWN* Projects

Answers will vary.

12-6   *HITTY: HER FIRST HUNDRED YEARS* Comprehension Test A

1. a	6. b
2. a	7. a
3. b	8. c
4. c	9. b
5. a	10. a

12-7   *HITTY: HER FIRST HUNDRED YEARS* Comprehension Test B

1. c	6. c
2. b	7. b
3. a	8. a
4. b	9. b
5. a	10. c

12-8   *HITTY: HER FIRST HUNDRED YEARS* Comprehension Test C

1. a	6. b
2. c	7. a
3. a	8. c
4. b	9. b
5. a	10. a

12-9   *HITTY: HER FIRST HUNDRED YEARS* Activity Sheet

Answers will vary.

12-10   *HITTY: HER FIRST HUNDRED YEARS* Projects

Answers will vary.

12-11   *NATIONAL VELVET* Comprehension Test A

1. a	6. a
2. b	7. b
3. a	8. c
4. b	9. c
5. b	10. a

12-12   *NATIONAL VELVET* Comprehension Test B

1. b	6. a
2. c	7. b
3. b	8. b
4. a	9. a
5. a	10. b

12-13 *NATIONAL VELVET* Comprehension Test C

1. a
2. b
3. c
4. b
5. a
6. a
7. c
8. a
9. b
10. b

12-14 *NATIONAL VELVET* Activity Sheet

1. Equus; Equidae
2. seventeenth
3. 58; 60
4. the Shetland; the Dales; the Welsh; the Dartmoor; the New Forest
5. Shetland; 42
6. turf; triangular
7. Epsom Derby; Saint Leger Stakes; Two Thousand Guineas
8. 1970s
9. 1920; racetrack
10. Jockey Club of Great Britain
11. Smithfield Track
12. 62; Manchester; Bedford; Mersey and Irwell Navigation Company; marshalling and towing barges; 1819
13. 21.25; 3,360
14. 21; $249,465
15. King Charles II

12-15 *NATIONAL VELVET* Projects

Answers will vary.

12-16 *THE RED PONY* Comprehension Test A

1. b
2. c
3. b
4. a
5. c
6. b
7. b
8. a
9. b
10. c

12-17 *THE RED PONY* Comprehension Test B

1. c
2. b
3. a
4. c
5. a
6. c
7. c
8. c
9. a
10. a

12-18 *THE RED PONY* Comprehension Test C

1. c		6. c
2. a		7. b
3. b		8. a
4. b		9. c
5. c		10. b

12-19 *THE RED PONY* Activity Sheet

Part I:
Answers will vary.

Part II:

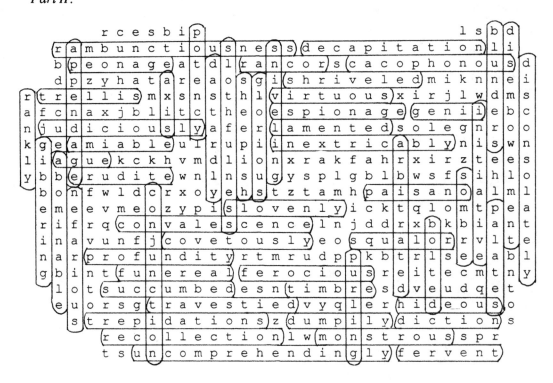

12-20 *THE RED PONY* Projects

Answers will vary.